Gaining Currency

GAINING CURRENCY

The Rise of the Renminbi

Eswar S. Prasad

OXFORD
UNIVERSITY PRESS

Oxford University Press is a department of the University of Oxford. It furthers
the University's objective of excellence in research, scholarship, and education
by publishing worldwide. Oxford is a registered trade mark of Oxford University
Press in the UK and certain other countries.

Published in the United States of America by Oxford University Press
198 Madison Avenue, New York, NY 10016, United States of America.

Library of Congress Cataloging-in-Publication Data
Names: Prasad, Eswar, author.
Title: Gaining currency : the rise of the renminbi / Eswar S. Prasad.
Description: New York, NY : Oxford University Press, [2017] |
    Includes bibliographical references.
Identifiers: LCCN 2016017263 | ISBN 9780190631055 (hardcover) |
    ISBN 9780190631079 (epub)
Subjects: LCSH: Renminbi. | Foreign exchange—China. | Finance—China. |
    China—Economic policy—2000–
Classification: LCC HG1285 .P73 2017 | DDC 332.4/50951—dc23 LC record
available at https://lccn.loc.gov/2016017263

9 8 7 6 5 4 3 2

Printed by Sheridan Books, Inc., United States of America

To Basia

My Muse, my love, my true friend
Zawsze i na zawsze

CONTENTS

LIST OF FIGURES AND TABLES

FIGURES

TABLES

PREFACE

I have only to beg that readers, who have been unaccustomed to see Chinese matters treated from a rational point of view, will believe that I am no Mandarin worshipper, and that I am quite alive to the great faults of the Chinese nation and Government. Their civilisation, like our own, has been in great part a failure, though perhaps not such a saddening one as ours, for it has not had such fine material to work upon; but we must at least understand it and treat of it as it really exists, if we would avail ourselves of its experience . . . It is desirable that we should know [the Chinese] system as it really is, and not as it has been fancifully represented—a subject of ridicule to amuse the passing hour, or a subject of abuse to justify dubious aggressions.

The 'Ever-Victorious Army': A History of The Chinese Campaign Under Lt.-Col. C.G. Gordon and of the Suppression of the Tai-Ping Rebellion, Andrew Wilson, 1868.

China's economy is now the second largest in the world. In 2015, its annual gross domestic product (GDP) was $11 trillion, accounting for 15 percent of world GDP, placing it second only to the United States, which has a GDP of $18 trillion. China is also an important player in international trade, accounting for 12 percent of global trade in goods. China's impact on the world economy is even greater when measured along other dimensions. The country holds about 30 percent of global foreign exchange reserves and has accounted for one-third of global GDP growth since the financial crisis. China is big (Figure P.1).

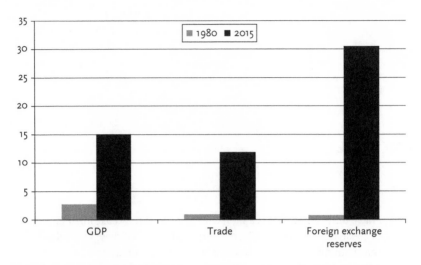

Figure P.1 China and the world (share of world total, in percent).
All data are for 2015. Gross domestic product is in market prices. Trade refers to merchandise trade (only goods). China's share of world trade in goods and services is 11 percent. Foreign exchange reserves data begin in 1989.
Sources: International Monetary Fund, People's Bank of China, and World Trade Organization.

Despite China's economic might, the international stature of its currency, the renminbi (RMB), does not quite match that of its economy. Among the currencies of the world's six largest economies, the RMB is only now beginning to emerge as a factor in the global economy. The others—the U.S. dollar, the euro (which covers two of the six largest economies—Germany and France), the Japanese yen, and the British pound sterling—all have well-established roles in global finance.

In recent years the Chinese government has taken a number of steps to elevate the RMB into this group of elite currencies by increasing its international use. The RMB's adoption in global markets is constrained, however, since the Chinese economy has neither a fully market-determined exchange rate nor an open capital account that allows for free cross-border capital flows. Nevertheless, given China's sheer size and its rising shares of global GDP and trade, the government's steps are rapidly gaining traction.

This book takes stock of China's progress in promoting the RMB as a major currency in international financial markets. While the currency has made remarkable progress in a relatively short period, it is far from assured that it will continue along the same impressive trajectory it has followed for the past few years. To be sure, the RMB will become a significant player even if its rise to prominence levels off, yet its full potential may remain unrealized unless the Chinese government undertakes a broad range of reforms.

STRUCTURE OF THE BOOK

Although China has used money in some form for more than two thousand years and was actually the first country to use paper money, the RMB came into being only in 1949. Chapter 1 provides a brief history of the evolution of Chinese paper currency, beginning with the Tang dynasty in the seventh century AD and tracing it to the present, following many twists and turns along the way. Even the tale of how present-day RMB notes came to look as they do reveals a colorful history.

There is a great deal of hyperbole surrounding the RMB, with some commentators arguing at the extreme that its displacement of the dollar as the dominant international currency is imminent. Such popular prognostications tend to conflate distinct elements of a currency's role in international finance. Chapter 2 unpacks three related but distinct aspects of the RMB's role in the global monetary system. First, *capital account convertibility* reflects the extent to which China restricts inflows and outflows of financial capital that are intermediated through transactions involving the RMB and foreign currencies. A fully open capital account has no restrictions on cross-border capital flows. The second aspect, *internationalization*, involves the use of the RMB in denominating and settling cross-border trade and financial transactions—that is, its use as an international medium of exchange. The third aspect is whether the RMB serves as a *reserve* currency, which is one that is held by foreign central banks as protection against balance of payments crises.

The remainder of the book evaluates these three elements within a unified conceptual framework and analyzes their implications along two dimensions: first, by reference to the balance and sustainability of China's own economic development; and second, by reference to the associated implications for the international monetary system, including the possible impact on the U.S. dollar and other existing reserve currencies.

Chapter 3 documents the evolution of China's capital account openness in terms of official policy changes to restrictions on capital flows as well as the actual levels of foreign investment in China and the country's own investment abroad. Why and how China has opened up its capital account is a story of some intrigue in itself.

Any mention of the RMB usually brings to mind the value of the currency relative to other currencies—in other words, its exchange rate. The RMB's exchange rate is the subject of considerable fulmination in many national capitals of Western countries. For instance, U.S. politicians and government officials are often incensed by what they see as China's willful attempts to cheapen its currency to boost its exports, thereby unfairly stealing jobs from the U.S. Chapter 4 digs deeper into the facts behind China's currency policy and how it has evolved over time.

Despite the constraints on capital flowing in and out of China, the RMB has begun playing a larger, although still modest, role in international finance over a relatively short period. Chapter 5 documents the areas in which the RMB has made progress, and cautions that the implications of these developments, while noteworthy, should not be blown out of proportion.

Chapter 6 turns to a discussion of the RMB's rise as a reserve currency. This topic might seem premature given that China has neither a flexible exchange rate nor an open capital account— two features once considered absolute prerequisites for a reserve currency. As in many other economic matters, China appears to have broken the traditional mold. The International Monetary Fund, the world's premier multilateral financial institution, has even recently designated the RMB as an official reserve currency.

Therein lies another matter of intrigue, with overt and behind-the-scenes machinations leading to this outcome.

After dispensing with traditional concepts, Chapter 7 turns to a concept that has become important in global finance: that of a "safe haven" currency, a concept transcending that of a plain vanilla reserve currency. Such a currency is one that investors turn to for safety during times of global turmoil, rather than for diversifying their stores of assets denominated in foreign currencies or seeking higher yields on their investments. This chapter advances a provocative argument: that China's economic strength alone is not sufficient for its currency to become a safe haven. A country seeking this status for its currency must have a sound institutional framework—including an independent judiciary, an open and democratic government, and robust public institutions (especially a credible central bank)—to earn the trust of foreign investors. This chapter provides a critical review of the Chinese government's approaches to broader institutional reforms and the implications of these approaches for the RMB's prospects of becoming a safe haven currency.

The RMB's path to global prominence depends to a significant extent on China's growing economic and financial power. A major growth slowdown or, worse, a collapse of the financial system could alter this trajectory. Chapter 8 discusses the potential risks China's economy faces that could derail the RMB's rise. In fact, some of the policies related to enhancing the RMB's international stature—including capital account opening and allowing the exchange rate to be determined more freely by market forces—could themselves expose China's economic and financial stability to a number of risks if these policy changes are mishandled.

Chapter 9 provides a broader geopolitical analysis that links the RMB's rising prominence to China's weight in international finance and its relationships with neighboring countries and other super-powers. China is using its financial clout to pull other countries and international financial institutions into the web of its influence. Eventually, this will allow China to start molding the rules of the game for international finance, which in turn could help level the playing field between the RMB and traditional reserve currencies.

In the U.S., China's rise is generating anxiety and fear, coupled with schadenfreude at China's recent economic troubles. China's exchange rate regime and trade relationship with the U.S. are featuring in the country's presidential politics during 2016 and will no doubt continue to do so in broader political discussions in the future. Chapter 10 reviews the implications of the increasingly prominent RMB for the international monetary system, including the implications for the U.S. dollar and the configuration of reserve currencies.

The main message of this book can be stated simply. The RMB is well on its way to becoming a significant international currency. If China plays its cards right, with suitable financial sector and other market-oriented reforms, the RMB will become an important reserve currency, perhaps eventually accounting for as much as 10 percent of global foreign exchange reserves (for comparison, the U.S. dollar and the euro now account for 64 percent and 21 percent of global foreign exchange reserves, respectively). For the RMB to become a safe haven currency, however, China will have to undertake broader reforms of its institutional framework that would ultimately alter its political, legal, and public institutions. Such changes are currently not in the cards.

The RMB has climbed to prominence on the international economic stage in the space of just a few years—a mere blink of the eye in the historical span of the evolution of China's currency. Indeed, a long time ago, it took a brave traveler from Venice to draw the attention of the Western world to the marvel of paper money, an invention that had its origins in China.

Gaining Currency

CHAPTER 1
A Historical Prologue

> At the end of the day's journey, you reach a considerable town named Pau-ghin. The inhabitants worship idols, burn their dead, use paper money, and are the subjects of the grand khan.
>
> *The Travels of Marco Polo the Venetian*, Marco Polo

Such was the strange behavior of the denizens of China in the thirteenth century, as narrated by Marco Polo. Clearly, using paper money was a distinguishing characteristic of the peoples the famed itinerant encountered during his extensive travels in China, one the explorer equated with what Europeans would have regarded as pagan rituals. Indeed, the notion of using paper money was cause for wonderment among Europeans at the time and for centuries thereafter; paper money came into use in Europe only during the seventeenth century, long after its advent in China.

That China pioneered the use of paper money is only logical since paper itself was invented there during the Han dynasty (206 BC–220 AD). Cai Lun, a eunuch who entered the service of the imperial palace and eventually rose to the rank of chief eunuch, is credited with the invention around the year 105 AD. Some sources indicate that paper had been invented earlier in the Han dynasty, but Cai Lun's achievement was the development of a technique that made the mass production of paper possible. This discovery was not the only paper-making accomplishment to come out of China; woodblock printing and, subsequently, movable type that facilitated typography and predated the Gutenberg printing press by about four centuries can also be traced back there. These two inventions, which occurred during the Tang (618–907 AD) and Song (96–1279 AD) dynasties, were also important technologies supporting production of paper money in large quantities.

Box 1.1 TIMELINE OF MAJOR DYNASTIES
AND GOVERNMENTS (QIN AND
LATER) IN CHINA

Qin dynasty:	221 BC–206 BC
Han dynasty:	206 BC–220 AD
Sui dynasty:	581–618
Tang dynasty:	618–907
Song dynasty:	960–1279
Yuan dynasty:	1260–1367
Ming dynasty:	1368–1644
Qing dynasty:	1644–1911
Republic of China:	1912–1949
(Kuomintang):	1928–1949
People's Republic:	1949–present

During the Tang dynasty, China began using a rudimentary form of paper money known as *Fei Qian*, which functioned essentially as certificates of deposit issued to merchants by deposit shops where the merchants left coins or goods as collateral. The name given to this money, which translates as "flying money," reflected the fact that it was printed on paper that, unlike metal coins, could be blown away by the wind. The name also signified the speed with which these certificates could be transported relative to metal coins. These certificates were tradable and accepted in some regions, but only in limited circulation.

It was three hundred years later, during the Song dynasty, that paper money came into widespread use. During the early period of that dynasty, modestly valued bronze coinage was in circulation as the principal form of money. However, the expanding scale of commerce in the Sichuan region and rising prosperity made it increasingly cumbersome and impractical to use these heavy coins for business transactions.

Around the tenth century, a type of banknote referred to as *Jiao Zi* (a rough translation is "exchangeable money") first appeared in Chengdu, the capital of Sichuan province. This currency was similar to the Tang dynasty's certificates of deposit. As the use of money permeated all levels of society and all spheres of economic activity, the rapidly growing demand for currency led to shortages known at the time as "currency famines" (*qianhuang*). Subsequently, a form of paper currency referred to as *Hui Zi* ("citadel money") was issued in 1160, but this time exclusively by the government, which had taken over from private deposit shops the role of issuing tradable currency. The Song court aggressively promoted the use of its currency, establishing several government-run factories to make paper money in the cities of Anqi, Chengdu, Hangzhou, and Huizhou. It is said these factories had large workforces by the standards of the time; records indicate that in the year 1175, the factory at Hangzhou employed more than a thousand workers.

MONETARY DEBATES IN ANCIENT CHINA

The Song government prohibited private issuance of currency on the grounds that only the government could ensure a reliable supply of a currency stable enough to support economic activity. This ruling, however, provoked controversy. The role of the state in issuing money had in fact been the subject of intense deliberation even during the Han dynasty, nearly a thousand years predating the Song, when only metallic money was in circulation. Those early discussions of the role of money in society and of who should have the prerogative of issuing it took place within the broader context of the "Salt and Iron Debates" of the Han era. These debates, held in the imperial court around 80 BC and featuring more than sixty scholars of various stripes and persuasions, focused largely on the role of the state relative to that of the private sector in managing the economy.

Many Confucian scholars at the time held that a state monopoly on the coinage of money was best avoided as it would allow the state to debase its own coin with impunity. As proponents of reduced state intervention in every aspect of the economy, they made the case that the market would compel private issuers of money to maintain its value, arguing "the sovereign provides for the people's welfare by not restricting the use of the natural resources of the mountains and the seas; he facilitates the use of currency by not prohibiting people from freely minting coin."

Government officials in charge of fiscal and financial matters were arrayed on the other side of the debate, enjoying the support of another set of scholars. This group contended that a state monopoly over the issuance of money was the best defense of sound money, which was seen as essential for economic prosperity. Even Sima Qian, a celebrated Chinese historian of the Han era and an ardent advocate of laissez-faire economic policies, argued that the issuance of money must remain a prerogative of the government. In his magnum opus entitled *Shi Ji* [Records of the Grand Historian]—covering almost three thousand years of history, written over twelve years, comprising some 520,000 Chinese characters, and written on about 21,000 bamboo slips (paper had not yet been invented)—Sima (in China, family names come first) used historical analogies to warn that allowing private citizens to "mint coins at will" would lead to manipulation of their value and related economic problems. Statesman Sang Hongyang defended the state's monopoly over coinage as follows: "If the currency system is unified under the emperor's control, the people will not serve two masters. If coin issues from the ruler, the people will have no doubts about whether it is genuine or not."

This Han–era debate was revived during the Song dynasty, although the government swept aside concerns about its paper currency monopoly by asserting that only it could ensure a stable ratio of value between metallic coin and paper currency.

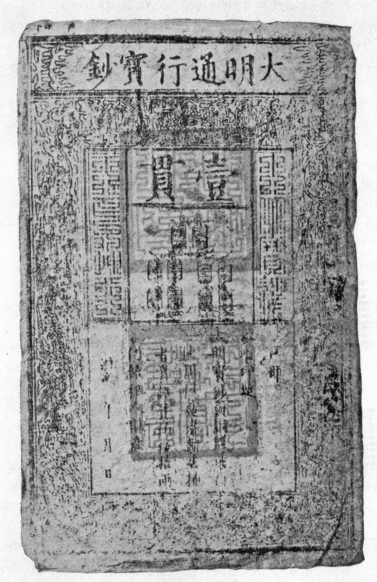

大明通行寶鈔

Bank-Note of the Ming Dynasty.   [*To face p.* 426.

Figure 1.3 Ming dynasty currency note.
The upper line shows the name of the banknote (*Da Ming Tong Xing Bao Chao*). The text in the middle block indicates that the note can be circulated in various provinces. The text in the bottom block states that counterfeiters of the note will be put to death; and that those who report counterfeiters to the authorities will be awarded 250 *tael* silver, along with the family property of the counterfeiters.

of the notes as merchants grew reluctant to accept them. Eventually, paper currency was abolished, with silver and coins becoming the only forms of payment acceptable for commercial transactions.

The Qing dynasty (1644–1911) resisted issuing paper money until 1853, when the government needed to raise substantial revenue to finance its efforts to suppress the Tai Ping Rebellion. This civil war lasted from 1850 to 1864 and ranks as one of the bloodiest in human history, with an estimated 20 million casualties. The currency notes issued by the Qing government during this period were backed by silver and bronze.

After the second Opium War (1856–1860), which China lost to Britain and France, various foreign governments set up banks in China's trading ports and issued their own banknotes. The Qing court initially did not resist these developments, but soon came to recognize that this represented, in effect, continued aggression by foreign powers. The nation's rights and interests were falling into the hands of foreigners, whose money was becoming the basis of commerce.

The eleventh emperor of the Qing dynasty, Guang Xu, eventually wrested monetary control from foreign governments. He approved the creation of a bank to be run by businessmen in Shanghai. The Tong Shang Bank (Commercial Bank of China) was established in 1897 and, the next year, it became the first modern bank to issue paper currency in China. The government then set up other banks as well to issue official banknotes, which made it difficult to maintain the stability of the monetary system while banknotes in various forms were being circulated simultaneously. To address this problem, in 1905 the Qing government set up a national bank in Beijing to regulate state finances and the monetary system more effectively. The Ta-Ching Government Bank was given the privilege of minting money, issuing paper money, and managing state funds. This ushered in some monetary stability, but only for a brief period.

A CURRENCY WAR

The 1911 revolution that swept the Qing dynasty out of power was followed by an extended period of turbulence in China's political and economic evolution. Provincial governments and financial institutions issued various paper currencies, with most of these enjoying, at best, limited acceptance.

In 1912, the Chinese Nationalist Party or Kuomintang, which had originally been conceived as a revolutionary league bent on overthrowing the monarchy, became a viable political party under the leadership of Sun Yat-sen. After Sun's death in 1925, Chiang Kai-shek took over the party's reins. By 1928, Chiang had succeeded in overpowering most regional warlords as well as the Communist Party, bringing most of China under the control of his government. In November 1928, the Kuomintang government established the Central Bank of China, with its headquarters in Shanghai, as the official national central bank. The bank was authorized to issue coins and banknotes, handle foreign exchange transactions, and issue government bonds. Various other private and government-owned banks' currencies circulated side by side. These currencies were backed by reserves of silver, i.e., the currency notes could be exchanged for silver at the banks that issued them. As worldwide silver prices rose in the latter half of 1934, legal and illegal exports of silver from China began to drain the reserves of banks. By early 1935, Chinese banks' silver reserves had shrunk markedly, depleting the national monetary base and pushing the country's financial markets to the brink of collapse.

In November 1935, the Kuomintang government implemented the "Fa Bi Reform," taking China off the silver standard and decreeing that only three banks could issue *Fa Bi* (legal tender). The Central Bank of China, the Bank of China, and the Bank of Communications were initially authorized to issue Fa Bi banknotes (Figure 1.4). The Bank of Agriculture, also known as the Farmers Bank, was subsequently added to this list, bringing to four the number of banks authorized to issue legal currency. To promote confidence in the currency, it was, in principle, made fully exchangeable into British pound sterling, which at the time was the dominant global reserve currency, as well as the U.S. dollar.

Meanwhile, Japan, which had invaded and occupied Manchuria in 1931, began to annex larger expanses of Chinese territory. The Japanese were eager to establish currency control as a tool for achieving economic dominance. In 1938, they set up the China

Figure 1.4 Kuomintang Fa Bi banknote.
Credit: Banknote printed by Waterlow & Sons Limited, London, for Central Bank of China. Scanned by Faka Handa, obtained through Creative Commons

Reserve Bank, which began to issue its own currency to compete with Fa Bi. In fact, some historians refer to the period of 1938 to 1941, when China Reserve Bank notes and Fa Bi were in direct competition, as a "currency war."

The convertibility of the Kuomintang's Fa Bi made them more widely accepted, giving them an edge over Reserve Bank notes. To counter this, Japan decreed that Fa Bi had to be exchanged for Reserve Bank notes in the territories it controlled; it then converted the Fa Bi it procured in this process into hard currencies through foreign banks operating in Shanghai. Facing possible erosion of the value of Fa Bi as the Shanghai banks started limiting such conversion to protect their hard currency reserves, the

Kuomintang government initially provided foreign exchange to the Shanghai banks to support its currency. This quickly drained the government's pound sterling and dollar reserves, weakening confidence in the currency. The Fa Bi was supported for a while with help from the British and U.S. governments, but the currency would not remain viable for long.

By 1941, the currency war between the Kuomintang government and the proxy government established in Nanjing by the Japanese, with Wang Jingwei as its head, had turned into an outright war of terror. In January 1941, the Nanjing authorities established the Central Reserve Bank, with a branch in Shanghai. This bank started issuing its own notes to compete with the Kuomintang's Fa Bi. Many Shanghai bankers were forced to cooperate with the Central Reserve Bank. Zhu Baoquan, a leading Shanghai banker, was asked to serve on its board. When he refused, he was kidnapped by agents of Wang's Nanjing government and held in captivity for ten days before he relented. A month later, Kuomintang agents attacked the Central Reserve Bank branch on the Bund in Shanghai with guns and homemade bombs, followed by assassination attempts against its officials (one of which was successful). The Nanjing government answered terror with terror, attacking pro-Kuomintang banks in Shanghai with hand grenades and executing some bank employees. In another incident, a bank building was dynamited, killing seven and wounding many more. This round was initially won by the Kuomintang, but it would prove to be a fleeting and Pyrrhic victory.

As the military conflict with Japan intensified, the Kuomintang government began printing money indiscriminately to finance military expenditures. The supply of Fa Bi shot up from about 1,400 million yuan in 1937 to 660,000 billion yuan in 1948. Needless to say, prices skyrocketed, multiplying—by one estimate—about 35 million times over this period, rendering Fa Bi worthless.

To counter the threat to the national economy of galloping inflation, the Kuomintang government issued gold yuan notes in 1948, ostensibly backed by gold. But, clearly, it had not learned much about monetary discipline. Within 10 months, there were 650,000 times more gold yuan notes in circulation, which could obviously not have been fully backed by the government's gold reserves. Despite government promises that the maximum denomination of these notes would be 100 yuan, denominations of 1 million gold yuan were in circulation within one year. Prices increased more than a millionfold during this period. Meanwhile, other provinces that had resisted the Japanese onslaught had begun issuing their own currencies called *Kangbi* (resistance notes) or *Bianbi* (border area notes). The end of Japanese influence, following Japan's surrender to Allied forces in 1945, did not unify these banknotes because by that time the revolutionary war between Chiang Kai-shek's Nationalists and the Communists was heating up.

THE RENMINBI APPEARS

A truce between the Nationalists and the Communists following Japan's surrender proved tenuous and brief, giving way to an all-out civil war that erupted in 1946. With stronger grassroots support and superior military organization, the Communists gradually began to gain the upper hand. As Communist control spread across China, a new currency, issued in banknote form only and denominated in yuan, was introduced. By the fall of 1948, most "liberated" areas had been unified under the control of Communist forces. On December 1, 1948, nearly one year before the People's Republic of China formally came into existence, the Communist Party of China (CPC) created a new institution called the People's Bank of China (PBC) to manage the country's monetary policy. Thus, the PBC became the country's central bank, similar to the Federal Reserve in the U.S. The PBC was formed through a merger of three banks: Beihai Bank, North China Bank (Huabei Bank), and Northwest China (Xibei) Peasant Bank. Its main location was initially in ShiJiaZhuang, the capital of Hebei Province, where Huabei Bank had been located.

Soon after its inception, the PBC began issuing its own currency, which was given the name *renminbi*—meaning, "the people's money." This designation was in keeping with the Communist fervor of the time, when everything was supposed to belong to "the people." At the same time, the PBC prohibited the circulation of foreign currencies, gold, and silver. It also swept away various banknotes issued during the Kuomintang government that remained in circulation, and called in currencies issued by other provinces. Upon the founding of the People's Republic of China in October 1949, the renminbi, henceforth generally abbreviated as "RMB" in this book, became China's sole legal currency.

There was a great clamor among the Communist Party leadership to see the portrait of Mao Zedong, regarded as the founding father of modern China, appear on the very first series of RMB banknotes issued by the PBC around early 1949. Mao rejected this. He is reported to have said, "Renminbi belongs to the entire nation. I am the President of the Communist Party, instead of the government, so it is inappropriate to print my portrait on the banknote." It was only in October 1949, upon the proclamation of the establishment of the People's Republic of China, that Mao became the

Figure 1.5 Chairman Mao Zedong announces the establishment of the People's Republic of China at Tiananmen Square, Beijing, on October 1, 1949. Dong Biwu is on his left (with hands clasped in front).
Credit: Pictures from History, Bridgeman Images

President of the Central People's Government (his formal title was changed to President of the People's Republic of China in 1954).

Dong Biwu was one of earliest leaders of the Communist Party and another of the founders of modern China (Figure 1.5). Like many of his comrades in the CPC leadership, including Mao himself, Dong had a keen interest in calligraphy and was considered to be highly skilled in this art. As the minister of finance and a skilled calligrapher, it was his responsibility to inscribe the characters for "People's Bank of China," which would appear at the top of all RMB currency notes. It is said he viewed his task as such a solemn and important one that he showered and put on new clothes before inscribing the six Chinese characters.

Mao was said to have been greatly excited when the first series of RMB was issued in 1948. He said "the Chinese people finally have their own army, their own regime, their own land, and now their own bank and currency! This is how a Republic mastered by the people should be."

Soon after the currency was issued, the *Renmin Daily* (the *People's Daily*) carried a front-page story emphasizing that the new currency represented a clean break from the Kuomintang regime:

> The unification of the currency this time is completely different from Jiang Jieshi's [Chiang Kai-shek's] currency reform. Jiang's goal was to inflate the currency so that the government could deprive its people, while the unification this time is to make our monetary system easier and more efficient, to promote the exchange of goods and materials, and to stimulate economic development. As a result, it contributes to the prosperity of the entire society. . . . Furthermore, holding the new renminbi, any person, at any time, in any market, can buy what they need.

There is a story that Deng Xiaoping, who was a key Party functionary at the time and would go on to become the paramount leader of China, went out for dinner with his colleagues Chen Yi and Luo Gengmo, the comrade in charge of the finance sector in Shanghai. They handed the new RMB to the vendor from whom they were purchasing food and asked, "Are you willing to receive this new currency?" The vendor was reportedly happy and responded: "I'm more than willing to receive this! Everyone wants this currency! Unlike the gold yuan note issued by Kuomintang, which could only be used as toilet paper, this currency has value so we can buy various goods with it." Such stories, whether apocryphal or not, were meant to instill confidence in the new currency and emphasize that the new government would not inflate away its value as so many regimes had done in the past.

When the People's Republic of China was formally established in 1949, Nan Hanchen, the governor of the PBC, is reported to have asked Mao again in person for his permission to include his portrait on RMB notes. Mao refused once more, apparently for two reasons: the first was that, throughout his life, Mao hated to touch money; second, Mao was firmly opposed to personality cults (which might strike contemporary readers, who are accustomed to seeing seemingly ubiquitous portraits of Mao in public spaces, as ironic), calling them "poisonous ideological survivals of the old society," and he stood firm in his commitment to collective leadership.

THE FACE OF THE RENMINBI

The first series of the currency consisted of denominations from 1 yuan up to 50,000 yuan. These large denominations became increasingly cumbersome for day-to-day use. In 1955, the new yuan, which was officially known as the RMB yuan, was introduced at the rate of 10,000 old yuan = 1 new yuan. This remains China's currency to this day. At that time, smaller denominations of the currency also appeared. One yuan is divided into 10 *jiao* and 1 jiao is in turn divided into 10 *fen*. The smallest denomination of the yuan is 1 fen, which may be considered the Chinese equivalent of the penny.

This second series of the currency consisted of denominations from 1 fen up to 10 yuan. The banknotes displayed the words "People's Bank of China" on the front of each note, and the denomination of the note in the Mongolian, Tibetan, and Uighur languages on the back. The Zhuang language was added to the third

Figure 1.6 Fourth series of RMB banknotes, first issued in 1987.

series that was issued, starting in 1962. This tradition of showing the denomination on the front of the note in Mandarin and on the back of the note in four other languages has continued to this day.

A fourth series of banknotes was first introduced in 1987. This set of currency notes displayed a variety of images. The 5 yuan note showed pictures of minorities, including a Tibetan woman and a Muslim man. The 50 yuan note featured images of an intellectual, a farmer, and an industrial worker. The 100 yuan note featured the profiles of four former Chinese leaders: Mao Zedong (who died in 1976), Zhou Enlai, Liu Shaoqi, and Zhu De (Figure 1.6).

In October 1999, during the celebrations staged to commemorate the fiftieth anniversary of the People's Republic of China, the PBC issued the fifth series of banknotes. Then, as described in the

Figure 1.7 Fifth series of RMB banknotes, first issued in 1999.
Credit: DnDavis

journal *Old Friend* (*Lao You*), "the Chinese people's long-lasting dream of putting Mao's portrait on the banknotes finally came true." Now every yuan note, whatever the denomination, bears the iconic full-face image of Mao Zedong.

An official from the Beijing bureau of printing indicated that, when the fifth series of banknotes was being designed, the portraits of historical figures such as Confucius, Li Bai, Yue Fei, and Li Shizhen were considered for the front side of the notes. However, it was decided that displaying a familiar image on banknotes could discourage counterfeiting, and what better image to accomplish this than the widely-recognized one of Mao (Figure 1.7). As one Chinese journal reports:

> There was an experiment showing that even for educated people, it is hard to tell the difference between Hua Mountain, Huang Mountain, Tai Mountain, and Heng Mountain. There are still many illiterate people in China, and there is a large literacy discrepancy among the population. But everyone recognizes Mao. So if Mao's portrait is shown on the banknote, it is easier for people to detect counterfeit money.

A ROSE BY ANY OTHER NAME?

Today you will find people discussing Chinese currency not just on the financial pages, but also in other sections of your daily paper and on television news shows. And no doubt you've noticed that some people refer to the currency as renminbi whereas others refer to it as *yuan*. In the previous section, I used both terms in describing the evolution of China's currency.

Is there a difference? These terms are often used interchangeably but they do not mean quite the same thing. Renminbi, which, as noted before, literally translates as "the people's money," is the name of the currency. The yuan is the unit of account for quoting prices.

If you happen to be at the Hong Qiao pearl market in Beijing and find yourself ensnared by an aggressive salesperson on the second floor, you will be offered, in broken English, a "genuine" Coach handbag for just 1,000 yuan (roughly 160 U.S. dollars). If you tear yourself away and head for the pearl shops on the third floor, a favored shopping destination for foreigners, your eager vendor will quickly drop the price to 300 yuan—a special price "just for you." It is unlikely you will hear the word renminbi.

The case is similar with "pound sterling," which is the name of Britain's currency. You will not see "pound sterling" on any of the signs at Marks and Spencer in London. If you happen to stop at a pub in Yorkshire for a pint or a few, the bartender will give you a tab denominated in pounds rather than sterling.

To make things more interesting and even more confusing, some people are accustomed to writing Chinese currency amounts in this manner: "RMB 100 million yuan." This is rather like writing "$10 dollars"—redundant, but harmless. Moreover, to add yet another layer of complexity, in colloquial usage *kuai* is often used in place of *yuan*. Expressing an item's price using kuai would be like saying "This costs 10 bucks" (or "quid," if you were in London rather than New York City).

The confusion about the name of the currency stems in part from popular media, where several styles have evolved as a matter of custom. *The Wall Street Journal* and newswire services such as Bloomberg and Reuters almost always use the word *yuan* when referring to Chinese currency. Searching for the word *yuan* on the *Journal*'s website for the period January 1 to December 31, 2015, yields 2,285 items. A search for the word renminbi over the same period yields only 149 items.

I once asked two *Journal* reporters about this and was told that their style guru had decided: "'Yuan' is what people know and our first choice, though 'renminbi' isn't banned." Similarly, *Bloomberg News* tends to use the word *yuan*. When a *Bloomberg* reporter uses the word renminbi, the article generally notes "it is another name for the Chinese currency."

The New York Times style guide suggests punting on the issue altogether. "In passing references, the Chinese terms can often be avoided altogether. Simply refer to China's currency, and give quantities in dollar equivalents." But then the guide adds, "When the name is necessary, use renminbi. . . . Generally confine *yuan* to quotations or to articles with multiple references to different quantities of renminbi. . . . Such cases may require a brief explanation that yuan is a shorthand reference to China's currency."

So *Wall Street Journal* readers know the yuan and need to be reminded of what the RMB is. *New York Times* readers know the RMB and need to be reminded of what the yuan is. No doubt all of this says something about the readers of these newspapers.

The style guide of *The Economist* magazine, after explaining the difference between the two terms, leaves no ambiguity about what its reporters should use: "Renminbi, which means the people's currency, is the description of the yuan, as sterling is the description of the pound. Use yuan." The *Financial Times* favors the use of renminbi over yuan by a six-to-one ratio. But *Financial Times* reporters seem to believe its readers are sophisticated enough to be able to shift back and forth between the two terms without further explanation.

In this book, I take the pedantic middle road of using renminbi, which as I have noted is generally abbreviated to RMB, as the name of the currency, while nevertheless using *yuan* when the occasion demands it.

In contrast, the dollar is just "dollar." My Australian and Canadian friends will no doubt object strenuously, noting that there is the

U.S. dollar, and then there are the Australian and Canadian dollars. In fact, there are 34 independent countries whose currency is named the "dollar," ranging from the Belize dollar to the Trinidad dollar, plus at least another six countries, including Ecuador and Panama, that use the U.S. dollar as their official currency.

In this case, I will be parochial, generally using the term *dollar* to refer to the U.S. dollar while explicitly identifying other types of dollars with the relevant country name.

No other country uses renminbi or yuan as the name of its currency. The old versions of the Japanese *yen* and Korean *won* were cognates of the yuan. All three words mean "round" (or circle) and originally shared the same Chinese character. In modern form, the characters for the three currencies are now written differently. Interestingly, the currency symbol for the yen and the yuan is the same: ¥. Perhaps surprisingly, the word *yuan* did not originate in the Yuan dynasty. In fact, coins known as *yuan qian* ("round money") existed as early as the third to fifth centuries BC, predating the Yuan dynasty by some sixteen centuries.

We have traced the origins of Chinese paper currency back to the seventh century and followed it through to its latest incarnation, with most of the developments described so far being relevant primarily to the Chinese economy. Since 1999, when the latest series of RMB was issued, the more interesting aspect of the currency's evolution has been its rising prominence in global trade and finance. Before analyzing the currency's evolution over the past two decades, it is important that we understand several salient concepts. We therefore shift from history to economics in the next chapter.

To borrow Marco Polo's subtle segue at the end of one of the chapters in his book, "Let us now change the subject."

CHAPTER 2

Currency Concepts

<blockquote>

Pointy-haired boss to Wally:	Our CEO wants to promote you to chief economist because nothing you say makes sense. He thinks that's the sign of a great economist. . . .
[Next day]	Our new chief economist, Wally, will tell us what to expect in the coming quarter.
Wally:	The exchange rate on derivatives will trigger a bubble in monetary policy and deflate the yen.
CEO:	I totally understand that and have no questions.
Pointy-haired boss:	Wow, he's good.

Dilbert comic strip, Scott Adams

</blockquote>

Currencies play into national psyches in complicated ways. They symbolize a country's strength or help it wield power in economic warfare. Debasing a currency's value by increasing the supply of money, which tends to generate inflation and erode the currency's purchasing power, is certainly not a sign of a well-functioning government with sound economic policies. In international trade and finance, however, the issue is not quite as simple, for it is not just the domestic value of a currency but also its value in world markets that matters. And here the opposite principles sometimes apply. Trying to cheapen a domestic currency's value relative to that of other currencies can actually help boost exports and, therefore, offset weak domestic demand and raise GDP growth.

The exchange rate—the international price of a currency—is a central element of that currency's role in global financial markets. Exchange rates can be confusing. I recall my PhD thesis supervisor at the University of Chicago, Robert Lucas, once mentioning in class that he often got exchange rates all mixed up. Lucas went on to win the Nobel Prize in economics in 1995, so how can the rest of us possibly hope to keep exchange rates straight? Lucas, of course, had his own elegant solution to the problem—writing a path-breaking academic paper on the subject so he could finally pin things down.

Writing a path-breaking research paper is not a widely available option, so let us instead take a short detour into the world of currency dynamics and exchange rates before plunging ahead with our discussion of the RMB.

A BRIEF PRIMER

The exchange rate is the price of a domestic currency relative to that of a foreign currency. This price is usually expressed as the number of units of the domestic currency needed to buy a unit of the foreign currency. The RMB–dollar exchange rate, now one of the most carefully scrutinized exchange rates, was 6.6 yuan per dollar in June 2016. Of course, the RMB has a bilateral exchange rate against every other currency as well.

The laws of supply and demand apply to currencies just as they do to apples and oranges. Indeed, because an exchange rate is a relative price, calculating an exchange rate does involve comparing apples to oranges, figuratively speaking. When the demand for a currency increases, its price rises. So when the RMB exchange rate moves from 6 yuan per dollar to 5 yuan per dollar, the RMB has become more expensive relative to the dollar. This appreciation in the RMB's value means that it takes fewer yuan to buy one dollar. Or, reciprocally, each yuan can now be exchanged for more dollars ($0.20 rather than $0.17).

Appreciation of a domestic currency—an increase in its value relative to those of other currencies—is good for consumers.

It makes foreign goods cheaper, raising the overall purchasing power of household incomes. In the above example, a Chinese tourist in New York City can now reserve a $400 hotel room in New York City for 2,000 yuan (at the rate of 5 yuan per dollar) rather than 2,400 yuan (at the rate of 6 yuan per dollar)—a nice discount.

There is, however, a downside to currency appreciation. Cheap imports from abroad hurt domestic producers, because they must choose between cutting prices to stay competitive and losing market share. Exporters find their profit margins shrinking when measured by the domestic currency; they, too, face the threat of losing market share for their products.

Consider a Chinese textile manufacturer who charges $10 (60 yuan) for a dress that is then shipped to the U.S. and sold at a Gap store in Manhattan for $75. If the RMB appreciates from 6 yuan per dollar to 5 yuan per dollar and the manufacturer keeps the export price of the dress at $10, her revenue drops from 60 yuan to 50 yuan. Since she cannot cut her worker's wages without hurting morale and, possibly, reducing worker productivity, and the interest she pays to the bank for her working capital remains the same, her profits shrink. She could raise her prices, but this would make her goods less competitive if there were alternatives from Bangladesh or Vietnam to which Gap could turn instead.

Exchange rates can be confusing and even knowledgeable people can struggle to put the right figures in the denominator and the numerator. One reason is the counterintuitive notion that a currency appreciates in value when the exchange rate declines (i.e., fewer units of a domestic currency are needed to buy a unit of a foreign currency). Currency talk can be even more complicated when foreign exchange traders follow conventions according to which the domestic currency's exchange rate is, in fact, *not* quoted in the traditional way (domestic currency per unit of foreign currency), but instead is quoted the other way around. The RMB–dollar rate is almost always referred to in terms of yuan per dollar whereas the pound sterling–dollar rate is generally quoted in dollars per pound.

A stronger currency is usually correlated with the strength of the domestic economy. In the long run, a currency's exchange rate tends to be driven by a country's productivity growth relative to productivity growth in its major trading partner countries. Higher productivity growth in the home country strengthens its currency. But this empirical relationship, which is predicted by a standard theoretical economic model, holds only over periods of a decade or longer. Over shorter time horizons, other factors such as capital flows, interest rates, and business cycle conditions can affect exchange rates. Moreover, since an exchange rate is the relative price of a financial variable (a country's currency), its value may also be determined by speculative forces that are not always anchored in economic fundamentals.

During the 2000s, when the Chinese economy was growing rapidly, it received large, private capital inflows. China also ran trade surpluses; it was exporting considerably more goods and services to other countries than it was importing from the rest of the world. When money comes into an economy either because of export earnings or investment flows from foreign investors, there is greater demand for the domestic currency. Exporters have to pay their workers' wages and suppliers' bills using the domestic currency. So, the Chinese textile exporter referenced earlier takes the dollars she receives from Gap and gets her bank to exchange them for RMB in the foreign exchange market. The same is true for investment projects; building materials, labor, and land all have to be paid for in the domestic currency. Hence, when domestic exporters and foreign investors bring money into China, demand for the RMB increases, driving up its price.

To offset currency appreciation, China's central bank, the PBC (Figure 2.1), can intervene in foreign exchange markets. This involves selling the domestic currency and buying "hard" currencies—currencies that are easy to trade and are widely accepted around the world—such as U.S. dollars. By selling the domestic currency, the PBC increases its supply to offset the

Figure 2.1 Beijing headquarters of the People's Bank of China, China's central bank.
Credit: AP Photo/Mark Schiefelbein

higher level of demand. This is not difficult to do because the PBC can, after all, print as much RMB as it needs to sell. Such an "intervention" in the foreign exchange market limits domestic currency appreciation and therefore improves a country's trade balance by limiting imports and propping up exports.

Following such foreign exchange market intervention operations, the PBC has to find safe and liquid (i.e., easily tradable) investments where it can park its foreign currency purchases. Investments that satisfy these criteria are typically government bonds issued by major advanced economies such as the U.S., the eurozone, Japan, the U.K., and Switzerland. These investments constitute a country's foreign exchange reserves. A country's reserve assets can include other liquid assets such as gold, but foreign exchange reserves now account for about 98 percent of China's total international reserves.

Foreign exchange market intervention can work in the other direction as well—to prevent a currency's value from depreciating. Although currency depreciation helps a country's exporters, it makes imports more expensive. For a country that depends heavily on imports, a sharp depreciation can be a problem. To offset such a depreciation, a country can sell its foreign exchange reserves and buy up its own currency, thereby driving up demand for its currency and stabilizing its price.

Managing a currency's value is a tricky business. Since the major currencies such as the dollar, the euro, and the yen trade freely among themselves, the RMB's value can be managed only against one of these currencies. China has long chosen to manage the RMB's value mainly against the dollar. Thus, the RMB's value rises and falls relative to the euro in tandem with the dollar's own movements against the euro. Similarly, the RMB's movements against the Japanese yen largely parallel the dollar's movements against that currency. China's decision is not unusual; most countries that manage their currencies, especially those in Asia, tend to use their own currency's value relative to the dollar as the benchmark—an indication of the dollar's importance in global finance.

The RMB–dollar exchange rate receives a great deal of attention within and outside China. From an economic perspective, however, it is an incomplete and sometimes even misleading measure of the currency's value. After all, the U.S. accounts for only about 18 percent of Chinese merchandise exports (goods). China's exporters do not benefit greatly if the RMB's value falls relative to the dollar yet rises relative to other major currencies. This is exactly what happened in the first half of 2015. With the U.S. economic recovery strengthening while other economies, especially Europe and Japan, remained weak, the dollar strengthened against virtually every other major currency in the world. The RMB rose along with the dollar. So, a mild depreciation of the RMB's value relative to the dollar still left the RMB stronger than all the other currencies, which meant that China's exporters were losing price competitiveness in about four-fifths of their export markets.

In principle, what really matters for keeping China's export prices and the domestic cost of its imports competitive depends on how much of China's trade is accounted for by each of its major trading partners and how the value of its currency moves against the currencies of each of those other countries. About 14 percent of China's overall merchandise trade (exports and imports of goods) is with the U.S., so that is a rough measure of how much the RMB–dollar exchange rate could directly affect the Chinese economy.

The trade-weighted *effective* exchange rate is designed to capture the change in the RMB's value in a more comprehensive manner. The effective exchange rate is an index that shows the evolution of China's currency against the currencies of all of its major trading partners, with each of those partner countries weighted by their respective shares of China's trade. Using this measure, then, the RMB–dollar rate has a weight of 14 percent to 18 percent in the index (depending on exactly which concept of trade—exports or the sum of exports and imports—is used in the calculations) whereas the RMB–euro rate has a weight of about 16 percent. These weights have shifted over time as China's trade patterns have changed. In 2000, the U.S. accounted for 16 percent of China's merchandise trade, compared to 14 percent in 2015.

The effective exchange rate described above is based on nominal exchange rates, such as RMB per dollar or RMB per euro. Hence, it is referred to as the trade-weighted nominal effective exchange rate (NEER).

The purchasing power of a currency can, of course, be affected by inflation. The NEER can be modified to take into account inflation rates in China relative to those of its trading partner countries. Economists have therefore created another index called the *real effective exchange rate* (REER) that does just that. The REER for China is a measure of trade-weighted bilateral exchange rates adjusted by a measure of the price level in China relative to a similarly weighted average of price levels in trading partner countries.

In an attempt to make these measures easier and more intuitive to interpret, institutions such as the International Monetary Fund (IMF) and the Bank for International Settlements (BIS) that calculate them have decided that increases in the NEER and REER should represent appreciation. This is in contrast to regular exchange rates, with respect to which a lower number (fewer units of domestic currency per unit of foreign currency) indicates appreciation.

Trade-weighted measures of the RMB's value, either the NEER or the REER, show that it has appreciated even more sharply over the past decade relative to the currencies of its trading partners compared with its appreciation relative to the U.S. dollar alone. This is because, since the global financial crisis, the dollar has strengthened significantly relative to other major currencies such as the euro and the Japanese yen. So an appreciation of the RMB relative to the dollar (over the past decade, notwithstanding the RMB's modest depreciation against the dollar since 2014) translates into even greater appreciation relative to the euro and the yen. Thus, concepts such as the NEER and the REER are of more than just academic interest because they have implications for the patterns of international trade.

To understand how China manages its exchange rate, at least relative to the dollar, we must look more closely at the trading system on which currency values are determined.

ONSHORE AND OFFSHORE EXCHANGE RATES

In April 1994, the PBC set up an interbank currency market, the China Foreign Exchange Trading System (CFETS), with headquarters in Shanghai, to facilitate currency trading on the Mainland. The CFETS initially had a trading system that focused mainly on the RMB–dollar exchange rate but has since expanded, with a broad range of foreign currency trading introduced in 2005. As of June 2016, fifteen currency pairs involving the RMB and another nine currency pairs not involving the RMB (such as dollar–euro and dollar–yen) could be traded on the CFETS.

Initially, the CFETS had only a small set of state-owned banks as market participants, making it easier for the PBC to manage the RMB–dollar exchange rate. In fact, many of these banks used to net out transactions between their own clients (some of whom wanted to sell dollars and buy RMB, and others of whom wanted to do the opposite). As a result, the number of trades actually executed between banks in the open market was quite low.

The system has been opened up considerably over the years, although it remains under the control of the PBC. In June 2016 there were 30 banking institutions, about one-third of them foreign owned, serving as market makers in the spot markets. Market makers serve the essential function of providing liquidity to a market. This means that, at any time during the trading day, these institutions post a bid and ask price for each currency pair traded on the CFETS and stand ready to fill a minimum number of buy or sell orders at those prices. The number of institutions licensed to trade on the CFETS is much larger than just this set of market makers, standing at more than five hundred in June 2016, with about one hundred of these being foreign-funded institutions.

The official value of the RMB is determined on this onshore market, where the currency's trading symbol is "CNY." However, there is also an offshore market where the RMB can be traded. These trades take place mostly on the Hong Kong Interbank Market. The RMB's trading symbol on this market is "CNH." The offshore market grew out of necessity to accommodate the demand for RMB trading before the CFETS was set up, and it continues to flourish because it is not subject to the tight control of Mainland authorities.

The onshore market is subject to the Mainland's capital account restrictions; therefore, the RMB's value on that market falls more squarely under the PBC's control. In contrast to the CNY (onshore) market, the CNH (offshore) market is not subject to direct official control or intervention. Consequently, at times the RMB has been worth more or less in the offshore markets compared with the onshore markets. When there is a strong demand for the RMB that the PBC tries to resist by intervening in the onshore market, the RMB exchange rate on the offshore market can be higher. Of course, such discrepancies tend not to last very long since financial market participants immediately jump in to try to make money by exploiting any such differential. Restricting capital flows makes it harder to exploit such differentials.

The CNY and CNH exchange rates relative to the dollar have moved in lockstep for much of the time since the end of 2010, reflecting the rising integration of China's onshore and offshore financial markets. Before this, RMB-related activities in the offshore market were quite limited, which contributed to a marked deviation of the CNH exchange rate from that of the CNY; the RMB was typically more valuable offshore.

THE INTERNATIONAL ROLES OF A CURRENCY

There is a great deal of hyperbole surrounding the RMB, with some commentators going so far as to argue that its displacement of the dollar as the dominant global currency is imminent. Before evaluating these claims, it is important first to clarify a few relevant concepts. Popular discussions of the RMB's emergence on the international stage tend to conflate three related but distinct aspects of a currency's role in international finance.

The first concept that pertains to a currency's international role is that of *capital account openness*. This term refers to the degree to which inflows and outflows of financial capital, which are intermediated through transactions involving the RMB on one side and various foreign currencies on the other, are restricted. A country with no restrictions on cross-border capital flows is said to have a fully open capital account.

Most countries in the world are members of the IMF, an international organization whose primary purpose is to ensure the stability of the international monetary system—the system of exchange rates and international payments that enables countries (and their citizens) to conduct business with each other. The IMF has 189 members who have all signed on to a charter stating they will not place any restrictions on the cross-border flows of payments related to trade transactions. This concept is referred to as *current account convertibility*—that is, the absence of restrictions on exchanging a domestic currency for foreign currencies, or vice versa, to pay for trade transactions. International trade transactions are recorded in the "current account" of a country's balance of payments, which accounts for the phrase *current account convertibility*.

Several decades ago, most flows of money across borders were, in some form or another, related to trade. China's exports of footwear and textiles to the U.S. would result in a flow of dollars from

U.S. importers to Chinese exporters. In today's world, financial transactions that have nothing to do with trade have become much more important. When a U.S. investor buys stock in a Chinese company listed on the Shanghai stock exchange or when a Chinese resident buys an apartment in San Francisco, that is a purely financial transaction that is not directly connected to trade.

Free conversion of currencies for transactions that are financial in nature is referred to as *capital account convertibility*. The capital account is the other side of the balance of payments, the first being the current account.

The IMF does not mandate capital account convertibility as a condition of membership. Most advanced economies have fully open capital accounts, so there are few restrictions on money coming into or leaving an economy, whether that is the result of domestic or foreign investor activity. In contrast, many emerging market economies such as China and India still maintain some controls on capital account transactions. Such countries do not have capital account convertibility.

The second concept relevant to understanding a currency's role in international finance is that of *internationalization*. This term refers to a currency's use in denominating and settling cross-border trade and financial transactions—that is, its use as an international medium of exchange.

Consider a widely traded commodity such as oil. Virtually all contracts for oil trading are denominated—that is, priced—in U.S. dollars. When an oil-producing country such as Saudi Arabia or Venezuela sells oil in world markets, the purchasers usually settle—that is, make payment on—those contracts in dollars. In principle, of course, the currency used to settle a trade contract can differ from the currency used to denominate that contract, but this is not often the case.

Some currencies are used more widely than others for settling trade transactions. When Argentina wants to import oil, foreign exporters typically demand payment in dollars rather than Argentine pesos because those pesos cannot be used as easily around the world as dollars, and because there is less confidence in the value of the Argentine peso. Where does Argentina turn to obtain dollars to pay for its imports? The country earns dollars when it sells soybeans and corn to foreign importers or when foreign investors buy stocks traded on the Buenos Aires stock exchange.

The denomination and settlement of purely financial transactions is now a more relevant aspect of a currency's internationalization. When a U.S. investor buys shares in Alibaba or Tencent on the Shanghai stock exchange, or when Walmart builds a store or a distribution center in China, these activities result in purely financial flows that are not connected directly to any trade transactions. Similarly, complex financial derivative contracts traded in London that can be purchased by both Chinese and U.S. investors, Yahoo's investment in the Chinese e-commerce company Alibaba, or the Chinese company Anbang Insurance Group's purchase of New York's iconic Waldorf Astoria hotel have no direct connection to trade. Even these financial contracts often have to be priced and settled in some currency, which is another aspect of what makes a currency international.

The third concept relevant to the analysis of a currency's international role is that of a *reserve currency*. This term refers to a currency that is held by foreign central banks as protection against balance of payments crises, which occur when a country runs out of internationally accepted currencies to meet its foreign debt obligations or to finance imports. Foreign currency reserves are typically accumulated through foreign exchange market intervention, as described earlier. The U.S. barely holds any such reserves because its currency is accepted around the world. The dollar's widespread acceptance means that U.S. consumers have no fear that other countries will refuse to sell them goods and services unless those consumers can pay in some currency other than the dollar. Moreover, the U.S. rarely intervenes in foreign exchange markets, allowing the value of the dollar to be determined by market forces.

In contrast, even advanced economies such as Japan and the eurozone maintain sizable foreign exchange reserves because their central banks often intervene in foreign exchange markets to prevent the value of their currencies from rising. Since euros and yen are widely accepted around the world, these economies do not use these reserves primarily for economic protection against crises. A country such as India, on the other hand, worries that it might have to reduce its oil imports drastically if foreign investors were to pull their money out of the country. For India, accumulating foreign exchange reserves through exchange market intervention not only helps prevent the currency from appreciating, but also buys protection from the fickleness of foreign investors.

Since the value of the dollar is not stable, countries that have considerable stocks of international reserves usually diversify their stocks with several reserve currencies. In recent decades, the world's major reserve currencies have been the dollar, the euro, the British pound sterling, and the yen. Some other reserve currencies, such as the Swiss franc and the Australian and Canadian dollars, account for a small fraction of global reserves. A country such as Japan would obviously not have financial assets denominated in its own currency, the Japanese yen, as part of its international reserves. Buying up assets in its own currency would drive up demand for yen, causing its value to appreciate. This would defeat the purpose of foreign exchange market intervention to keep the value of the yen from rising.

The three concepts discussed in this chapter are distinct but related. Their interrelationships are useful to keep in mind, even though the evolution of the RMB along each of these dimensions is explored in separate chapters.

A currency's international use differs from its convertibility (the openness of its home country's capital account) and neither is a necessary or sufficient condition for the other. That is, a country may have an open capital account but its currency may not play a prominent role in international finance. By the same token, the presence of a significant international currency does not necessarily imply that the country issuing that currency has an open capital account. The RMB is a prime example of a currency that is being used increasingly in international transactions, although China keeps capital flows restricted.

An additional wrinkle in all this is that a fully open capital account does not necessarily imply a freely floating market-determined exchange rate. Hong Kong, for instance, has an open capital account, but its currency is, in effect, pegged to the U.S. dollar at a fixed rate. Therefore, market forces have no role in determining the level of the exchange rate between the Hong Kong dollar and the U.S. dollar.

All these conditions—capital account convertibility, a floating exchange rate, and internationalization—are, in principle, necessary for a currency to become a reserve currency. China, of course, does not play by conventional rules. It has taken a unique approach to each aspect of the RMB's role in global finance, starting with capital account opening. The results have been dramatic and surprising.

CHAPTER 3
Capital Account Opening

> Freud tells us to blame our parents for all the shortcomings of our
> life, and Marx tells us to blame the upper class of our society. But
> the only one to blame is oneself. That's the helpful thing about the
> Indian idea of karma. Your life is the fruit of your own doing. You
> have no one to blame but yourself.
>
> *The Power of Myth*, Joseph Campbell

apital account openness is gauged by the degree of freedom or
the ease with which foreign and domestic investors can move
financial capital into or out of a country. By this definition, most
advanced economies have operated mostly open capital accounts
for at least two or three decades. Emerging market economies, in
contrast, mostly have not. This situation is changing fast, and many
of these economies now have relatively open capital accounts.
Importantly, though, the two major economies that continue to
impose significant capital controls are China and India.

On paper, China still places a large number of restrictions on the
free flow of capital across its borders. The gatekeeper for China's capital account is the State Administration of Foreign Exchange (SAFE),
which is an arm of the PBC. From 2009 to 2015, the SAFE was headed
by Yi Gang, a monetary policy expert who is now a deputy governor
of the PBC (he held that rank even while heading the SAFE) (Figure
3.1). Yi Gang is one of the most thoughtful policymakers in China and
an academic at heart; during his initial years working at the PBC, he
continued to teach and advise students at Peking University. Under

Figure 3.1 Yi Gang, Deputy Governor of the People's Bank of China and former head of the State Administration of Foreign Exchange.
Credit: Imaginechina via AP Images

his guidance, China's capital account has become increasingly open. The process has continued under Pan Gongsheng, the new head of the SAFE (since January 2016) and also a deputy governor of the PBC. China has gone about the process in its own unique way, making it harder to interpret the results using just conventional metrics.

HOW OPEN IS CHINA'S CAPITAL ACCOUNT?

Two factors determine how open a country's capital account is to inflows and outflows. The first is related to legal requirements on flows, which can range from simple registration or reporting stipulations to more severe restrictions on certain types of flows. Such restrictions are called *capital controls*. For instance, visitors or U.S. citizens coming into the U.S. from abroad must declare at the border if they are carrying $10,000 or more in cash. This is an administrative reporting requirement. In contrast, a capital control applies, for example, when China restricts foreign investments into its equity markets or when India restricts foreign investors' purchases of domestic firms in certain sectors or prevents those investors from setting up new firms in those sectors.

The second factor that determines capital account openness is less about regulations than about the reality on the ground. Although there may be formal capital controls on the books, the strictness of enforcement can vary, and how strictly such controls are enforced affects whether capital moves more or less freely across borders. On the other hand, the strictness of capital controls tells only part of the story. A country may have a fully open capital account but foreign investors, despite the lack of restrictions, may have no interest in that country, perhaps because of political instability or a volatile economy. Hence, to fully understand capital account openness we must understand how it operates both in *principle* and in *reality*.

I refer to these concepts as *de jure* and *de facto financial openness*. De jure financial openness reflects the extent of legal restrictions on the flow of financial capital. De facto financial openness measures how much an economy is actually integrated into global financial markets.

De Jure Financial Openness

De jure measures of capital account openness typically rely on binary indicators from the IMF's *Annual Report on Exchange Arrangements and Exchange Restrictions* (AREAER). These binary measures reflect the presence of restrictions on many categories of inflows and outflows. Such measures change only when there is a relatively major policy shift related to specific capital account items. The AREAER indicates that, as of 2014, China placed restrictions of some sort in fourteen of fifteen broad categories of capital inflows and in fifteen of sixteen categories of capital outflows.

Conventional measures of de jure financial openness constructed using the AREAER data show little, if any, change in China's policy during the past decade. For example, a widely cited index devised by Menzie Chinn of the University of Wisconsin and Hiro Ito of Portland State University has registered almost no change in

China's de jure openness since 1993. The index, which is based on a statistical procedure that aggregates information from multiple categories covered by the AREAER, ranges from 2.4 (most financially open) to –1.9 (least financially open). A higher value corresponds to a greater degree of de jure capital account openness.

The major advanced economies—such as the U.S., the U.K., and Japan—have the same index value of 2.4, which is the maximum and indicates a fully open capital account. In contrast, the value of this index for China in 2013 (the latest year for which these data are available) was –1.2, the same as India but well below the average of –0.2 for emerging market economies. China's index jumped from –1.9 to –1.2 in 1993 and has not changed since then. This value indicates a relatively closed capital account characterized by capital controls that are, on paper, extensive and stringent.

De Facto Financial Openness

We can also evaluate an economy's financial openness by analyzing de facto measures of integration into global financial markets. Economists use the sum of imports and exports, expressed either in overall dollar amounts or as a percentage of national GDP, to measure an economy's openness to international trade. An analogous measure of financial openness that has come to be used widely in the academic literature involves adding an economy's external assets and its external liabilities—a measure that one can express either in levels or as a ratio to GDP.

External assets in China's case comprise the total foreign assets of Chinese households, corporations, financial institutions, and the government. External liabilities comprise the total value of foreign investments in China, along with financial obligations (such as debt) of Chinese households, corporations, and the government to foreign entities. These assets and liabilities together constitute China's international investment position (IIP), which is essentially a country's balance sheet in relation to those of the rest of the world. Over the past decade, both assets and liabilities have risen sharply—China now has $6.2 trillion in foreign assets and $4.6 trillion in foreign liabilities (see Figure 3.2).

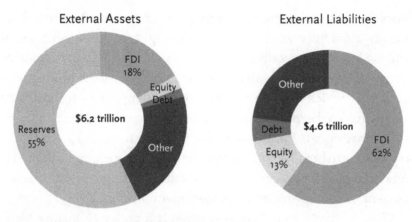

Figure 3.2 China's external assets and liabilities.
Data shown here are for the end of 2015.
Source: The State Administration of Foreign Exchange.

China's gross external position, the sum of its external assets and liabilities, has grown rapidly. At almost $11 trillion, it is roughly six times larger than it was just a decade ago. This figure exceeds the gross external positions of other key emerging markets as well as that of Switzerland. One can also measure the size of a country's external position relative to the size of its economy. The ratio of China's gross external assets plus liabilities to GDP is now about 100 percent. Measured by this ratio, China lags behind the traditional reserve currency economies such as Japan, the U.K., and the U.S. in financial openness, although it comes in ahead of most other emerging markets.

A closer examination of China's IIP reveals many striking features. The structure of external liabilities, representing the stock of foreigners' investments and other assets in China, is quite distinctive. Foreign direct investment (FDI) accounts for 62 percent of China's external liabilities, a higher fraction than in most other emerging market economies. Portfolio equity liabilities, which represent foreign investors' ownership of stocks in China, amount to only 13 percent of external liabilities. Portfolio debt and other investments (which typically represent bank loans and trade credit) account for the remaining 25 percent.

China's external balance sheet reflects how the capital account was managed in the past. The government welcomed FDI, often seen as the most favorable type of capital inflows. Inward FDI typically involves substantial investment in a new or existing domestic firm, ranging from full ownership to a smaller equity stake but with a controlling interest (typically at least 10 percent of a company's tradable shares). FDI investors have an incentive to increase the productivity of firms in which they are investing by bringing in new technologies and managerial expertise as well as better corporate governance and risk management. This raises the bar for other firms in a given industry, leading to broader spillover effects of FDI. For example, domestic retail chains have adopted some of Walmart China's product development, sales, and inventory management practices.

China's government has also made it a policy to ensure technological spillovers from foreign to domestic manufacturers. In September 2015, Boeing trumpeted a massive order of three hundred jets by China. The deal included Boeing's investment in a jet completion center in China, along with an agreement to build a parts manufacturing center there. The agreement also required Boeing to allow Chinese firms to cooperate in manufacturing the jets. Similarly, in the mid 2000s, Siemens of Germany and Kawasaki of Japan invested in Chinese state-owned train manufacturing companies, collaborating in the production of high-speed trains and transferring technology to those companies. Now the Chinese companies are exporting their own high-speed bullet trains, competing with German and Japanese manufacturers.

For a number of years, the Chinese government welcomed FDI not just by cutting red tape and bureaucracy, but also by using more direct economic incentives. The income tax rate on firms funded through FDI was about half the rate faced by domestically funded firms (15 percent vs. 33 percent). This large differential was an open invitation to Chinese entrepreneurs to exploit it. A significant amount of Chinese investment was "round-tripped" through foreign channels, especially Hong Kong, to take advantage of this tax differential. That is, Chinese entrepreneurs would find ways to move money to Hong Kong and then bring it back in as foreign investment. In 2008, the differential in income tax rates that favored FDI over domestically financed investment was removed, but China continues to have an open-door policy regarding FDI investment. With its economy—especially the size and income levels of the middle class—expanding rapidly, there has been no dearth of foreign investors eager to pour FDI into China.

With the exception of FDI, however, the Chinese government has viewed other types of capital inflows with disfavor. Having seen many other emerging market economies encounter trouble because their corporations borrowed too heavily from foreign lenders, the government severely restricted Chinese corporations' ability to borrow from foreign lenders. This explains why the country's external debt level is low (about 13 percent of GDP in 2015).

The government was also not keen on seeing foreign investors participate in China's fledgling stock markets for fear that they might increase volatility. The stock market in China is split into the A-share and B-share markets. There are two main stock exchanges in China—Shanghai and Shenzhen—and these two classes of shares trade on both markets. A-shares are denominated in RMB and, until 2002, foreign investors could not purchase these shares. B-shares have a face value in RMB but are listed for trading primarily to foreign investors in foreign currency (in U.S. dollars on the Shanghai exchange and in Hong Kong dollars on the Shenzhen exchange). Local Chinese companies can issue both types of shares, although B-shares tend to trade at a discount relative to the same company's A-shares. This is, in part, due to the A-share market's much larger trading volumes.

In 2001, the B-share market was opened to domestic investors with foreign currency accounts. Since 2002, foreign investors have had access to the A-share market, although this access has been limited until recently, a point discussed later in this chapter. (With government approval, Chinese companies can also list on the Hong Kong exchange, where their share prices are quoted in Hong Kong dollars. These instruments are called H-shares.)

The structure of China's external assets is also revealing. Foreign exchange reserves account for 55 percent of the country's external assets. In the period just before the global financial crisis, this share was even higher—amounting to nearly two-thirds of external assets—because the government was wary of private capital outflows, so it had imposed a number of restrictions on individuals' and corporations' ability to move money out of the country. This policy was motivated in part by a desire to protect the domestic banking system. The country has traditionally had a high savings rate, evidenced by massive household and corporate deposits. These deposits have provided a cheap and captive source of funds for the state-owned banking system, and the government has been keen to support these banks.

Outward FDI, representing Chinese companies' substantial direct investments in foreign companies, accounts for 18 percent of external assets, up from barely 5 percent a decade ago. In recent years, Chinese corporations have been expanding into foreign countries, buying up foreign firms and setting up their own subsidiaries. China's total FDI abroad now tops $1.1 trillion. Chinese households have had little opportunity to diversify their savings portfolios by investing in foreign equities or bonds, leaving China's external assets in portfolio equity and debt modest, at less than $300 billion in 2015.

The data analyzed so far indicate the occurrence of some important changes in the size and structure of China's external balance sheet. But, since this balance sheet represents stocks rather than flows, it changes relatively slowly. There are even bigger changes on the way as China frees up restrictions on capital flows.

WHY LIBERALIZE THE CAPITAL ACCOUNT?

It is worth pausing at this juncture to consider why China is liberalizing its capital account. After all, a more open capital account exposes an economy to the fickleness of foreign investors. China has not needed foreign capital flows for its development because it has a high national saving rate. Indeed, through its massive accumulation of foreign exchange reserves, China has in fact been exporting some of its savings to the rest of the world. And when it comes to such capital outflows, surely it seems safer for the government to manage them. So why open the capital account?

A conceptual framework that Ayhan Kose of the World Bank, Kenneth Rogoff of Harvard University, Shang-Jin Wei of Columbia

University, and I developed when we were all at the IMF may help to make sense of China's approach to capital account policies. Standard economic models posit that open capital accounts should allow capital-poor developing countries to obtain foreign financing, invest more heavily in physical capital such as plants, machinery, and infrastructure, and thereby grow faster. In earlier work, the four of us had found that the empirical evidence was not consistent with this view. Developing economies that borrowed more heavily from abroad did not grow more rapidly than those that did not depend as much on foreign finance. Moreover, many researchers at the time were making the case that more capital account openness simply exposed developing economies to greater capital flow volatility and even to crises related to overborrowing.

We did agree with many skeptics of capital account liberalization on one point: our research showed that bringing in greater capital inflows is not necessarily the main benefit of capital account opening for an emerging market economy. However, rather than dismissing this as a misguided policy, we argued that there are important, and potentially quite powerful, indirect or "collateral" benefits of capital account liberalization. We also acknowledged that, although the risks can never be eliminated fully, a controlled approach to liberalization could improve the cost–benefit calculus substantially and make this a worthwhile proposition for emerging market economies.

What are these potential collateral benefits? Consider equity market liberalization. There is a significant body of evidence showing that opening a country's equity markets to foreign investors increases trading volumes and improves the overall performance of those markets. Foreign investors often have a sharper eye for how well domestic companies are managed and how effective these companies' corporate governance and business models are. This provides an incentive for domestic firms to improve their governance and transparency so they have better access to foreign funds. Foreign investors are certainly not omniscient and often make colossal investment mistakes, but on average they bring greater discipline to equity markets.

Similarly, the entry of foreign banks increases competition in the banking sector, which in turn benefits private savers and borrowers. Foreign banks from advanced economies entering emerging market economies can bring in better products and services, a broader set of risk management tools, and other innovations. For instance, the entry of foreign banks in India helped to spur improvements in the service levels and efficiency of domestic banks. Of course, as the global financial crisis showed, banks in advanced economies are also capable of wreaking mayhem on a massive scale. Still, the overall evidence is that, in general, foreign bank entry can catalyze improvements in the domestic banking system of an emerging market economy.

This is a playbook to which China had already resorted. In 2007, frustrated with the slow pace of corporate governance reforms in the major state-owned banks, the PBC invited foreign banks to take modest equity stakes in these banks. China certainly had enough resources of its own if the sole objective was to add to these banks' capital. But, the idea of bringing in foreign banks as "strategic investors" was that, since these investors would have an incentive to enhance the profitability of their investments in the Chinese banks, they would prod these banks and give them the expertise needed to improve their risk management systems and corporate governance structures.

Other parts of China's financial system could also benefit from a more liberal foreign investment policy. For instance, the insurance sector has depended on capital controls and other entry restrictions to stay competitive. These segments will face greater competition with more open inflows. This is not to say that foreign institutions are uniformly well managed and need less regulatory oversight. As long as there is consistent and effective regulation of both domestic and foreign financial firms, opening these sectors to foreign investment could significantly improve efficiency.

In related research building on this framework, Raghuram Rajan (a University of Chicago professor who is now the governor of India's central bank) and I made the case that controlled liberalization of outflows would be good for China. Liberalizing outflows provides Chinese households with opportunities to diversify their savings portfolios internationally and stimulates domestic financial reforms by creating competition for domestic banks that currently have a captive domestic source of funds. Initiatives encouraging corporate outflows would allow Chinese corporations to expand their operations abroad and diversify their sources of revenue.

Capital account liberalization could also bring broader benefits to China. An open capital account would spur progress toward the objective of making Shanghai an international financial center. More importantly, if it did spur financial sector reforms, capital account opening could serve as a catalyst for promoting a more efficient allocation of resources in the economy—shifting capital into the more dynamic and productive sectors of the economy rather than primarily to large state-owned enterprises.

CONTROLLED CAPITAL ACCOUNT LIBERALIZATION

China's government has created a number of schemes that allow for controlled opening of its capital account to both inflows and outflows. These schemes have been designed to generate many of the collateral benefits of financial openness in a cautious and calibrated manner that allows freer movement of capital but without full capital account liberalization. A unifying theme across these schemes is that they allow the government to pick and choose the sorts of investors that are allowed to take advantage of capital account opening and also to maintain control of the volumes of flows in either direction. Each scheme is designed to start small and, after the kinks have been worked out and the government has attained a level of comfort, they are usually expanded in scope and volume.

LIBERALIZING INFLOWS

Although China has long been open to FDI, it is only recently that China has ramped up schemes to promote other types of capital inflows.

Qualified Foreign Institutional Investor Scheme

The qualified foreign institutional investor (QFII) scheme, introduced in December 2002, allows qualified foreign institutions to convert foreign currency into RMB and invest in A-shares and a variety of other RMB-denominated financial instruments. The scheme seeks to attract high-quality and long-term foreign portfolio investments while deterring short-term speculative inflows of foreign capital. One of its main objectives is to promote the development of China's securities markets.

The broader objectives of the QFII program line up well with the collateral benefits framework. At a press conference held in 2006, a spokesman for the China Securities Regulatory Commission (CSRC) took stock of the program, articulating its guiding principles and the potential benefits:

> The histories of many developing countries demonstrate that, when the economy grows to a certain level, limited and stepwise liberalization of the local capital market not only helps attract foreign capital inflows through the capital market, but is also conducive to systematic improvement in the capital market and local enterprises as well as an increase in the efficiency of resource allocation. . . . Entry of QFIIs into China's capital market has . . . improved international influence [on] our capital market, increased long-term capital supply to the market, brought to [the] Chinese capital market well-established investment philosophies and cutting-edge investment risk management technologies, and played a positive role in causing domestic listed [companies] to improve the corporate governance structure and boost system reform and mechanism innovation of the capital market.

QFIIs (pronounced "cue-fees" among the cognoscenti!) are typically foreign fund management institutions, insurance companies, securities companies, and other asset management institutions. Foreign central banks and sovereign wealth funds can also apply to be QFIIs. As is typical in China, there are administrative hoops through which these entities must jump. An aspiring QFII has to apply for a license from the CSRC, the agency that decides which institutions can participate in China's equity and other securities markets and also regulates how these markets function. A licensed QFII then has to apply for an investment quota from the SAFE, which is the gatekeeper for capital inflows and outflows.

Chinese regulators have been cautious about which foreign institutions can qualify for a license under this program, setting the bar for qualification high. Institutions applying for QFII status are required to meet minimum eligibility criteria related to the number of years of operation, the dollar value of total assets under management, sound financial status, and corporate governance. They are further required to be domiciled in countries with sound legal and regulatory systems whose securities market regulators have entered into memoranda of understanding for maintaining regulatory cooperation with China's securities regulator. These criteria have the explicit goal of blocking short-term, speculative capital inflows of foreign capital and inviting investors that have long-term investment horizons. It is interesting that foreign institutions are held to higher standards than domestic ones.

The QFII program started out modestly with just a dozen licenses and a total quota of barely $2 billion allotted during its first year. By 2008, the program had entered a phase of more rapid expansion. The SAFE has made it clear that it wants to liberalize foreign portfolio investment via this channel by increasing the aggregate amount available for allocation as QFII quotas and also by relaxing the maximum quotas for individual institutions. This has meant progressively weakening the eligibility criteria related to the minimum number of years of operation and the minimum total assets under management to allow an increasing number of foreign institutional investors—smaller and lesser known—to undertake portfolio investment in China.

Over time, the SAFE has also increased the maximum amount that each QFII can be granted in quotas. Before 2009, each institution could be granted a maximum amount of $800 million across all quota allocations. This limit was increased to $1 billion that year. Until recently, only a handful of sovereign wealth funds, central banks, and monetary authorities were allowed to invest more than $1 billion. In March 2015, the $1 billion investment quota limit for overseas fund management companies was lifted.

Despite the progressive liberalization of the QFII scheme, the government continues to impose restrictions on how these institutions allocate their assets. In the early stages of the program, each foreign institution was required to hold no less than 50 percent of its total assets in equities or equity-related instruments and no more than 20 percent of its assets in cash. These restrictions were intended to prevent institutions from placing the bulk of their assets in bonds and cash to speculate on RMB appreciation. The first restriction was eliminated in 2012; QFIIs are now allowed to hold flexible configurations of assets balanced between equities and fixed-income securities. However, the restriction on cash holdings remains unchanged. In addition, investments by a QFII in any single company listed in China cannot exceed 10 percent of its total shares, and the cumulative shares held by all such institutions in any single company cannot exceed 30 percent of that company's total shares. These restrictions serve to keep foreign investors from gaining control of Chinese companies.

The government further expanded the scope of the QFII scheme and liberalized investment restrictions on QFIIs during 2016. In February, the PBC announced that the country's government and corporate bond markets would be opened to QFIIs, with no quota restrictions and few administrative barriers to investing in bonds. The notice did not immediately generate much attention or excitement because of limited investor interest at the time due to widespread concerns about the state of China's economy and its financial markets. But, within a few days, stories about how this policy shift could be a game-changer over time, potentially attracting trillions of dollars in foreign investments into China's bond markets, began appearing in the international press.

In March 2016, the SAFE further liberalized the QFII scheme. First, it lifted the upper limits on QFII quotas and indicated that basic quotas of up to $5 billion would be allocated in proportion to the size of an institution's assets or assets under management. Second, these basic quotas would be approved more or less automatically, with the SAFE's formal approval needed only for quotas above $5 billion (as noted, there are no quota restrictions anymore on investments in bonds). Third, there would be no deadline on inward remittances following a QFII's quota approval. Moreover, investments by QFIIs could be repatriated anytime after three months (compared to a previous one-year "lock-up period"). In May 2016, the SAFE announced that foreign institutions would be able to sell and repatriate their investments in China's bond markets at any time without having to secure regulatory approval.

It is interesting to note that many of the steps taken in 2016 to liberalize QFII inflows into China's equity markets fall straight out of a playbook set out by Morgan Stanley Capital International (MSCI), a firm that creates stock market indexes used as benchmarks by investment managers around the world. China has been keen to have its A-shares included in the MSCI emerging markets index as that would cause more foreign investments to flow into its stock markets. In June 2015, MSCI had declined to include China in this index, citing various restrictions on foreign investors who wanted to purchase stocks and other securities in China. Chinese financial regulators responded by asking for a check-list of items that MSCI wanted to see progress on and then set about systematically ticking off the elements on that list. However, in its June 2016 review, MSCI concluded that not all steps had been completed and again declined to include Chinese A-shares in its index.

As of May 2016, the total investment quota awarded under the QFII scheme was $81 billion, covering roughly three hundred institutions. Total QFII investments in the A-share market have remained small compared with the overall size of that market. A-shares held by foreign institutions account for less than 2 percent of the tradable capitalization of the A-share market. Thus, any effects of the QFII scheme on securities market development have so far been largely catalytic rather than directly substantive in nature.

Renminbi Qualified Foreign Institutional Investor Scheme

The renminbi qualified foreign institutional investor (RQFII) program was launched in late 2011. The key difference relative to the

QFII program is that RQFIIs can use offshore RMB directly to invest in mainland markets. In contrast, QFIIs have to first convert their foreign currency funds into RMB before purchasing equities and securities in onshore markets.

This scheme, like its precursor, requires financial institutions to apply for licenses from the CSRC and for investment quotas from the SAFE. Approved institutions need to open special RMB accounts separately for investment in stock markets, interbank bond markets, and stock index futures in domestic custodian banks. As is typical of most avenues for capital account opening that involve financial institutions, various restrictions apply to movements of funds under the RQFII scheme.

Under this scheme there are, for example, tight controls on funds that can be moved into or out of China. Funds that can be remitted inward include the investment principal as well as amounts required to pay the relevant taxes and fees. Funds that can be remitted outward include income from the sale of domestic securities as well as cash dividends and interest.

Initially, only Hong Kong subsidiaries of Chinese financial institutions were eligible for RQFII licenses. Since 2014, the scheme has been expanded to additional Hong Kong banks and asset managers, and subsequently also to financial institutions in the U.K., Singapore, South Korea, France, Germany, Australia, Canada, Luxembourg, and Switzerland. As of May 2016, 165 financial institutions, including foreign institutions and foreign branches of China's financial institutions, had been granted a total quota of $76 billion under this scheme. Financial institutions from Hong Kong, many of which are branches of Mainland financial institutions, remain the major players. Hong Kong now accounts for $41 billion of the allocated RQFII quota while South Korea accounts for $11 billion.

LIBERALIZING OUTFLOWS

We can summarize the philosophy of capital outflows by a phrase that appears in the 2014 SAFE report, which notes that recent changes in the structure of external financial assets reflect a "philosophy of 'holding foreign exchange by the people.'" That is, the

PBC (which manages the SAFE) is keen to have private citizens and corporations hold foreign exchange on their balance sheets rather than acquiring more foreign exchange reserves on its own balance sheet.

The large stock of foreign exchange reserves has created complications for the PBC over the years. First, finding safe and liquid investments that also yield more than negligible returns has been a major challenge for the PBC. Second, the large stock of reserves means that the PBC has taken on considerable exchange rate risk. When the RMB rises in value relative to currencies such as the dollar, the euro, and the yen, the RMB value of China's foreign exchange reserves falls. If the exchange rate were to appreciate from 6 yuan per dollar to 5 yuan per dollar, the value of $1 trillion of reserves held in dollars would fall from RMB 6 trillion to RMB 5 trillion. This matters because the PBC's balance sheet is denominated in RMB, including its liabilities that are matched against these foreign assets. Moreover, even when the RMB has stayed stable relative to the dollar but appreciated relative to the euro and the yen (because of those currencies' depreciation against the dollar), the value of China's reserves reported in dollars per international convention has fallen. The PBC finds it challenging to explain either of these circumstances to China's leaders and its people.

One might argue that the PBC's desire to burden households and corporations with the exchange rate risk that comes from holding foreign currency assets reflects mercenary motives. In fact, this approach is fully consistent with the notion of giving Chinese households and corporations the opportunity to diversify their portfolios through international investments rather than having to rely solely on domestic investments.

The Chinese government has, in fact, been quite aggressive in creating channels for capital outflows from major financial institutions and individual investors.

Qualified Domestic Institutional Investor Scheme

The qualified domestic institutional investor (QDII) scheme allows Chinese domestic financial institutions to invest in offshore financial products such as securities and bonds. (Interestingly, while the QFII program is referred to as "cue-fee," the QDII program is referred to as just that—Q, D, I, I—rather than as "cue-dee.") The program was officially launched in 2006 and permits selected commercial banks, securities companies, fund management companies, and other large institutional investors such as insurance companies to invest in foreign capital markets, subject to certain restrictions.

QDIIs gather funds from retail investors, pool those funds, and then invest them abroad. There is, of course, some risk involved in foreign investments, but since QDIIs presumably have better information and, in principle, invest more wisely than the average retail investor, the risk–benefit tradeoff may tilt to the benefits side. More importantly, the QDII approach gives the government control over when and how much money can be moved offshore as the QDIIs are given specific investment quotas.

It is not easy to be qualified as a QDII, and the government clearly intends to weed out unsavory financial operators in favor of clean ones. An institution applying for a license under this program must exhibit financial stability and good credit, employ qualified personnel with the requisite asset management and risk assessment expertise, operate with a sound governance structure and robust internal control system, and have no record of any major penalty levied by the relevant regulatory authority. In other words, it must have a clean record.

To avoid fly-by-night operators who are able to set up new firms with clean records and low levels of capital, the government has put in place additional specific requirements depending on the type of institution involved. For example, an eligible fund management company needs to have net assets of at least RMB 200 million ($30 million), at least two years of active participation in the fund management business, and more than RMB 20 billion ($3 billion) or assets of equal value under management at the end of the latest quarter.

The scope of an investment under this program is subject to certain restrictions. Investments in bank deposits, debt securities, stocks, bonds, and basic derivatives are allowed, whereas investments in real estate and precious metals are forbidden. Approved investment destinations for QDIIs include Hong Kong, the U.K., the U.S., Singapore, Japan, Korea, Luxemburg, Germany, Canada, Australia, and Malaysia. It is interesting to note these are mostly advanced economies, and all of them have well-developed financial markets, good property rights protection, and sound financial sector regulatory frameworks. Thus, China encourages financial institutions to invest in countries that have the attributes its own financial markets lack. In addition to tilting investments toward safer destinations, this approach may also have the collateral benefit of enabling investors to acquire knowledge of other countries' practices and standards in these areas.

By May 2016, 132 institutions had been granted QDII licenses and the total allocated quota stood at $90 billion. The breakdown of quotas by institution type was as follows: securities companies, $38 billion; insurance companies, $31 billion; banks, $14 billion; and trust companies, $8 billion.

Qualified Domestic Individual Investor Scheme

The PBC has also been studying ways to allow individual investors to invest abroad more directly. The proposed scheme, commonly known as *QDII2*, will expand the QDII scheme from institutional to individual retail investors. It is to be launched initially in six Chinese cities: Shanghai, Tianjin, Chongqing, Wuhan, Shenzhen, and Wenzhou. News reports indicate the pilot scheme will allow individuals with at least RMB 1 million in assets (roughly $160,000) to invest directly overseas in securities, stocks, and real estate. At present, the maximum amount in local currency that individuals can exchange for foreign currency is subject to an annual cap of $50,000.

That the State Council discussed a plan to open up channels for individual overseas investment was first revealed in a document on the development of capital markets issued in May 2013. In April 2015, Zhou Xiaochuan (Figure 3.3), the governor of the PBC, confirmed in a speech to the IMF's International and Monetary Financial

Figure 3.3 Zhou Xiaochuan, Governor of the People's Bank of China.
Credit: China News Service

Committee that China would launch the pilot QDII2. In June 2015, a Shanghai government official indicated the city would launch a trial of the program by the end of the year. The plan was also discussed in a report on RMB internationalization released by the PBC in July 2015. However, as of June 2016, the specific framework and timeline of the program had yet to be announced.

LIBERALIZING TWO-WAY FLOWS

China has also been creating channels that allow capital to flow in both directions across its borders. In this process, too, the government has taken a nontraditional approach.

Islands of Integration: Free Trade Zones

China's experimental, learning-by-doing approach to capital account liberalization has manifested uniquely in its free trade zones (FTZs), which function as islands of full capital account convertibility within China. FTZs are designed to allow for a greater degree of capital account openness, but they are limited to specific geographic areas.

The Shanghai FTZ was officially launched on September 29, 2013. It was expanded in 2015 to include Lujiazui, the city's financial district. In early 2015, China launched three new FTZs—in Guangdong, Tianjin, and Fujian—each of which covers only a few specific sectors.

Companies and financial institutions located in the FTZs can raise capital from abroad with fewer restrictions and reporting requirements. In principle, however, this money cannot be moved outside such zones. Companies in FTZs are allowed to borrow RMB offshore so long as these funds are not used outside the zones and are not invested in securities or used to extend loans. Foreign financial institutions can set up operations with fewer restrictions than in the rest of the Mainland and can operate more freely inside the zone. So long as they meet some basic requirements, foreign-invested banks are allowed to set up subsidiaries or branches within the zones. Private investors can also enter the banking sector in FTZs and set up banks, finance leasing companies, consumer finance companies, and other financial institutions as long as their operations remain within the zones.

Despite its name, an FTZ is not fully open to foreign investors. Foreign investment in FTZs is restricted to sectors that do not appear on a "negative list," a list of sectors that remain off limits to foreign investors. Investment in sectors not on the list is mostly unrestricted, although some administrative procedures must still be followed. The approval process for establishing a foreign-funded enterprise in an industry that is not on the negative list has been simplified. Moreover, the negative list has shrunk over time, helping make the case that FTZs are becoming increasingly open to foreign investors. The negative list is not exhaustive, however, when it comes to prohibitions on foreign investment; it applies only to those industries in which domestic and foreign investors are treated differently. Industries such as weapons and ammunition are not on the list because even domestic nongovernment firms are not allowed to invest in them.

In practice, the extent of capital account liberalization that China has achieved through the FTZs amounts to less than meets the eye. For instance, in areas such as oil and natural gas exploration, rare earths smelting, and airplane design, foreign investors are required to form joint ventures with domestic companies. In these areas, the government clearly wants to ensure that domestic companies do not cede ground to foreign enterprises. Moreover, foreign companies in FTZs are subject to national security reviews if they seek to invest in certain "sensitive industries, technologies, [or] locations." Foreign companies must undergo such a review if they acquire a controlling stake in a firm that operates in "the military industry, major energy and resources, major infrastructure projects, [or] telecommunications, [or produces] certain agricultural products that may affect national security."

Interestingly, national security reviews consider more than just an investment's impact on national security, Internet security, and sensitive technology for use in national defense. Other considerations include the impact of an investment on the stability of the economy, basic social order, and culture and social morality. No doubt these are purposefully broad and vague terms that give the Chinese government wide latitude in triggering security reviews. During President Xi's visit to the U.S. in September 2015, China committed to limiting the scope of the national security reviews. It remains to be seen how this will work in practice.

FTZs provide a significant channel for two-way capital flows through the banking system as well as through corporations, although there is, in principle, a firewall between each FTZ and the rest of the Mainland. Over time, these walls are likely to erode since multiple financial institutions and corporations operate on both sides of those walls. Nevertheless, in the interim, the FTZ approach provides the government with another controlled approach to capital account opening.

The Shanghai–Hong Kong Stock Connect

China has initiated an alternative approach to selective and calibrated capital account liberalization through a "stock-connecting" program that creates another channel for cross-border equity investments by a broad range of investors, including retail investors. The Stock Connect link between the Shanghai and Hong Kong stock exchanges was officially launched in November 2014. The program allows Mainland Chinese investors to purchase shares of selected Hong Kong and Chinese companies listed in Hong Kong (Southbound investment), and lets foreigners buy Chinese A-shares listed in Shanghai (Northbound investment) in a less restrictive manner than had previously been the case.

Trading under this program in either direction is subject to a maximum cross-border investment quota (i.e., an aggregate quota), together with a daily quota. The Southbound aggregate quota has been set at RMB 250 billion ($38 billion), with the daily quota set at RMB 10.5 billion ($1.6 billion). The aggregate quota caps the total amount of investment undertaken by Chinese investors in Hong Kong equity markets through this channel. Once that quota is reached, no further investment is allowed through the program unless an existing investor reduces his or her investment. The corresponding Northbound investment quotas are RMB 300 billion (aggregate, $45 billion) and RMB 13 billion (daily, $2 billion).

The Stock Exchange of Hong Kong and the Shanghai Stock Exchange monitor compliance with these quotas, with each responsible for investment in its direction. Trades are settled through the Hong Kong Securities Clearing Corporation and the China Depository and Clearing Corporation. With these mechanisms in place, regulators have real-time information on trading volumes in both directions as well as the quota balances. The Mainland's political control over Hong Kong thus allows it to manage these experiments with capital flow liberalization easily.

This investment channel has been used quite extensively. The Northbound daily quota was met on the launch day and was consistently high in the months following the launch, reflecting foreign investors' interest in Mainland equity markets. That interest waned sharply when Mainland markets began to fall sharply in the summer of 2015. The Southbound daily cap was hit for the first time in April 2015. The government has indicated that it plans to set up more stock-connecting schemes that link other mainland cities to Hong Kong, but no specific dates have been announced.

Mutual Fund Connect

The Mutual Fund Connect program, launched in July 2015, allows eligible Mainland and Hong Kong funds to be distributed in each other's markets through a streamlined vetting process. Along with the Stock Connect, this program substantially increases the range of equity investment products available to investors on both sides and provides yet another channel for bidirectional flows of capital. The major difference between the two schemes is that Stock Connect allows retail investors to invest directly in equities whereas Mutual Fund Connect allows funds to sell their products to investors on both sides. The initial investment quota for the scheme is RMB 300 billion ($45 billion) for fund flows in each direction.

Eligibility is limited to general equity funds, bond funds, mixed funds, unlisted index funds, and physical index-tracking, exchange-traded funds. Institutions that are viewed as more "speculative" in terms of their investment strategies—such as gold exchange-traded funds and structured funds—are not eligible. Mutual funds hoping to take advantage of the program face additional requirements. For instance, there is a minimum fund size and a minimum period for which a fund needs to have been in existence. Another criterion is that a fund must be a publicly offered securities investment fund registered with the CSRC in China or the Securities and Futures Commission in Hong Kong. Thus, only legitimate and carefully vetted funds are permitted to use this program.

China has opened up a variety of channels for both inflows and outflows of financial capital. Typically, developing economies tend to be more interested in obtaining foreign capital than in letting domestic savings seep out. Why has China been so eager to create channels through which capital can flow out from its economy? Therein lie two interesting tales—both of which are as much about domestic politics as they are about economics.

One of the great ironies of the structure of China's external balance sheet is that the country has been paying the rest of the world for the privilege of holding more assets than liabilities.

The difference between a country's earnings on its investments abroad (i.e., its external assets) and foreigners' earnings on their investments in that country (external liabilities) is its net investment income. A country with more external assets than external liabilities should, logically, have positive net investment income. That is, the country should see higher investment income inflows (earnings on its assets) compared with its investment income outflows (the income it provides to foreign investors).

At the end of 2014, China was a net creditor (i.e., lender) to the rest of the world—to the tune of $1.6 trillion. How much money did the country earn during the course of 2015 as a result of having more assets than liabilities? Remarkably, its net investment income in 2015 was *minus* $73 billion. That is, China paid out far more to foreign investors than it earned on its investments abroad.

China is certainly special in this regard. Most other net creditors, such as Germany and Japan, have positive net income flows. For instance, at the end of 2014, Japan had a net asset position of $3 trillion (its foreign assets exceeded its foreign liabilities by that amount) and a net investment income of $172 billion during 2015.

It was not that 2015 was an unusual year for China. Its net income flows have been either negative or essentially zero every year over the past decade, even as the country's net asset position was growing from $400 billion in 2005 to four times that amount in 2015. In contrast, Japan, which has also been a net creditor over the past decade, earned a positive net investment income in every one of those years.

The U.S. is also special, but its situation is exactly the opposite of China's. The U.S. has been a net debtor to the rest of the world for the past three decades. In 2007, its net liabilities stood at $1.3 trillion. The global financial crisis of 2008–2009 and its aftermath, including the eurozone debt crisis, precipitated a surge of capital inflows into the U.S. By the beginning of 2015, the U.S, had a net foreign liability position of $7 trillion. Foreign investor ownership of U.S. Treasury securities alone had risen by $4 trillion since 2007.

And how much does the U.S. pay out to foreign investors? Interestingly, it turns out that during 2015, the U.S. made a better return on its $25 trillion worth of foreign assets than foreign investors made on their $32 trillion worth of investments in the U.S. During 2015, its net investment income was a *positive* $193 billion, and 2015 was not an unusual year for the U.S. in this regard. Its net international investment income has been positive every year for the past decade, despite its large and growing net foreign liability position.

Reflect on this for a moment. China is a creditor to the rest of the world but has a negative net income flow while the U.S., a debtor, has a positive net income flow.

For another perspective on this issue, consider the rates of return on a country's external assets and its external liabilities. One simple way to measure the gross returns on China's external assets is to see how much inward investment income flows (i.e., earnings) were generated in a given year by the total stock of external assets measured at the beginning of that year. For instance, with a stock of external assets amounting to $6.4 trillion at the beginning of 2015 and an inward investment income flow of $194 billion during the course of the year, the return on China's assets for 2015 was 3 percent. Using a similar procedure, one can compute the approximate gross returns on China's foreign liabilities—in other words, the gross investment income earned by foreign investors on their investments in China. At the beginning of 2015, China's external liabilities amounted to $4.8 trillion and its outward investment income during the year was $267 billion, implying a return of 5.5 percent. In other words, in 2015 the rate of return on China's external assets was 2.5 percentage points lower than the return on its external liabilities. These calculations do not account for changes in assets or liabilities during the year or the effects of shifts in currency values on returns. Still, although returns estimated using this procedure are crude approximations, the patterns they reveal

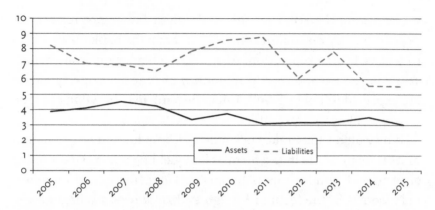

Figure 3.4 Returns on external assets and liabilities (measured as a percentage). Return on investment is the investment income inflow (or outflow) in a given year, expressed as a ratio of the stock position of external assets (or external liabilities) at the end of the previous year.
Source: The State Administration of Foreign Exchange.

are striking and unlikely to be overturned by more sophisticated calculations.

Figure 3.4 shows that, in every year over the past decade, China has received a substantially lower return on its foreign assets than it has paid out on its foreign liabilities. The average annual difference between the gross return on liabilities and the gross return on assets is 3.6 percentage points.

In contrast, during the past decade, the returns earned on U.S. assets have been 1.3 percentage points higher than the returns paid on U.S. liabilities—4 percent versus 2.7 percent—which is why net returns have been positive despite the U.S.'s net liability position.

China is in the odd position of being a banker to the world but a generous one that provides a better interest rate on money deposited with it than the rate it charges on money it lends out to other countries. To appreciate the oddity of this situation, consider the following scenario. You would no doubt consider it quite a deal if you could get a better interest rate on money deposited at your local bank compared with the lower interest rate you paid on a mortgage taken from the same bank. This scenario would make sense if your deposit in the bank were risky, which might cause you to demand a higher average rate of return in exchange for accepting the risk that the bank might fail or not repay your deposit for any reason. In contrast, perhaps the bank views a loan to you as a safe proposition. After all, the bank can always repossess your house and recoup its money as long as property values are expected to hold up well. Thus, the bank may be willing to lend to you at a low interest rate.

Why would China take such a deal? China holds a large portion of its foreign assets in the form of low-yielding advanced economy government bonds. This is because a large fraction of its external assets is in the form of foreign exchange reserves held on the balance sheet of its central bank. In managing foreign exchange reserves, the PBC, like all other central banks, favors maintaining the safety and liquidity of its investments over increasing yields. Reserves are seen as a country's rainy day fund, and a central bank cannot afford to take risks with these investments. They must not only be kept safe, but also be easy to liquidate quickly if necessary. Safer assets typically yield lower returns on average than riskier ones.

In contrast, foreign investors in China, including those from the U.S., have focused on higher return investments, although these are, in principle, more risky. Still, with China's sustained and remarkable growth over the past three decades, these bets have, in general, paid off handsomely.

The flip side of this situation is what gives the U.S. a much better outcome on its investment income. A significant portion of foreign investments in the U.S. is in the form of debt securities, especially U.S. Treasury securities that pay a low rate of return because they are considered safe and highly liquid (easy to trade). So, outward investment income flows from the U.S. are modest. In contrast, about 60 percent of U.S. investments abroad are in the form of FDI and portfolio equity, which typically yield higher average rates of return. So inward investment income flows are, on average, higher.

For China, the prospect of financing U.S. government debt and putting so much of its savings into advanced economies, with these yields generating miniscule returns, no doubt stings, as does the fact that foreign investors seem to have been far more savvy about their investments in China. This uncomfortable situation may be one of the motivations driving China to try to diversify its international asset portfolio by investing its foreign exchange reserves in higher yielding assets and through private investment.

The PBC cannot deviate far from the safety and liquidity criteria as it needs access to liquid reserves and would face political blowback if it registered significant losses on its balance sheet. Hence, the government has relied on other state-owned agencies, including the national sovereign wealth fund, to undertake more aggressive, high-yielding investments. More substantively, it has turned increasingly to the private sector to take on the responsibility of generating higher returns on the external asset portfolio by allowing, and indeed encouraging, households, corporations, and financial institutions to invest abroad directly.

SHIFTING STRUCTURE OF CAPITAL OUTFLOWS

China's capital account policies have led to a marked shift in the pattern of its overall exports of financial capital, which include not only the gross capital flows mentioned earlier (such as outward FDI and portfolio equity investments abroad), but also the PBC's accumulation of foreign exchange reserves. To explore changes in the composition of overall capital outflows, I divided them into two categories: (1) reserve accumulation by the PBC and (2) gross private and nonreserve official outflows plus (the negative of) net errors and omissions (NEOs). The latter category includes foreign investments made by the China Investment Corporation, China's sovereign wealth fund, as well as by other state-owned financial and corporate entities. Negative NEOs in the balance of payments reflect unrecorded outflows through unofficial or illegitimate channels, so they must be added to gross outflows.

Figure 3.5 shows the trailing three-year moving averages of shares of gross capital outflows accounted for by these two components. There is a discernible trend over time in the composition of gross outflows, which has shifted markedly from reserve accumulation to official and unofficial flows from both the private and

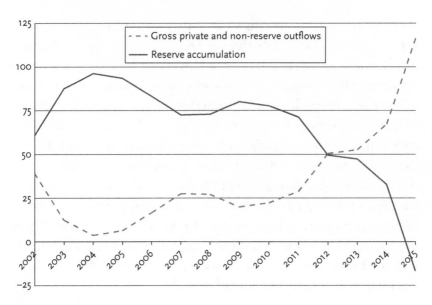

Figure 3.5 Structure of capital outflows (measured as a percentage).
This figure shows three-year trailing averages of the shares of China's gross capital outflows accounted for by (1) net reserve accumulation and (2) all other outflows, which comprises private outflows as well as foreign investments by Chinese official agencies, including its sovereign wealth fund.
Sources: The State Administration of Foreign Exchange and CEIC.

state sectors. In 2014-2015, China started to run down its stock of official reserves while other outflows surged. This shift is consistent with the SAFE's stated objective of shifting foreign exchange risk from the central bank's balance sheet to those of households, corporations, and state-controlled entities such as the sovereign wealth fund. Earning better returns on China's external assets, which the SAFE cannot do because it is constrained to invest the reserves it manages in safe and liquid financial assets, is another potential benefit.

The objective of "foreign exchange holdings by the people" (rather than by the PBC/SAFE) will have a significant impact on the composition of future capital outflows from China. China's demand for low-yielding advanced economy government bonds is likely to remain muted whereas the country's investments in foreign equity and corporate bond markets, along with hard assets such as real estate, will continue to rise. This approach is not without risks. Although the government is providing channels for international portfolio diversification, which is a positive development, there is a risk that lack of effective oversight of domestic securities markets and institutional investors that enable such diversification could portend risks for household and corporate balance sheets. Moreover, as we shall see in Chapter 8, a rapid loss of foreign exchange reserves is not entirely a benign or desirable phenomenon.

A TROJAN HORSE

There is another subtle reason—beyond generating better returns on China's overseas investments—that has prompted the PBC to place high priority on opening the capital account. Over the past decade, the PBC has been an aggressive advocate for financial market liberalization and reform. Notwithstanding the top leadership's support for the PBC's reform efforts, the pathway to a better financial system has been strewn with roadblocks. The big banks, in tandem with the large state-owned enterprises and provincial governments that they bankroll, have been fierce and powerful opponents of reforms. The system, as it is structured, works well for these groups, which hardly makes them eager for greater liberalization as that would mean more competition and fewer opportunities to feed at the public trough.

Large-scale reforms usually require either a crisis, which makes them unavoidable, or a framework that builds popular support along with an effective advocate to convert that sentiment into concrete actions. Without a crisis at hand, the PBC took the latter route. The idea that a great economic power should have a currency to match its clout in global finance resonated well in the CPC and among China's citizens, leading to a convergence of populist sentiment around this idea.

The objective of making the RMB a global reserve currency thus had a subtler and broader motivation: to promote domestic reforms essential for improving the level and sustainability of China's growth. Uniting the country's citizens behind this nationalistic objective has helped built support for, or at least reduced resistance against, reforms needed to make it a reality. Such reforms include a better banking system, broader financial market development, a more flexible exchange rate, and greater ease of entry for new firms in hitherto protected sectors of finance such as insurance. All these reforms will be good for China's economy, regardless of how much international prominence the RMB eventually attains.

The notion of elevating the RMB in international finance has created both a framework and a sense of urgency that the PBC has exploited to the hilt, especially with its methodical opening of the capital account. Once the taps for capital flows in both directions have been opened, it becomes difficult to shut them off. The PBC was, therefore, clearly eager to push forward with capital account opening, as those reforms are difficult to reverse and would also catalyze other reforms. For instance, without captive deposits (since depositors can now invest more easily abroad), Chinese domestic banks are being forced to elevate their game and become more efficient to remain profitable.

As PBC Governor Zhou Xiaochuan put it in an interview:

> To press ahead with reform, one should take decisive actions when windows of opportunities open up ... advancing reform should pick good windows of opportunities and requires art in timing, cooperation and skills of execution. Some reforms will lose momentum if suspended and the "once bitten, twice shy" mentality should be avoided.

But Governor Zhou also indicated the PBC would not put the speed with which reforms are enacted above all else, highlighting the need to "refrain from reckless moves in the absence of such windows [of opportunity]." He noted the government was willing to be patient and, when necessary, create favorable conditions for reform before pressing ahead.

With a clear objective (promoting the international role of the RMB) as well as an enthusiastic and effective advocate (the PBC), China's capital account has become more open at a faster clip than most had anticipated. The PBC has effectively countered the broadly held assumption that the global financial crisis would put a damper on any moves toward opening up of emerging market economies' capital accounts. This is certainly not to say that China's capital account is anywhere near fully open, raising an obvious question: What is the government's end game?

THE END GAME

China's selective and calibrated approach to capital account liberalization has been effective at promoting the RMB's international presence without risking the potential deleterious effects of complete capital account liberalization. China's approach has, however, limited its currency's international use, the full potential of which cannot be realized without more active onshore development. It will be difficult, for instance, to fully develop China's foreign exchange and derivatives markets in the absence of a more open capital account.

It is interesting to consider whether China's goal is to formulate a policy concerning the capital account that provides a better benefit–risk tradeoff than it associates with complete capital account convertibility. Joseph Yam, the former head of the Hong Kong Monetary Authority, has argued that China's long-term objective ought to be full capital account convertibility, which he defines as relaxing capital controls while maintaining "soft" controls in the form of registration and reporting requirements for regulatory purposes. He draws a careful distinction between this and an entirely unfettered capital flow regime, referred to as *free* capital account convertibility. This is a subtle but important distinction that appears to have resonated well with the Chinese leadership, given that full convertibility by this definition provides a path to an open capital account without entirely ceding control to market forces.

During the early 2000s, including in meetings with my team when I was head of the IMF's China Division, government officials indicated that capital account liberalization would be achieved within a decade. The official position remained the same year after year, indicating a marked degree of consistency around a moving target. By 2015, the objective and the time frame for its achievement had become more concrete. The thirteenth Five-Year Plan, issued in early 2015, contained more specific language. Although the words in the plan seemed like the usual bromides, *The Wall Street Journal* reported that the "proposal ... called for making China's currency, the yuan, 'freely convertible and usable' over the next five years, setting a new timetable for the long-promised and delayed capital account convertibility—whereby money can move freely across borders—in an orderly manner."

At a press conference, Premier Li Keqiang (Figure 3.6) stated that "China is working towards full convertibility of renminbi

Figure 3.6 President Xi Jinping and Premier Li Keqiang of China.
Credit: Reuters/Carlos Barria

under capital accounts. This shows that China is taking further steps to open up its capital market." In a subsequent interview, President Xi Jinping reiterated that objective, but noted that it was simply a continuation of long-standing policy:

> China put forward the goal of convertibility of the RMB under the capital account back in the early 1990s. Over the past 20 years and more, China has been working toward this goal. Currently, there are only very few transactions that are still banned under the RMB capital account. China is advancing the convertibility of the RMB under the capital account in a steady and orderly manner.

We can perhaps find a definitive indication of the Chinese government's intentions in a statement PBC Governor Zhou made at the IMF in April 2015. He argued that the concept of capital account convertibility had changed since the global financial crisis, and that China was not trying to achieve the traditional concepts of full or free convertibility. Rather, he said:

> China will adopt a concept of managed convertibility. After achieving RMB capital account convertibility, China will continue to manage capital account transactions, but in a largely transformed manner, including by using macroprudential measures to limit risks from cross-border capital flows and to maintain the stable value of the currency and a safe financial environment.

Zhou went on to say that China would continue practicing capital account management in four cases. First, cross-border financial transactions would be monitored to deter money laundering, financing of terrorism, and the use of tax havens to evade taxes. Second, the external debt-raising activities of banks and corporations, especially debt denominated in foreign currencies, would be controlled through regulations. Third, China would place controls on short-term speculative capital flows when they posed risks to financial stability, whereas medium- and long-term capital flows that support the real economy would be left largely unfettered. Fourth, balance of payments statistics and monitoring would be strengthened in order to "adopt temporary capital control measures when there are abnormal fluctuations in the international markets, or there are balance of payments problems."

In sum, China has an extensive capital control regime in place but it is dismantling these controls selectively and cautiously. Many of the restrictions on cross-border capital inflows and out-flows have been made less stringent, but few have been eliminated entirely. The country's capital account is nevertheless becoming increasingly open, in terms of both fewer restrictions on capital flows and more de facto openness even when there are some controls in place.

The government seems intent on allowing capital to flow rather freely, even if not to the full extent that is typical of the traditional reserve currency economies. This raises the issue of the effects of capital account opening on the level and volatility of the RMB's value in international markets. I turn to this topic in the next chapter.

CHAPTER 4
The Exchange Rate Regime

"How would it be," said Pooh slowly, "if, as soon as we're out of sight of this Pit, we try to find it again?"

"What's the good of that?" said Rabbit.

"Well," said Pooh, "we keep looking for Home and not finding it, so I thought that if we looked for this Pit, we'd be sure not to find it, which would be a Good Thing, because then we might find something that we weren't looking for, which might be just what we were looking for, really."

"I don't see much sense in that," said Rabbit.

"No," said Pooh humbly, "there isn't. But there was going to be when I began it. It's just that something happened to it on the way."

The House at Pooh Corner, A.A. Milne

On August 11, 2015, at a campaign event in Michigan, Donald Trump, then the leading contender for the Republican presidential nomination in the U.S., let loose, venting his apparent anger at China: "[China] continuously cuts their currency, they devalue their currency. They've been doing this for years; this isn't just starting." Republican senator Lindsey Graham, another candidate for the Republican presidential nomination, added, "Today's provocative act by the Chinese government to lower the value of the yuan is just the latest in a long history of cheating." The same day, Senator Charles Grassley, head of the Senate Finance Committee, released a statement: "China has manipulated its currency for a long time. This is just the latest example, and it's past time to do something about it."

It wasn't just the Republicans fulminating against China that day. Charles Schumer, an influential Democratic senator from New York said, "For years, China has rigged the rules and played games with its currency, leaving American workers out to dry. Rather than changing their ways, the Chinese government seems to be doubling down." Bob Casey, another Democratic senator, added, "It's time for the administration to focus more intensively on China's cheating and label the county a currency manipulator."

What were Trump, Schumer, and other members of the U.S. Congress complaining about? Remarkably, on that day, China's government had done just what the Americans had been asking it to do for a long time: ease up on its management of the RMB's value and let it be determined more freely by market forces. What the U.S. and the world had not anticipated was that China would, cleverly, do the right thing at a time when it was convenient for it but difficult for the rest of the world. Rather than changing its policy at a time when the RMB might appreciate, which would hurt China's exports, the government picked a time when market forces were, in fact, pushing the RMB downward, which would help China's exports. The notion that China must be doing something underhanded—even when it was, ostensibly, doing the right thing by letting market forces work—was behind much of the outrage directed at China.

Currency policy in China has come a long way over the past two decades. To understand this evolution better, we need to step back into recent history to a turbulent period in Asia.

STABILITY AS A VIRTUE

In 1997, the Asian "tigers" were defanged. The so-called *tigers* were a group of Asian economies—Hong Kong, Indonesia, Malaysia, Singapore, South Korea, Taiwan, and Thailand—that had grown by leaps and bounds for a number of years. It turned out, however, that the foundations of their growth were shaky. The first of the tigers to fall was Thailand, which, in July 1997, gave up the fight to manage the value of the Thai baht and devalued it sharply against the dollar. Other currencies in the Asian region depreciated sharply; foreign investors grew nervous about the entire region and pulled out. For many of these economies, the fall in their currencies was, in principle, a mixed blessing but would in fact turn out to be a devastating blow.

The Asian tigers' currency depreciation meant their exports were cheaper when measured in foreign currencies and could, therefore, be sold more easily to the rest of the world. However, when times had been good and these economies were growing rapidly, their corporations and governments had taken on large amounts of debt denominated in U.S. dollars. As a consequence, when their currencies fell sharply, they faced a big problem: a currency mismatch. Their corporate and government revenues, which flowed in largely in domestic currencies, were now matched against a level of dollar debt that was ballooning rapidly in terms of their domestic currencies (when a domestic currency depreciates, more units of it are needed to buy one unit of a foreign currency). Corporations would have to generate higher sales in domestic markets to meet their debt service obligations, which was even more challenging when their economies were collapsing. Similarly, to pay off their own foreign currency debts and to help their strapped corporations, governments were forced to raise taxes and cut expenditures, pushing growth down further.

Financing dried up as foreign investors refused to roll over the debt and started calling in the loans they had provided earlier. As a result, even many solvent companies faced a liquidity problem; their cash flow from sales was insufficient to meet their repayment obligations. This set off a chain reaction of falling currency values leading to corporate bankruptcies, squeezing government finances and pushing currency values down even further.

Amid all this turmoil in Asia, China faced a weighty decision. With little external debt, it was sorely tempted to devalue its currency. Otherwise, China risked losing export market share to its Asian competitors, whose currencies had now become cheaper. For the other Asian economies, this was a troubling prospect as it meant that they would suffer the costs of having their currencies fall but gain none of the benefits. The world awaited China's decision with bated breath, knowing that if it chose the logical option to protect its own narrow interests, the crisis could wreak more prolonged havoc and pain in the region.

China chose to stand tall. While economies and currencies in its neighborhood were collapsing, the Chinese RMB's value stood pat against the U.S. dollar. At the October 1998 IMF–World Bank meetings, PBC Governor Dai Xianglong noted that, "since the eruption of the Asian financial crisis [in] the interests of regional stability and growth, we have maintained the stability of RMB and pursued a non-devaluation policy."

China's Ministry of Foreign Affairs wanted to make sure the world would not fail to give China due credit. It issued a statement underlining the noble nature of the currency inaction:

> The Chinese Government, with a high sense of responsibility, decided not to devaluate [sic] its Renminbi in the overall interest of maintaining stability and development in the region. It did so under huge pressure and at a big price. But it contributed considerably to financial and economic stability and to development in Asia in particular and the world at large.

The IMF agreed that China's decision not to devalue the RMB was critical to restoring stability in the region. When asked about China's decision, U.S. Treasury Secretary Robert Rubin noted, "They were very prescient, and they are getting and deserve a great deal of respect in the world for this decision." He further praised China for being an "island of stability" in a region buffeted by economic turmoil. British Prime Minister Tony Blair added, "We paid tribute to the role that China has played in the aftermath of the Asian crisis."

STABILITY BECOMES A VICE

The scars of the Asian financial crisis ran deep but, by the early 2000s, capital had started flowing back to the region. Then, as the new millennium got underway, there was another major event that would prove to be a game-changer in the world economy.

After complex and protracted negotiations, China became a member of the World Trade Organization (WTO) in 2001. This deal meant that exports from China would have greater access to markets around the world, especially in developed economies such as Europe, Japan, and the U.S.

China's exports began to pick up soon thereafter, which meant more foreign currency coming into the country. As the economy started registering strong growth and also began opening up its capital account, foreign capital flowed in increasingly, putting further upward pressure on the RMB. China did not want its export machine to lose momentum, so it started intervening in foreign exchange markets to prevent the value of the RMB from rising. With China's manufacturing sector registering strong productivity growth, the RMB should have appreciated markedly. The PBC's intervention made the RMB increasingly undervalued—in other words, kept it a level that was lower than it would have been had it been subjected to unfettered market forces. The increase in manufacturing sector productivity, in tandem with low domestic wages and an undervalued exchange rate, made Chinese exports very competitive in world markets. Consequently, the trade surplus grew by leaps and bounds, forcing the PBC to intervene even more aggressively, buying up dollars, euros, yen, and other currencies that were flooding into China as payments for its exports. This maneuver was intended to offset the rising demand for RMB in exchange for those currencies that would otherwise have driven up the price of the RMB (i.e., the exchange rate).

China's foreign exchange reserves amounted to a mere $300 billion in 2000. By 2008, when the collapse of Lehman Brothers triggered the global financial crisis, the stockpile had grown to nearly $2 trillion. The world economy went into a tailspin in 2009 as the major advanced economies fell into recession. China's government unleashed a massive burst of credit and a fiscal stimulus that maintained the economy's growth at a remarkable 9.2 percent in 2009 and 10.6 percent in 2010. This pace of growth kept China's demand for imports strong while exports fell, since foreign demand was weak. Consequently, China's trade surplus declined sharply, from a peak of 8.7 percent of GDP in 2007 to 4.3 percent of GDP in 2009, and then averaged 2.8 percent of GDP from 2010 through 2014. Still, appreciation pressure on the RMB remained strong because China continued to attract capital inflows as it was by far the fastest-growing major economy in the aftermath of the crisis. As the PBC intervened even more intensively to prevent RMB appreciation, China's reserves kept growing rapidly, hitting a peak of $3.99 trillion in June 2014.

That month, when China's reserves were a hair's breadth away from the $4 trillion mark and seemed on an unstoppable rise, would prove to be a turning point. Before analyzing how and why the economic picture for China changed, we must first examine the PBC's approach to exchange rate management and trace its evolution over time.

THE TRAJECTORY OF A CURRENCY (OSTENSIBLY) BREAKING FREE

To tell the history of currency management in China, one has to go back to the 1980s and early 1990s. This was a period when Deng Xiaoping and other reformers were trying to shift the economy away from state domination. Although the government still controlled most aspects of the economy, the reformers recognized the benefits of liberalization and argued that free enterprise, within bounds and under the paternalistic oversight of the state, could be consistent with the core principles of the CPC. China still remained largely closed to the outside world, especially in terms of financial flows, although international trade was beginning to build some momentum.

At that time, China had an official exchange rate and a separate rate in officially sanctioned swap centers where the forces of demand and supply were given freer rein to determine the currency's value. The official exchange rate relative to the dollar was overvalued (i.e., it was cheaper to buy dollars using yuan at the official rate than it was to buy them at the market exchange rate). Importers who needed to pay their foreign suppliers with dollars or other hard currencies could buy yuan at the more favorable official exchange rate (i.e., at fewer yuan per dollar), but the amounts were limited and few others had access to yuan at this exchange rate. By 1994, this dual exchange rate system had become untenable as the discrepancy was large and the PBC was running out of hard currency reserves.

In early 1994, the Chinese government devalued the official exchange rate so it matched the swap market rate and then unified the two exchange rates. From 1994 onward, the value of the RMB was pegged to the U.S. dollar—meaning that the RMB–dollar exchange rate was held fixed. The peg held up through the Asian financial crisis of 1997–1998.

After maintaining an unchanged peg for over a decade, in July 2005 the PBC announced that it was eliminating the RMB's peg to the dollar. In principle, the PBC began implementing a managed floating exchange rate mechanism, with the currency's value determined by market demand and supply, and with reference to a basket of currencies rather than just the dollar. This certainly made good economic sense as the U.S. was accounting for a declining share of China's trade.

The PBC did not indicate which currencies would be in the basket. It was only a month later, at a public event in Shanghai in August 2005, that PBC Governor Zhou Xiaochuan stated that "the United States, [the] European Union, Japan and the Republic of Korea are China's most important trade partners, so their currencies naturally become the main currencies in the basket." In an article reporting on the speech, an official newspaper, *The People's Daily*, noted that "Singapore, Britain, Malaysia, Russia, Australia, Thailand and Canada also have important roles in China's foreign trade, so their currencies are important for the RMB exchange rate as well." Despite all these statements, however, in practice the dollar remained the main benchmark for managing the currency's value.

The new system, based on a managed floating exchange rate, was designed to work as follows. Before the start of currency trading on a given day, the PBC would announce the reference rate (relative to the dollar) at which the RMB would begin trading, with intraday volatility of ±0.3 percent permitted. That is, during any given day the currency's value in the Shanghai foreign exchange market could rise or fall by up to 0.3 percent relative to the reference rate, called the *central parity*. This presumably meant that the RMB could rise by 0.3 percent each day, which would amount to a significant appreciation over a few days or weeks. In reality, the practice of managing the value of the RMB relative to the dollar did not stop. The central parity each day was usually set close to the central parity rather than closing price of the previous day, no matter how much the previous day's closing price and central parity differed from one another. Still, through this mechanism of fixing the central parity, the RMB was allowed to appreciate gradually relative to the dollar (Figure 4.1).

In May 2007, the floating band of the yuan was widened to ±0.5 percent around the central parity. The PBC used customary language to describe the move:

> In order to improve the managed floating exchange rate mechanism—
> managed floating exchange rate regime based on market supply and

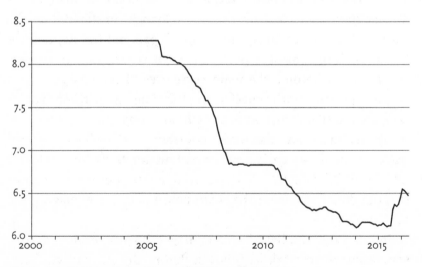

Figure 4.1 RMB per dollar (January 2000 to April 2016).
A decrease denotes appreciation of the RMB (fewer RMB per dollar).
Source: The State Administration of Foreign Exchange.

demand with reference to a basket of currencies—facilitate the development of the exchange market, and strengthen financial institutions' ability of pricing and risk management, [the People's Bank of China] has decided to widen [the] yuan's band.

This move received a cautiously positive response from the IMF and the U.S. Treasury, but the overall skeptical reaction was summed up by a foreign exchange trader interviewed by *The Wall Street Journal*, who said that "it 'means nothing' for yuan appreciation. We don't even use half of the current band. This is just to impress [U.S. Treasury Secretary] Henry Paulson."

By the summer of 2008, the RMB had risen in value by 17 percent relative to its level in June 2005, and was trading at 6.84 yuan per dollar. Then, in September 2008, the Lehman moment arrived and the world economy stood on the brink of financial cataclysm. Unannounced, the PBC quietly repegged the RMB to the dollar, not wanting currency fluctuations to add to an already volatile environment.

In June 2010, with the world economy slowly getting back on its feet, the PBC decided to relax the currency peg. There was no formal announcement of this move, which was understandable since there had been no formal announcement of a change in policy two years prior. Rather, a PBC spokesman hinted that the change would do the following:

[F]urther facilitate the renminbi exchange rate mechanism. Increase the elasticity of [the] Chinese exchange rate. During the recession, many other currencies have depreciated a lot against [the U.S. dollar], but the renminbi was stable, playing an important role in confronting the international recession. Now the global economy is gradually resurging, so it's necessary to further facilitate the exchange rate mechanism announced in 2005, increasing the elasticity of the renminbi's exchange rate.

The IMF took a positive view, welcoming the PBC's announcement that it would increase exchange rate flexibility and return to the managed floating exchange rate regime that was in place before the global financial crisis. U.S. President Barack Obama called it a "constructive step that can help safeguard the recovery and contribute to a more balanced global economy." U.S. Treasury Secretary Timothy Geithner added, "We welcome China's decision to increase the flexibility of its exchange rate. Vigorous implementation would make a positive contribution to strong and balanced global growth."

FLEXIBILITY WELCOME, BUT ONLY ONE WAY

Note that these official statements referred mostly to exchange rate flexibility rather than to an appreciation of the currency, which was what the U.S. and China's other trading partners really wanted, as that would put a dent in the price competitiveness of China's exports. The presumption was that a more flexible RMB could go just one way: up. Only a statement by the IMF referred explicitly to a stronger RMB as being helpful in rebalancing the Chinese economy. The idea behind the IMF's statement was that a stronger currency would increase the purchasing power of Chinese households, causing them to save less while consuming more. This would help shift the balance of China's GDP growth away from depending on investment and exports, instead increasing the contribution of household consumption to growth. Rebalancing the economy in this manner was a stated objective of the government.

In April 2012, the floating band was widened to ±1 percent around the central parity. The IMF welcomed the shift as underlining China's commitment to rebalancing its economy toward domestic consumption and allowing market forces to play a greater role in determining the exchange rate. To fend off criticism that any praise was premature, IMF Managing Director Christine Lagarde remarked, "It is not a baby step; it is a very good step in the right direction." The U.S. Treasury was less enthusiastic, issuing a statement to the effect that, "while we welcome the progress to date, the process of correcting the misalignment of China's exchange rate remains incomplete, and further progress is needed."

In March 2014, the floating band was widened further to ±2 percent around the central parity. At a press conference, a PBC official made this statement to signal another move toward a more flexible exchange rate and why it was good for China:

The communiqué of the third plenary session of the 18th central committee put forward the idea that the market should play a decisive role in the allocation of resources. As the important price of the factor market, the exchange rate is one of the decisive factors in allocating the domestic and international resources. Widening the band is good for increasing the elasticity of the exchange rate, higher efficiency in resources allocation, further [strengthening] the decisive role of the market, and [facilitating] the economic development transformation and structural adjustment.

The IMF and the U.S. Treasury endorsed the move. However, just a month later, the RMB experienced a bout of weakening relative to the dollar, which was widely seen as having been engineered by the PBC to scare off speculators who were betting heavily that the currency would have to appreciate. The U.S. Treasury hit back with a strong admonishment:

The Chinese authorities have been unwilling to allow an appreciation large enough to bring the currency to market equilibrium, opting instead for a gradual adjustment which has now been partially reversed. China should disclose foreign-exchange market intervention regularly to increase the credibility of its monetary policy framework and to promote exchange-rate and financial-market transparency.

For all of America's complaints about the RMB, though, from June 2005 to June 2014 it had in fact risen in value by nearly 25 percent relative to the dollar. On a trade-weighted basis, the RMB's nominal appreciation over that period was even larger, at almost 30 percent (Figure 4.2). However, the U.S. administration faced the uncomfortable fact that the bilateral trade deficit the U.S. ran with China had climbed to an all-time high of nearly $350 billion in 2014. In other words, even with the RMB appreciating slowly but steadily, the U.S. was importing more goods and services from China than it was exporting to that country, and that ratio was increasing. With the U.S. economy experiencing weak employment growth at that time, China was too tempting a target for U.S. politicians.

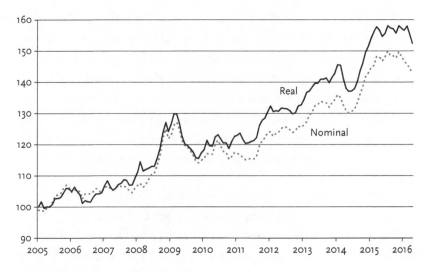

Figure 4.2 Effective exchange rates.
Indexes set to 100 in June 2005. An increase denotes appreciation of the RMB; a decrease denotes depreciation.
Source: Bank for International Settlements.

THE TIDE BEGINS TO TURN

Meanwhile, the world economy was itself becoming unbalanced. During the second half of 2014 and into 2015, there was a growing divergence in business cycle conditions between the U.S. and other major advanced economies. The U.S. economic recovery was strengthening while Europe and Japan were battling recession. The European Central Bank (ECB) and the Bank of Japan (BOJ) were not only trying to support economic growth, but were also trying desperately to stave off deflation. By the summer of 2015, it seemed as though it was just a matter of time before the U.S. Federal Reserve would start raising interest rates while the ECB and BOJ were still trying to pump money into their economies and weaken their currencies. During this period, the dollar strengthened substantially against all other major currencies. Except one.

The RMB alone weakened only marginally against the dollar since the PBC was still managing the currency's value relative to the dollar. With the dollar gaining strength, the RMB was rising along with it against all other currencies even as China's economy was weakening and its exports were suffering from weak demand around the world. From July 2014 to July 2015, the RMB depreciated by a modest 0.8 percent relative to the dollar. But, on a trade-weighted basis, the RMB *appreciated* by 14 percent against the currencies of its major trading partners despite the slowing of China's growth momentum.

International pressure for the RMB to appreciate further had eased off by this time. In May 2015, the IMF declared that the currency was no longer undervalued, a significant shift after more than a decade of making the case that a stronger RMB would be good for China and the rest of the world. In addition to the substantial appreciation of the currency since 2005, China's current account surplus (which comprises its trade surplus and net factor income from abroad) had averaged just 2 percent from 2011 to 2014, down sharply from 10 percent in 2007 (Figure 4.3). Moreover, with China's economic growth having slowed, it would be unreasonable to expect the RMB to continue appreciating. Given the pressure it faced from the U.S. Congress, the U.S. administration was less gracious, acknowledging the RMB's appreciation but not conceding the currency was no longer undervalued.

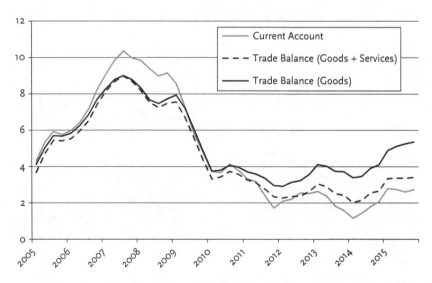

Figure 4.3 Current account and trade balances (as a percentage of the gross domestic product [GDP]).
The current account balance (light solid line), the goods and services trade balance (dashed line), and the merchandise trade balance (goods only; dark solid line) are shown as ratios to nominal GDP. The figure shows four-quarter trailing moving averages for all three variables.
Sources: The State Administration of Foreign Exchange and the National Bureau of Statistics.

The U.S. administration's economic case against China for keeping its currency artificially undervalued was becoming increasingly difficult to sustain. One of the main indicators of China's foreign exchange market intervention—accumulation of foreign exchange reserves—had turned around sharply since June 2014. From the peak level of $3.99 trillion in June 2014, reserves had fallen to $3.65 trillion by July 2015 (Figure 4.4).

Currency valuation effects accounted for part of this decline of $350 billion. It is widely believed that China holds about two-thirds of its reserves in financial assets denominated in U.S. dollars, although this has never been confirmed officially. The remainder is likely to be kept largely in assets denominated in euros and yen, with smaller amounts in a few other currencies. Since the dollar appreciated against virtually every other major currency during this period, the value of China's reserves held in other currencies but reported in terms of U.S. dollars would have fallen even if there were no actual change in the holdings of various assets. This is the result of simple accounting; the same amount in euros is worth fewer dollars when the euro depreciates relative to the dollar.

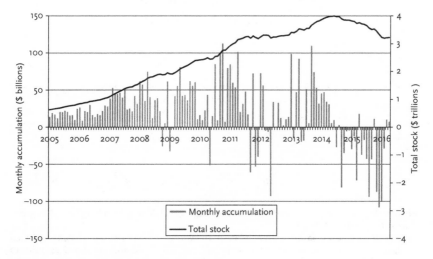

Figure 4.4 Foreign exchange reserves.
Source: The People's Bank of China.

Adverse market valuation effects compounded these unfavorable currency effects. Financial markets around the world performed poorly during this period, driving down the market value of many financial assets, especially equities. It is likely that many of China's foreign assets lost some of their notional market value.

The currency and market valuation effects on China's reported reserve position cannot be estimated precisely because China does not make public the currency and asset composition of its foreign exchange reserves. Official data indicate that valuation effects explain only about one-third of the loss in the book value of China's reserves during 2015, similar to the estimates of many private sector analysts.

Instead, China had expended reserves trying to maintain the stability of the RMB exchange rate relative to the dollar. This was exactly the reverse of the operations the PBC had been conducting in foreign exchange markets for more than a decade. China's trade surplus had narrowed. Less financial capital was coming into the country because of concerns about the economy. Moreover, with more channels for international portfolio diversification available as a result of capital account opening, outflows of domestic capital from China were also picking up. All of this meant that demand for RMB was falling and the corresponding demand for foreign currencies was rising.

Now that the RMB was facing depreciation pressures, the PBC was selling the dollars it had accumulated on its balance sheet and buying up RMB in order to preserve its currency's value relative to the dollar. Although a $350 billion loss in reserves in just one year sounds ominous, it was less than 10 percent of China's stock of reserves. It looked as though the PBC might continue gently guiding down the value of the RMB relative to the dollar, perhaps losing some additional reserves when making this process smooth. Concerns about the state of the economy were growing, and the tumble in Chinese stock markets since their peak in June 2015 was undermining the confidence of domestic and foreign investors. Yet, there was no inkling of panic in the foreign exchange markets.

The calm in China's currency markets would prove all too fleeting.

GOOD INTENTIONS BACKFIRE

On August 11, 2015, China rocked financial markets worldwide. The PBC created such tumult simply by doing what the world had been asking it to do for a long time: free up the currency and allow it to be determined by market forces. It is equally important to understand what China did not do, and why it implemented this shift in currency policy in the manner in which it did.

China's foreign exchange rate management has three elements: first, the reference pricing mechanism, whereby the PBC sets the opening RMB–dollar price for trading on the Shanghai CFETS each morning; second, the 2 percent trading band around the central parity, which determines the maximum amount of intraday volatility in the RMB–dollar exchange rate; and third, a "dirty float" to prevent excessive exchange rate volatility when the PBC determines that the exchange rate is overshooting or shifting too rapidly in one direction or the other.

On August 11, 2015, with no advance notice, the PBC changed the first element of the exchange rate management mechanism, combining it with a 1.9 percent devaluation of the RMB relative to the dollar. The first step in this action meant that the opening RMB–dollar reference rate on the Shanghai foreign exchange market would tightly track the closing price at the end of the previous day's trading, although it could also be affected by trades on U.S. and European markets while the Shanghai market was closed. Or, to put it in the PBC's terminology, the objective was to "improve quotation of the RMB central parity." The key point is that, in principle, the PBC would no longer arbitrarily set the morning reference price at a level that was not consistent with conditions in the foreign exchange market. The other two elements of the exchange rate management system, which allow the PBC to intervene in foreign exchange markets to reduce intraday volatility or "excessive" currency movements in one direction or another, were left unchanged.

It appeared the PBC had astutely combined a move to weaken the RMB with a shift to a more market-determined exchange rate. This should have blunted criticism that the move was, in fact, just a case of orchestrated currency devaluation since, technically, all the PBC was doing was reducing its foreign exchange market intervention to prop up the RMB's value as part of a shift to a more freely floating currency. China's currency move could also have been interpreted as a relatively modest and defensive one. The move was aimed at signaling that the PBC would not persist in supporting the RMB's value relative to the dollar if the dollar were to keep rising against other major currencies. Indeed, as noted before, in the year before this move, the trade-weighted effective exchange rate of the RMB had appreciated sharply even while economic growth was slowing, largely because the dollar had appreciated relative to virtually every other major currency. It simply did not make sense for China to have an appreciating currency while its economic growth momentum was slipping away.

However, the shift in China's currency policy set off a negative reaction in stock markets around the world, including the U.S., as it was taken as a response to domestic economic weakness rather than as a market-oriented reform. The move also reverberated in currency markets worldwide, where it was interpreted as an indication that China had joined other central banks such as the ECB and the BOJ in trying to use a weaker currency to prop up exports and counter weak domestic demand. In the next two days, the RMB's value relative to the dollar fell by another 2 percent. The PBC then had to step in because it was beginning to look like the currency was in free fall.

Why did China implement the reform in such an infelicitous manner that forced it to backtrack so quickly on letting the currency float more freely? Subsequent statements by PBC officials indicate they believed it was necessary to adjust the level of the currency to prevent speculators from taking advantage of the currency reform by placing one-way bets. If the RMB were allowed to float more freely and most market participants expected it to depreciate, it *would* depreciate, but perhaps by too much and too quickly. The initial devaluation was intended to avoid giving that gift to currency speculators, and the PBC seemed to believe it could then let the currency float more freely around its new level, at which the pressures would be balanced evenly. As assistant governor of the PBC Zhang Xiaohui put it later in that fateful week: "The three percent depreciation pressure has been released, and the deviation correction is almost done." China's official news agency *Xinhua* quoted PBC Chief Economist Ma Jun as saying, "The shift is a one-off technical correction and should not be interpreted as an indicator of future depreciation."

The PBC's lack of an effective communications strategy certainly made matters worse. If there is one thing that central bankers around the world have learned, it is that unclear communications, especially close to major policy changes, can lead to a frenzy in markets. The PBC's communication strategy amounted to a press release announcing the move, followed by two question-and-answer (Q&A) posts on the PBC's website. A press conference to explain the move more fully was not held until 36 hours after the initial announcement on the PBC's website—an eternity in financial markets and by which time a great deal of damage had been done in terms of worldwide perceptions of the motives behind the move and the PBC's competence at managing the shift in policy.

Subsequently, the PBC made a determined effort to correct the perception that the currency move was just a cover for devaluing the RMB. At the press conference on the morning of August 13, PBC Deputy Governor Yi Gang dismissed this view: "It's nonsense to report that [the PBC] wants to initiate an eventual 10 percent depreciation of the currency in an effort to help exporters." He also emphasized that the key objective was to increase exchange rate flexibility because that would be good for China: "It's a good news for renminbi because though a fixed exchange rate looks stable, it hides accumulated problems. The effect of the change to the internationalization of renminbi is positive as well. . . . The elastic exchange rate is in favor of the more stable capital inflow and outflow."

In a separate statement, Prime Minister Li Keqiang added:

The process of the internationalization of renminbi will be decided by the market, and it also depends on Chinese economic development. But one thing [is] for sure, the continuous depreciation of [the] yuan is not in favor of the internationalization of [the] yuan. It's not what our policy favors. China is not the origin of worldwide economic risk, but is the origin and motivator of world economic development.

The U.S. Treasury was caught in a bind. Rather than applauding the policy change that it had called for over many years, the U.S. Treasury reserved judgment:

> We will continue to monitor how these changes are implemented and continue to press China on the pace of its reforms, including additional measures to transition to a market-oriented exchange rate and its stated desire to move towards an economy that is more dependent on domestic demand, which is in China and America's best interests. Any reversal in reforms would be a troubling development.

The absence of huzzahs from the U.S. administration and negative reactions from U.S. politicians led the PBC back to intervening in the currency market, this time to keep the RMB from *depreciating* relative to the U.S. dollar. With President Xi Jinping due to undertake his first state visit to Washington just a few weeks later (in late September), China wanted "peace and quiet" on the currency front. Indeed, in his remarks at a joint press conference with the Chinese leader in the Rose Garden of the White House, President Obama brought up the currency issue more directly than in the past, eschewing oblique references to exchange rate flexibility: "President Xi discussed his commitment to accelerate market reforms, avoid devaluing China's currency, and have China play a greater role in upholding the rules-based system that underpins the global economy—all of which are steps we very much support."

At a speech in the U.S. in late September, Chinese President Xi Jinping tried to set the record straight on the Chinese government's intentions and dispel fears that China was initiating a round of competitive devaluation:

> Given the economic and financial situation both domestically and abroad, there is no basis for the continuous depreciation of the RMB. We will stick to the purpose of our reform to have market supply and demand decide the exchange rate and allow the RMB to float both ways.

> We are against competitive depreciation or currency war. We will not lower the RMB exchange rate to boost export. To develop the capital market and improve the market-based pricing of the RMB exchange rate are the direction of our reform.

It was not just ruffled political feathers that needed smoothing. The shift in the currency regime on August 11, 2015, also set off a sharp divergence between the onshore (CNY) and offshore (CNH) RMB–dollar exchange rates. The RMB was, for much of the remainder of the month, worth less in offshore than onshore markets, reflecting downward pressures on the RMB as markets appeared to have interpreted the government's move as possibly being the first in a series of devaluations intended to support the weak economy by boosting exports. By intervening in the CNY market, the government was able to limit the downward pressures on the RMB–dollar exchange rate, but at the cost of opening up a spread between the onshore and offshore rates.

By mid September 2015, this gap between the CNY and CNH exchange rates had been closed. Press and analyst reports suggested that the PBC and Chinese state-owned commercial banks intervened directly in the CNH market to facilitate this outcome. It remains to be seen over time if such attempts to force convergence of the two rates can be sustained or if the PBC will, in fact, allow the onshore rate to float more freely and thereby lead to a natural, market-led convergence of the two rates.

Actions taken by the PBC to stabilize the currency's value led to a drain on foreign exchange reserves. The PBC was, in effect, selling assets in dollars and other hard currencies and using the proceeds to buy RMB on the open market to support the RMB's price. In August alone, the stock of foreign exchange reserves fell by $94 billion. From July to December 2015, reserves fell by a total of $415 billion. This depletion of reserves caused consternation in China, where the stock of reserves was viewed as the national patrimony earned by the blood, sweat, and toil of its workers, who were manufacturing the exports that earned hard currency revenues.

In an interview with *The Wall Street Journal* in September 2015, President Xi Jinping sent a message of reassurance to both his domestic and foreign audiences.

> There has been a recent drop in China's foreign reserves. This actually reflects improvement to the mix of local currency as well as foreign exchange assets and liabilities of domestic banks, enterprises and individuals.... These changes are part of normal capital flows, which are moderate and manageable. Foreign investors who aim at long-term gains are still investing in China. China's foreign exchange reserves remain abundant and are still very large by international standards.... With improvement to the RMB exchange rate regime and progress in RMB internationalization, it is quite normal that China's foreign reserves may increase or decrease, and there is no need to overreact to it.

On October 18, a terse statement was posted on the State Council website under the slightly patronizing title "How to Treat the Recent Drop in China's Foreign Reserves More Rationally." The statement was intended to allay fears about the depletion of foreign exchange reserves, making the case that it was part of a normal process:

> The shrinkage of the foreign exchange reserves is to a small extent due to the balance of payments deficit ([the PBC's] intervention), and to a large extent because of the decrease in asset values (stronger dollar and loss on investment). But there is no need to panic because the impact on the general public is very limited. With the better RMB exchange rate mechanism, and its internationalization, the future rise/drop of the foreign exchange reserves will be normal and not surprising.

PLUS ÇA CHANGE ... THE BASKET REEMERGES

On December 11, 2015, the PBC signaled another change in policy in its own inimitable way. Late that evening Beijing time, the PBC posted an article on its website by a "guest commentator of CFETS." The article, "The Launch of RMB Index Helps to Guide Public View of RMB Exchange Rate," indicated that the CFETS would begin publishing a set of trade-weighted exchange rate indexes on its website.

The piece laid out the logic behind this move, noting:

> [F]or quite long, market participants have used [the] bilateral exchange rate of RMB against [the U.S. dollar] to assess RMB exchange rate movements. However, as fluctuations of [the] exchange rate serve to adjust trade and investment activities with multiple trading partners, the bilateral RMB–USD exchange rate is not considered a good indicator of the international parity of tradable goods. Therefore, it is more desirable to refer to both the bilateral RMB–USD exchange rate and [the] exchange rate based on a basket of currencies.

The piece made it clear that the objective of publishing the index was to "bring about a shift in how the public and the market observe RMB exchange rate movements."

This approach would certainly have made more sense even before December 2015. For instance, the increase in the trade-weighted exchange rate of the RMB from July 2014 to July 2015, while the Chinese economy was losing growth momentum, was clearly not desirable. This appreciation was the result of the PBC keeping the currency's value from falling significantly relative to the dollar even as the dollar was appreciating against other major currencies. This outcome could have been avoided if the PBC had, in fact, been managing the currency's value relative to the trade-weighted basket of currencies rather than the dollar, for then the RMB's value would have been stable against that basket.

In any event, after the August 11 communications debacle, this was a welcome change in the PBC's strategy regarding both practice and communications. First, by putting into practice a policy that had in principle been in operation since 2005, this move would make it easier for the PBC to delink the RMB from the dollar. Second, by hinting at the policy change before it took effect, the PBC was preparing the market for further RMB depreciation relative to the dollar in the short run—if the dollar were to strengthen further—and a more sensible benchmark for future movements in the currency.

The apparent increase in transparency regarding policy actions did not extend to making public the weights that various currencies would have in the currency basket against which the PBC would manage the RMB. The CFETS indicated it would publish three exchange rate indexes—one based on thirteen of fourteen currency pairs with the RMB trading at that time on the CFETS (excluding the Kazakhstani tenge), one on the much larger set of currencies used by the Bank for International Settlements (or BIS) to calculate its indexes, and a separate index based on the four major reserve currencies (the dollar, the euro, the yen, and the British pound sterling). The crucial point was that the RMB–dollar exchange rate would receive a weight of, at most, 42 percent in these indexes. In fact, in the BIS index, the dollar would have a weight of only 18 percent, consistent with the portion of China's trade accounted for by the U.S. By reporting three indexes, including one widely used by academics and analysts (the BIS index), the PBC was also hoping to deflect criticism that it was cherry-picking an index to suit its own convenience.

Of course, as with any move the PBC made, there were critics. Many market analysts from Western financial firms noted dismissively in their research reports that this form of oblique communication by the PBC only fueled unnecessary speculation about its true intentions and added to confusion about how the exchange rate would actually be managed.

Interestingly, there was no formal statement from the PBC itself or any of its officials about a shift to managing the currency's value relative to a basket. To dispel the confusion, on December 14, 2015, the PBC posted another guest commentary from the CFETS. This commentary reiterated the official view that the exchange rate system had been essentially the same since 2005. The article noted:

> First, the managed floating exchange rate regime has been in place for a long time, which is based on market supply and demand and with reference to a basket of currencies. Since the exchange rate regime reform in 2005, most of the time [the] RMB exchange rate fluctuated under this regime, except for [a] few periods when management was enhanced due to China's international responsibility as a major economy.

The article went on to clarify that managing the currency's value relative to a basket would not be a mechanical process, instantly generating multiple interpretations among market analysts of the weights the PBC would attach to the several currencies in the basket. The article noted that managing the RMB "with reference to a basket of currencies does not mean pegging to a basket of currencies or adjusting [the] RMB exchange rate mechanically in line with the movements of the exchange rate index of the currencies in the basket. Market supply and demand is another important reference. The floating and flexible exchange rate is an outcome of these two factors combined with necessary management." This did not quite reach the level of clarity that participants in the currency markets were looking for.

Compounding the confusion about what exactly had been accomplished through the August 11 currency reform, the PBC indicated through a Q&A posted on the SAFE website that it was continuing to use the onshore RMB–dollar exchange rate at 4:30 p.m. as the closing price, although trading hours on the Shanghai exchange had been extended to 9:30 p.m. local time. The stated logic was that the volume of trading past 4:30 p.m. was relatively thin, and the RMB–dollar exchange rate could therefore be unduly volatile in the remaining trading hours, "making it easy for the exchange rate to be misstated and even be manipulated."

Moreover, the CFETS noted "[t]he RMB/[U.S. dollar] central parity will keep reflecting the characteristics of 'previous close + movements of a basket of currencies.'" In other words, the central parity quotation for the RMB–dollar rate on the morning of the next trading day could deviate from the actual 9:30 p.m. closing price on the onshore market, and even from the 4:30 p.m. closing price, based on the movements of the RMB relative to an unspecified basket of currencies. Reassuringly, the CFETS statement noted that between August 12, 2015, and December 31, 2015, the deviation between the central parity on any given trading day and the 4:30 p.m. closing rate on the previous trading day had been reduced to an average of barely 0.1 percent. This was much lower than the average deviation of almost 1 percent between the closing prices on one day and opening prices on the next day during the trading period of January 1, 2015, through August 11, 2015. The CFETS statement used this as evidence that the "rationality of the central parity's quotation has been enhanced." During the latter half of February 2016, this deviation rose to 0.2 percent on average—a small number but still a significant one in the context of currency markets, where there is money to be made on even smaller differentials. Thus, the notion that the RMB central parity has become a market-determined exchange rate might count as at least a modest overstatement.

NEITHER GOD NOR MAGICIAN

On February 15, 2016, *Caixin* magazine published a remarkably detailed and wide-ranging interview with PBC Governor Zhou Xiaochuan. He took on critics who had argued that the PBC's communication strategies had been inept, adding to market confusion and unnecessary volatility in the RMB exchange rate. After acknowledging the importance of an effective communication strategy for a central bank, he said:

> Good communication is never an easy thing. Currently, there are many uncertainties in the global financial market, which have led to the divergence of opinions and many debates. In these days of stress, everybody hopes for a person of foresight or an authoritative voice that could turn uncertainties into certainties. But uncertainties do exist in the market, which cannot be simply eliminated by some words of assurance. The central bank is neither God nor magician that could just wipe the uncertainties out. Therefore, sometimes the central bank has to say "Excuse us, but we have to wait for new data inputs." . . . Debates are unavoidable at times, and even within central banks there is sometimes internal divergence of viewpoints. At these particular times, the signals sent by forward guidance cannot give the market much relief.

Governor Zhou added in the interview that the PBC had developed specific communication strategies for specific constituencies. Its aim was to communicate with the general public about its monetary policy framework and the way it conducted policy. For those who used foreign exchange, especially importers and exporters, the

PBC focused on guiding and stabilizing their expectations. But, the PBC had no desire to be transparent to currency speculators: "For speculators, however, the central bank views them as rivals in a game, and it is unimaginable for the central bank to reveal its operational strategies to them. This is like a player who will never reveal his next moves to the opponent in a game of chess."

Both political and economic constraints have hindered the PBC's communication strategy. The PBC takes orders from the State Council and cannot deviate from the official CPC stance on any major issue. Moreover, with a decrepit financial system and an economy that is still under extensive and direct state control, the PBC's actions can have unpredictable effects, even more so than in the case of a central bank operating in a market economy. Nevertheless, as its actions reverberate with greater force within the Chinese economy and in global financial markets, the PBC is at a juncture where it has to improve its communications—both the message itself and the clarity with which it is delivered—if it is to be a source of stability rather than volatility. This is particularly true in the case of foreign exchange markets and will determine the level of confidence with which foreign investors approach investments in RMB-denominated assets.

A STEEL SHIELD TURNS INTO SPONGE

The RMB has taken a strange and convoluted journey during the past two decades. In 1998, China's government was praised for keeping the RMB stable and not letting markets determine its value as that could have meant a sharp depreciation in the currency, hurting Asian economies already in the midst of a crisis. During the 2000s, the IMF and the U.S., along with many other of China's trading partners, railed against the PBC's tight management of the currency. They wanted China to let the RMB's value be determined by market forces, rather then keep it artificially undervalued. Then, in 2015, when the Chinese government caved in to a long-standing demand of the international financial community—freeing up the currency's value to be determined by market forces—it was reviled. Could one blame China for asking the rest of the world to make up its mind?

This would, of course, be a disingenuous view, as the Chinese government has in fact been quite canny. Its policy moves, in substance and timing, have suited its own best interests every step of the way. But, China has clearly been able to take a longer-term view of its self-interest, as evidenced by its actions during the Asian financial crisis when it resisted the temptation to devalue the RMB, which could have further damaged the economic and financial stability of its trading partners in the region.

The reality is that China's shift toward a more market-determined exchange rate is going to be difficult to reverse, particularly as the capital account becomes more open. This does not mean that, as in the case of many other major central banks, the PBC will not intervene in foreign exchange markets to smooth out excessive market volatility or to try, at least temporarily, to push the currency's value in one direction or another as part of its monetary policy strategy. Nevertheless, the persistent tight management of the currency's value relative to the U.S. dollar is most likely a thing of the past, especially since that policy often led to destabilizing speculative flows of capital in one direction or another. As PBC Governor Zhou put it: "If the fixed exchange rate in the past was considered an unmovable steel shield, the more flexible exchange rate could be considered a sponge shield, with which we could better manage excessive speculation."

The opening of the capital account and the increasing flexibility of the exchange rate—although both are modest in scope and gradual in pace—are helping to promote the international role of the currency, as we see in the next chapter.

CHAPTER 5

The RMB Goes Global

> He was not a risk-taker. The stakes did not lure him. What lured him
> was the game itself, the rolling of the balls, the calculation and the
> execution, the possibility each game presented ... He was simply
> proud of the fact that it lay within his power to choose the rules of
> the game, loved to follow the unraveling of a necessity that he had
> himself created—here lay the humor for him.
>
> *The Execution of Justice*, Friedrich Dürrenmatt

The plumbing of international finance, it turns out, is not apolitical.

The Russian military intervened in Ukraine in February 2014, setting off rising tensions with the West that would peak with the Russian annexation of Crimea a few weeks later. With few good military options available, Europe and the U.S. chose to strike back with economic sanctions. The European Union and the U.S., along with other NATO allies such as Canada, imposed a broad range of sanctions. Some were symbolic, such as restricting the travel and business activities of individuals seen as close to the Russian leadership and complicit in the takeover of Crimea. An EU statement expanding these sanctions as tensions with Russia continued to rise struck directly at President Putin's associates, referring to "the recently expanded listing of persons and entities undermining Ukrainian territorial integrity and sovereignty, including the so-called 'cronies.'" Exports from the West to Russia involving high-technology oil exploration and production equipment as well as certain military goods were embargoed.

The financial sanctions were the most substantive measures and included restrictions on access to Western financial markets and services by designated Russian state-owned enterprises in the banking, energy, and defense sectors. These sanctions quickly bit into the Russian economy, which was already hurting from the decline in oil prices, a key source of export and tax revenues. Although only selected Russian firms and financial institutions were covered by the sanctions, the practical effect was to cut off Russian industry and finance from access to Western financial markets. Russian corporations could no longer raise capital abroad and faced difficulties completing financial transactions with foreign partners. Credit cards issued by Russian banks could no longer be used abroad because their payments would not be processed by the payment networks operated by firms such as Mastercard and Visa.

Russian President Vladimir Putin lashed out:

> We have never thought about it before, we believed that all our partners—Visa and MasterCard—are depoliticized economic entities. It turns out that they are strongly affected by political pressure and tend to succumb to it.... Payments within the country are made with Visa and MasterCard, and to a large extent this is done on servers located in the United States—this is crazy! ... now we have moved to practical measures to set up a national payment system.... We have to be completely certain that whatever happens in the world—in politics, the economy or in the world of finance—payments within the major industries will be conducted without a glitch, without any problem.

Russian Prime Minister Dmitry Medvedev elaborated on the risks his country faced because of its reliance on payment systems controlled by Western powers: "It is obvious that all foreign systems are convenient and everybody is used to them, but certainly they do not provide privacy and are vulnerable in terms of other risks, in particular politically."

By June, Elvira Nabiullina, Governor of the Central Bank of Russia, was able to declare: "Recent legislative amendments were passed making it possible to establish a full-fledged national payments system so that people here who use bank cards and are already used to this way of doing things will know that they are safe from any unfriendly action taken by parties outside Russia."

As would soon become apparent, however, even the Russian empire could not set up a smoothly functioning payment system, let alone one that was well integrated into the international financial system, in such a short period. About a month after Russia's National Payment System came into effect, it crashed and stayed down for a while during the early morning hours. A spokesman for the company did little to assuage concerns about the system's stability, unwittingly damning it with faint reassurance: "I can only say that it isn't a system failure. The crash wasn't caused by hardware or software-related problems." With tensions in Ukraine still simmering and the economic sanctions having been extended into 2016, Russia remains hobbled by the sanctions and the restrictions on its access to global payment and financial systems.

Clearly, having control of payment systems bestows both economic and geopolitical power. Recognizing this, China has taken notice and has recently started paying attention to the plumbing of the international financial system. No doubt it might have more benign motives related simply to increasing the efficiency of cross-border payments, but it is hard to imagine that China's leadership has not been paying close attention to the leverage that the U.S. and other Western economies gain from having control of the choke points in international finance.

A key building block for creating a cross-border payment system, and one that has given added momentum to the process, has been the RMB's rising prominence as an international currency. Indeed, many of the breathless pronouncements about the unstoppable advance of the RMB refer to its growing role as a currency for intermediating and settling cross-border trade and finance transactions. This chapter describes how, along this dimension, the RMB has come a long way in a short period and how the Chinese government has used these developments to gradually take control of its own financial destiny.

HONG KONG AS A STARTER PROJECT

In the mid 2000s, China began promoting the international use of the RMB, using its customary cautious and gradual approach. Hong Kong, with its sophisticated financial markets along with strong supervisory and other institutions, provided a perfect testing ground for these policy reforms during the initial stages of the RMB's path to becoming an international currency. It allowed the Chinese government to experimentally promote the RMB's international use without losing control. Not only could China keep the Mainland financial markets insulated from what was happening in Hong Kong, but the Chinese government also knew it could shut things down easily if the reforms created conditions too volatile for comfort. Meanwhile, its status as an international financial center meant that Hong Kong could help to actively build up the RMB's role, at least in Asia. The rule of law and the quality of the regulatory framework meant international investors felt more comfortable using Hong Kong as a center for RMB transactions because they had access to legal protections they could not take for granted on the Mainland.

As early as 2004, personal RMB business had been initiated in Hong Kong by allowing residents there to open deposit accounts denominated in RMB. In 2007, China began to take a number of additional steps to promote the international use of its currency, in most cases using Hong Kong as the platform.

TRADE SETTLEMENT

Given China's rapidly expanding trade volumes, promoting greater use of the RMB in trade settlement was a logical first step in the currency's internationalization process. In a relatively short period, cross-border trade settlement in the Chinese currency expanded substantially. Trade settlement in RMB reached $1.1

trillion in 2015, accounting for 30 percent of China's total external trade (exports plus imports). Considering that the amount of trade settled in RMB was essentially zero in 2000, this was a dramatic increase in the absolute amount as well as the share of China's trade that did not require an alternative "vehicle currency"— another currency used solely as an intermediating currency—to denominate and settle trade transactions.

It is important that we not be overly impressed by the RMB's progress as a trade settlement currency. Virtually all of the trade settled using the RMB involves China, either as an importing or exporting country. That is, the RMB is far from becoming a "vehicle currency" used in trade transactions between other countries.

Additionally, the rise in the share of China's trade settled using RMB plateaued starting in early 2014. This may be related to the dissipation of appreciation pressures on the currency since that period. The notion that the level of interest in settling trades in RMB is related to movements in the value of the currency is consistent with a breakdown of the settlement data by the direction of trade flows.

For the first couple of years after RMB trade settlement was initiated, data for these settlement transactions were available separately for imports and exports. This breakdown showed that most of the RMB trade settlement involved transactions that represented imports into China. Payments by Chinese importers in RMB allows foreign traders to acquire the currency, which at that time was difficult to acquire offshore through other channels. In contrast, payments for China's exports were being settled using RMB to a very limited extent, suggesting that recipients of exports from China either had limited amounts of the currency or were disinclined to reduce their holdings.

Some interpreted this one-sided pattern of trade settlements as reflecting the desire on the part of foreign traders to bet on the RMB's appreciation by acquiring as much of the currency as possible. By the middle of 2014, the RMB had started weakening modestly against the dollar and currency traders saw further depreciation as more likely than appreciation. Around this time, interest in settling trade transactions with RMB leveled off.

These developments in trade settlement illustrate how China's rising trade volumes and financial integration into global markets will make it increasingly difficult to tightly manage the currency's external value. As volumes of goods and services trade increase, the demand for RMB for trade settlement will fluctuate with broader appreciation or depreciation pressures on the RMB and will act as a conduit through which to intensify those pressures even if the government restricts capital flows. It may be worth noting that, reflecting official sensitivities about the matter, when analysts began paying closer attention to the breakdown of the trade settlement data and what they meant for pressures on the currency, the government stopped publishing the disaggregated data.

Hong Kong banks handle about 95 percent of RMB trade settlement. Settling trade transactions in RMB requires access to that currency. To support RMB settlement, the Hong Kong Interbank Market initiated an RMB settlement system in March 2006, providing a variety of services such as check clearing, remittance processing, and bankcard payment services. There were virtually no RMB clearing transactions until mid 2010, when financial institutions in Hong Kong were allowed to open RMB-denominated accounts.

RMB activities in Hong Kong are supported by a sizable pool of liquidity in that currency. As of March 2016, RMB customer deposits and certificates of deposit issued by banks in Hong Kong together amounted to RMB 759 billion ($115 billion), a modest amount and a drop from the previous year's level of RMB 850 billion. RMB financing is also available in Hong Kong in the form of bank loans. The outstanding amount of RMB loans in Hong Kong was RMB 294 billion ($45 billion) in October 2015, up 56 percent from the beginning of the year.

DIM SUM AND PANDA BONDS

Another notable development is the rising issuance of RMB-denominated bonds, better known as *dim sum bonds*, in international financial markets. These bonds were first issued in Hong Kong, which remains by far the largest RMB bond market outside the Mainland. The outstanding stock of these bonds issued in Hong Kong was RMB 367 billion ($56 billion) in October 2015 (starting from a minuscule level in 2010). This was slightly lower than the stock in 2014. Issuance of these bonds started slowing in the middle of 2014, possibly reflecting shifting expectations about changes in the RMB's value. The likelihood of RMB depreciation reduces the incentive for firms to raise funds in that currency as a means of currency speculation.

Mainland government agencies, banks, and enterprises accounted for 40 percent of the outstanding stock of RMB bonds as of October 2015, but it is not just Chinese institutions that are using this instrument to raise funds. A similar proportion of RMB bond issuers in Hong Kong are entities incorporated overseas (outside the Mainland and Hong Kong). Multinational companies from countries such as Germany, South Korea, and the U.S. apparently view these bonds as an affordable way to raise RMB funds that can then be used to fund investments and other operations in China. Hong Kong banks and enterprises account for the remaining 20 percent of these bonds.

The initiation and rapid expansion of various elements of the offshore RMB market has given the currency a significant foothold in the Asian region's trade and financial transactions. By this measure, the RMB is also beginning to gain traction outside Asia.

Sovereign governments in other regions have started, in a small way, to issue RMB-denominated bonds. The U.K. was the first Western government to do so, selling RMB 3 billion (roughly $470 million) in government bonds in London in October 2014. The bond issued by the U.K. was the first by a national government; but, in 2013, the Canadian province of British Columbia had already become the first foreign governmental entity to issue an RMB-denominated bond. In December 2015, there were indications that the Russian government was planning to issue $1 billion in RMB-denominated sovereign bonds in Moscow.

In October 2015, the PBC, for the first time, issued offshore one-year RMB bonds in London in the amount of RMB 5 billion (approximately $760 million). The PBC noted that this was its first ever offshore RMB bond issuance and it would help promote the offshore use of the currency as well as cross-border trade and investment. In May 2016, China's finance ministry announced plans to issue RMB bonds with a total face value of RMB 3 billion (roughly $450 million) in London.

In December 2015, South Korea became the first country to issue RMB-denominated sovereign debt in China's domestic market. The RMB 3 billion ($450 million) issue of so-called *panda bonds* was substantially oversubscribed, indicating strong interest in these financial assets. Previously, only a handful of foreign firms and Chinese companies incorporated overseas had issued such bonds. By early 2016, there was a small but growing list of foreign governments and companies that were getting ready to issue more such bonds. Panda bonds are seen as a way to deepen bond markets in China, promote the internationalization of the RMB, and give domestic investors opportunities to diversify their portfolios (since the bonds are issued by foreign governments and firms) while keeping their money in onshore markets. Foreign investors also seem to find these bonds an attractive option for investing in Chinese debt markets. These investors may have better information about foreign companies and governments issuing these bonds, obviating the need to seek hard-to-obtain information on the credit profiles of domestic Chinese issuers.

THE RMB'S ROLE AS A PAYMENT CURRENCY

One indicator of the RMB's rising international role that has received considerable attention is its evolution as a payment currency (i.e., a currency used for clearance and settlement of cross-border financial transactions). Data on the RMB's role as a payment currency are based on information compiled and provided by the Society for Worldwide Interbank Financial Telecommunication (SWIFT). The SWIFT is an interbank communications system that was developed in 1973 for the purpose of providing a standardized means of sharing financial information more rapidly and efficiently between institutions around the world. While SWIFT transports financial messages, it does not perform the service of clearing or settling transactions. Because financial institutions have multiple means of exchanging information about their financial transactions, SWIFT statistics on financial flows do not represent complete market or industry statistics. Nevertheless, the majority of international interbank messages use the SWIFT network.

SWIFT data on RMB usage provide a gauge of the number of financial institutions using the RMB for payments, both inbound and outbound, throughout the world. The data can also be used to show the share of the RMB in terms of the value of all payments transacted over the SWIFT network. The RMB's share has risen significantly in recent years, from 0.3 percent at the end of 2011 to a peak of 2.8 percent in August 2015. This share, which had been rising gradually but steadily for four years, then declined over the subsequent six months and stood at 1.8 percent in April 2016. The volatility in the exchange rate since the August 11, 2015 exchange rate reform appears to have reduced interest in making payments using RMB.

Although the RMB's share of payments still seems modest, it has vaulted the currency from ranking twentieth in terms of importance at the end of 2012 to becoming the fifth most important payment currency (sharing that rank with the Canadian dollar). That leaves just four currencies—the U.S. dollar (44 percent), the euro (29 percent), the pound sterling (9 percent), and the Japanese yen (3 percent)—ahead of the RMB by this metric. In August 2015, the RMB jumped ahead briefly into fourth place ahead of the yen, but lost that spot a month later. It is likely, based on past trends and the continued rise of China, that the RMB will regain this rank in the near future.

Hong Kong accounts for the dominant share of RMB payment transactions in 2015, with a share of 70 percent of such transactions over the SWIFT network. This share has declined marginally over time, from 80 percent in 2012, as other financial centers increasingly intermediate RMB payments. Singapore and the U.K. account for 7 percent and 5 percent, respectively, whereas China itself accounts for less than 5 percent. Most of the countries on this list are also designated as RMB clearing centers. The U.S. is an important exception; it does not have a clearing center for RMB transactions but still accounts for nearly 3 percent of RMB payments over the SWIFT network.

Although the SWIFT data on the RMB's rising international role have attracted great interest, we must bear several caveats in mind. First, SWIFT estimates its market share to be around 80 percent of all cross-border payment flows by volume (correspondent banking); the remaining transactions flow through channels other than SWIFT. Second, SWIFT does not capture all intrainstitutional flows since financial institutions may use their own proprietary networks or systems. Third, SWIFT does not capture a large share of domestic flows. For instance, transactions intermediated through the Fedwire Funds Service in the U.S. are not on SWIFT. Fourth, the financial flows track bank-to-bank activity rather than the underlying commercial flows. For instance, a commercial transaction between China and South Africa that is intermediated through a U.S. bank could involve two messages—one between South Africa and the U.S., and the other between the U.S. and China. This could result in double counting of some financial transactions (relative to the value of the underlying commercial transactions). Notwithstanding these caveats, the SWIFT data reveal the rising prominence of the RMB as an international payment currency.

LIMITED USE IN INTERNATIONAL FINANCIAL TRANSACTIONS

The pace of the internationalization of China's currency depends on its use in international financial transactions as well. The choice of currency for denomination and settlement of trade flows depends on the extent to which that currency can also be used in international financial transactions. The BIS conducts a survey of central banks around the world once every three years to gather data on foreign exchange market turnover, derivatives markets, and currency denomination of international debt securities. The last survey, which was published in 2014, covers the period through 2013. The RMB has no doubt made progress in its international use since 2013, but the data discussed here indicate how far it still has to travel on the path to becoming a major international currency.

Foreign exchange market turnover is a good indicator of a currency's potential for developing into a vehicle currency in international trade. The RMB now accounts for just over 2 percent (of 200 percent, as each transaction involves two currencies) of all turnover in foreign exchange markets. While this is a small share, it is higher than that of any other emerging market currency and also represents a considerable increase over a relatively short period, especially for a currency that is not freely convertible. The U.S. dollar is dominant along this dimension, accounting for 87 percent of turnover in 2013. The four major reserve currencies (the dollar, the euro, the yen, and the pound sterling), along with the Australian dollar and the Swiss franc, together account for 169 percent of total turnover.

In terms of the geographic distribution of foreign exchange turnover, however, China has the advantage of having Hong Kong as an important financial center for settling foreign exchange transactions. Hong Kong accounts for 4 percent of global foreign exchange market turnover (compared with 41 percent for the U.K. and 19 percent for the U.S.). This puts the RMB on a competitive footing, at least relative to other emerging market currencies, in terms of attaining the role of an international currency.

When one breaks down foreign exchange trading into its several components, it is clear that trading in the RMB has advanced to a significant extent but remains far below that of the traditional reserve currencies. Still, the RMB has made considerable progress—especially in its share in the worldwide volumes of trades in foreign exchange derivatives, outright forwards, and foreign exchange swaps.

Another indicator of the currency's potential use in international financial transactions is the relative size of international debt securities (i.e., debt issued outside the home country) in various currencies of issuance. The traditional reserve currencies dominate, with the U.S. dollar and the euro accounting for more than four-fifths of outstanding international bonds and notes. The top five reserve currencies combined account for 95 percent of these instruments. Only a modest 0.5 percent of international debt is denominated in RMB. The same is true for other major emerging market currencies.

In short, China has made some headway in promoting the international use of its currency, although it may have a long way to go to match the stature of the traditional reserve currencies. To be sure, though, China's government has been far from passive in promoting the international use of the RMB, recognizing that it has to build up an international infrastructure for this purpose.

OFFSHORE CLEARING CENTERS

The RMB's broad international use will be determined to an important extent by how much RMB liquidity is available offshore and how many financial centers are authorized to serve as clearing centers for RMB transactions. Hong Kong and Macao have, for a long time, been designated as RMB offshore centers, but these two centers by themselves cannot carry a rising load, especially in regions outside Asia. Since 2012, the Chinese government has promoted the RMB's international use by increasing the number of international financial centers authorized to do RMB business and by making it easier to settle transactions abroad in RMB.

Other than Hong Kong and Macao, seventeen new financial centers now serve as Chinese government-approved offshore centers for clearing RMB transactions. The list spans a wide geographic distribution of countries, with only five of them located in Asia (Singapore, Taiwan, Thailand, South Korea, and Malaysia). Three major European financial centers—Frankfurt, London, and Paris—joined the list in 2014. Two Latin American countries—Chile and Argentina—are the latest additions, which also include Australia, Canada, Luxembourg, Russia, South Africa, Switzerland, and Qatar. Japan and the U.S. are prominent absences. At the bilateral U.S.-China Strategic and Economic Dialogue in June 2016, the two countries agreed that an offshore RMB clearing center would soon be set up in the U.S.

The offshore financial centers will make it easier to transact in RMB financial assets, especially for investors who prefer to conduct their transactions closer to home or in financial centers backed by strong regulatory frameworks and the rule of law. China has also been astute in seeking a wide geographic distribution of the financial centers where RMB trades are officially sanctioned. Indeed, China has effectively played the major international financial centers against each other by dangling before them the alluring prospect of attracting RMB business, which has the potential to grow rapidly.

SETTLING ACCOUNTS DIRECTLY

China is also taking steps to promote the use of its currency through bilateral trading arrangements between the RMB and the currencies of its major trading partners. Such arrangements allow these currency pairs to be traded directly without being intermediated through the dollar. The arrangement not only reduces transaction costs for traders and investors that conduct business between the two countries whose currencies are involved, but also bypasses the dollar. This latter aspect is an added bonus for Chinese officials who have long chafed at their reliance on the dollar to intermediate China's international transactions.

In December 2010, the Moscow Interbank Currency Exchange opened direct trading between the RMB and the Russian ruble. A spokesman for the Russian exchange declared "we are pioneers," noting that this was the first time the RMB had been directly listed and traded on an offshore exchange. An exchange for rubles and RMB was opened in Shanghai at about the same time. In June 2011, the central banks of the two countries signed a formal agreement to promote bilateral local currency settlement. These steps have facilitated settlement of trade transactions between the two countries in their own currencies rather than the dollar. The amounts involved have been small so far, but that could change soon. China's voracious appetite for energy and Russia's energy exports could lead to a rapid expansion of trade and local currency settlement of that trade between the two countries, bypassing the dollar as the settlement currency.

In December 2011, China and Japan signed a pact to promote the use of their currencies for bilateral trade and investment flows. In

June 2012, the two countries started direct trading of their currencies on the Shanghai and Tokyo foreign exchange markets. The Japanese yen was the first major international currency with which the RMB's direct trade in an offshore market was sanctioned officially.

In principle, such an agreement between the two largest economies on the Asian continent could be transformative for Asian finance. However, trade between the two economies amounted to only about $300 billion in 2015, and annual bilateral financial flows are estimated to be less than $100 billion. Assuming that most of these transactions are currently settled in dollars and will eventually be settled in the two countries' currencies, the effect on switching from dollar-intermediated transactions would still be relatively modest at the global level. Over time, the effects could be larger if the reduction in currency transaction costs and exchange rate uncertainty were to boost trade and financial flows between the two countries.

In April 2013, China signed a direct currency agreement with Australia—a source of its commodity imports. For Australia, this was a big deal since China is its major trading partner. Hence, being able to conduct trades using the two countries' currencies, without having to use an intermediary currency such as the U.S. dollar, counts as a significant benefit.

In December 2014, direct trading between the RMB and the Korean won was launched in Seoul. This occurred even before a formal currency pact between the two countries, which are major trading partners, was announced in October 2015. The agreement indicated that a reciprocal direct exchange-trading mechanism between the RMB and the Korean won would be set up on the CFETS. The agreement included a statement by the PBC that it would support Korea's issuance of RMB-denominated sovereign debt in China, while Korea would facilitate Chinese institutions' bond issuance in the Seoul market.

In November 2015, the Swiss franc became the seventh currency that could be traded directly with the RMB on the CFETS (in addition to the U.S., Australian, and New Zealand dollars; the British pound sterling; the Japanese yen; and the euro). The Swiss National Bank (SNB) was not shy about its eagerness to promote

RMB business in Switzerland: "Direct trading between the currencies of China and Switzerland is an important step in strengthening bilateral financial and trading relations, and in establishing a renminbi hub in Switzerland." The SNB's press release also noted that the currency agreement and a separate memorandum of understanding it had signed with the PBC would facilitate the establishment of such a hub in Switzerland.

CROSS-BORDER INTERNATIONAL PAYMENT SYSTEM

The interbank payment system serves as the basic infrastructure—as I've been calling it, the plumbing—of financial markets because it is necessary for interbank funds transfer and currency clearing in most countries. Individual financial institutions can always find corresponding banks to fulfill their specific needs for funds transfer and payments. However, this method is inefficient and costly, especially with the large volume of transactions occurring each day, many of them involving cross-border activities. The payments system provides a central platform that helps clear interbank financial transactions in a standardized manner both domestically and internationally.

China's domestic RMB payments system, called the China National Advanced Payment System (CNAPS), is not aligned with international standards and its operation has been limited by its incompatibility with foreign language codes. This had been a significant stumbling block in promoting the international role of the RMB.

To remedy this situation, in October 2015 China launched a new cross-border RMB payments system—the China Cross-Border International Payment System (CIPS)—that is organized to be aligned more closely with internationally accepted standards. This will help facilitate settlement and clearing of cross-border RMB transactions, including trade and investment flows, and bolster the international role of the RMB. The CIPS will initially use SWIFT for interbank messaging, but the system has the capability of eventually serving as an independent channel for secure transmission of payment messages. In cooperation with SWIFT, the PBC will adopt international (ISO 20022) standards and support both Chinese– and English–language transactions, allowing for easier transmission of domestic and international payments. By addressing the problems inherent to the CNAPS, the CIPS is expected to reduce transaction costs substantially and increase the international use of the RMB.

The construction of the system is being carried out in two steps. Phase one focuses on real-time gross settlement, serving primarily cross-border trade, cross-border direct investment, and other cross-border RMB settlement business. Phase two will expand to support other forms of cross-border movement of RMB and settlements of offshore funds. Nineteen banks have been authorized to use the CIPS, including eight Chinese subsidiaries of foreign banks such as Citigroup, Deutsche Bank, HSBC, and Standard Chartered. The system operates from 9 a.m. to 8 p.m. Beijing time, which will cover business hours in Africa, Asia, Europe, and Oceania, increasing the accessibility of cross-border RMB settlements.

Questions remain about how the new infrastructure will change the existing rules of the game. As discussed earlier, the PBC has designated seventeen RMB offshore clearing centers (in addition to Hong Kong and Macao), along with the overseas branches of the major state-owned commercial banks (the Industrial and Commercial Bank of China, the Bank of China, and the China Construction Bank) that are authorized to operate clearing business. In theory, the designated offshore centers will lose many of their privileges once the CIPS is fully established, as qualified financial institutions, regardless of their location, will have direct access to the onshore correspondent clearing banks or the central platform. In practice, however, the CIPS is starting in the typical Chinese fashion in a modest way with tests and trials among a limited number of designated institutions before expanding its membership gradually. It is also not clear whether the existing overseas clearing branches of China's stated-owned banks in offshore clearing centers will be incorporated into the CIPS. In practice, the CIPS is likely to be a supplement to rather than a substitute for existing offshore clearing arrangements.

It is no surprise that the Chinese government will manage the CIPS, but this is not necessarily standard practice. Although a payments system serves as a public good, it is not always owned and run by a government. For example, there are two coexisting interbank payment systems in the U.S. The first is the Clearing House for Interbank Payments System (CHIPS), which is operated by the New York Clearing House, an association of private banks. The other is the Federal Reserve Wire Network, commonly known as *Fedwire*, a part of the Federal Reserve Bank System. Fedwire has a domestic focus, providing transfer services to all banks within the Federal Reserve Bank System, whereas the CHIPS focuses on both the domestic and international arenas, and has only forty-seven large financial institutions as members. Historically, the CHIPS specialized in settling the dollar portion of foreign exchange transactions, although its focus has gradually shifted to the domestic market as well. It appears the CIPS will be modeled largely after the CHIPS, although control is likely to remain with the government.

To understand the scope of the CIPS, it is worth emphasizing the distinctions between SWIFT and other national payment systems. SWIFT provides a communication channel for banks and is not a funds transfer system. So, in general, the national and international payment systems launched by particular countries do not act per se as substitutes for SWIFT, although the payment system does have to rely on SWIFT and has to be consistent with its standards. However, the CIPS has been designed as a system that could eventually also serve as a conduit for interbank communications concerning international RMB transactions that operates independently of SWIFT. This would make it not only a funds transfer system, but also a communication system, reducing the SWIFT's grip on interbank communications related to cross-border financial flows. China's government is astute enough not to challenge SWIFT until the CIPS has matured, but no doubt one day the challenge will come.

However the CIPS ultimately evolves, the main point is that it is the adoption of international standards that makes the new payment system a meaningful move in facilitating the international use of the RMB. In a speech given shortly before the CIPS was launched, Premier Li Keqiang China said that it would "support the further development of offshore RMB market and the 'going global' strategy of Chinese equipments [sic]." PBC chief economist Ma Jun added, "As the cross-border renminbi settlement framework approaches completion, it will inevitably stimulate greater renminbi demand from market participants."

The CIPS gives China a valuable tool it can use to reduce its reliance on Western payment systems and financial markets, even as it expands its currency's reach into those markets. While the economic considerations are important by themselves, it is intriguing to speculate about how China's policymakers may also have been influenced by the desire to counterbalance U.S. and European dominance of payment systems. As is evident in the example of the sanctions on Russia mentioned at the beginning of this chapter, the control of payment systems confers enormous economic and geopolitical power. Such control does not even require direct ownership by government-owned entities, just legal jurisdiction. As one lawyer put it, "China wants to facilitate cross-border international business transactions, but you also have to wonder if there's another angle here. They're currently relying on a payments system that is highly susceptible to being accessed by intelligence agencies from the U.S."

The CIPS builds on other steps China has taken to gain control over financial transactions. In 2002, China established a bankcard association called UnionPay, which is under the purview of the State Council and the PBC. It operates an interbank transaction settlement system for interbank, cross-region, and cross-border use of bankcards by its member banks. In 2003, the association launched the UnionPay card, which allows its members to issue cards to their customers under its brand, similar to MasterCard and Visa. UnionPay has aggressively developed its international acceptance network and its cards are now accepted in most countries around the world. This has been a boon for Chinese citizens—increasing numbers of whom are traveling abroad for business, education, and tourism—as it allows them to draw cash from their Chinese bank accounts directly in local currencies of countries they visit. Many foreign institutions also now offer UnionPay cards, which can be used in China by foreigners.

The UnionPay website makes it clear that, in addition to commercial considerations, a key objective of the association and its activities is to "safeguard the economic and financial security of China." With the rapid expansion of UnionPay, Western governments will certainly face a diminished ability to make threats of financial sanctions against China, similar to those imposed on Russia in 2015–2016 by cutting off its access to international payment systems. In fact, China wields some of that power itself now that UnionPay cards have proliferated widely around the world. UnionPay is managed by the state, giving the Chinese government direct control, unlike the case of Western bankcard systems that are owned and managed privately, and can only be co-opted by Western governments through legal procedures.

THE BIGGER PICTURE OF THE RMB'S INTERNATIONAL ROLE

Promoting the RMB's international role is tied up with many complex domestic and geopolitical considerations. As with all of its policies, China is working toward multiple objectives. For now, China will continue promoting the international use of the RMB using Hong Kong as a platform. When the Chinese government determines that its financial markets are finally strong enough to allow for a more open capital account, it is likely that promotion of Shanghai as an international financial center could take precedence, especially as that would fit better with the objective of domestic financial market development.

While using Hong Kong as the main staging ground for the internationalization of the RMB, the Chinese government is also working to promote competition among financial centers eager to engage in RMB business. Regional and international financial centers such as Bangkok, Frankfurt, London, and Singapore are all being given opportunities to engage in RMB transactions. This competition enables Beijing to continue its program of internationalizing the RMB without having to open its capital account fully.

In the next chapter I consider whether this strategy is sufficient for the RMB to make the leap from being an international currency to a reserve currency.

CHAPTER 6

Reserve Currency

As a boy, I accepted those facts of ugliness as one accepts all those incompatible things that only by reason of their coexistence are called "the universe."

There Are More Things, Jorge Luis Borges

In the fall of 2015, there was high drama in the world of international finance. The IMF was getting ready to determine whether the RMB would be included in the basket of currencies that constitute the IMF's artificial currency unit called the *Special Drawing Rights* (SDR). Since 2001, the SDR's value had been based on a basket of the four major reserve currencies: the dollar, the euro, the Japanese yen, and the pound sterling. This was a momentous decision because inclusion in the SDR basket would, effectively, grant the RMB official recognition as a reserve currency by the world's premier international financial institution.

China had made it clear it wanted this prize. The official news agency *Xinhua* reported that, when IMF Managing Director Christine Lagarde (Figure 6.1) visited Beijing in March 2015, Premier Li Keqiang made a strong pitch for the IMF to include the RMB in the SDR basket. According to the agency, he told Lagarde China would do whatever was necessary to make this happen, including speeding up liberalization of the capital account and providing more channels for cross-border investment flows. He

Figure 6.1 IMF Managing Director Christine Lagarde and People's Bank of China Governor Zhou Xiaochuan.
Credit: Xinhua News Agency

remarked that adding the RMB to the SDR basket would benefit not just China, but the rest of the world as well: "China hoped to, through the SDR, play an active role in the international cooperation to maintain financial stability and promote the further opening of China's capital market and financial area."

Lagarde, wanting to maintain the support of a key member of the IMF, left no doubt about her institution's leanings. "The authorities have . . . expressed interest in having the RMB included in the SDR basket. We welcome and share this objective, and we will work closely with the Chinese authorities in this regard." In other words, the IMF would find a way to make it happen, as long as China held up its end of the bargain.

On November 30, 2015, the IMF announced that "the Executive Board . . . today decided that the RMB met all existing criteria and, effective October 1, 2016 the RMB is determined to be a freely usable currency and will be included in the SDR basket as a fifth currency, along with the U.S. dollar, the euro, the Japanese yen and the British pound."

And with that, the RMB was on a clear path to attaining the status of an official reserve currency. Why did the Chinese government care so much about seeing the RMB recognized as a reserve currency?

THE BIG BOYS CLUB

Prestige matters when it comes to achieving reserve currency status, especially for a country that has only recently come to be recognized as a major economic power. Being included in the SDR basket signals, in particular, the RMB's ascendance into the big boys club of leading global reserve currencies.

Another benefit of this status is that of *seigniorage revenue*, a source of revenue that any central bank issuing its own currency can earn. Seigniorage is the difference between the value of money and the cost of producing it. An additional source of revenue is the *inflation tax*. An increase in the money supply tends to drive up inflation. This reduces the inflation-adjusted value of the debt a government incurs when it finances its purchases of goods and services by issuing debt rather than using current tax revenues. In other words, the government can pay for goods and services now or in the future simply by printing money to pay down its debts. Printing too much money can, of course, generate inflation; but, within limits, some inflation may actually be helpful in lubricating the machinery of an economy.

Revenues from seigniorage and the inflation tax can accrue to any government whose central bank issues its own currency. A reserve currency economy enjoys an added benefit in being able to collect some of these revenues from foreign citizens. In principle, reserve currency status makes it more likely that foreign citizens will hold a country's currency. The U.S. had $1.38 trillion worth of currency notes in circulation at the end of 2015. It is estimated that about three-fifths of dollar banknotes, worth roughly $800 billion, are held outside the U.S. The value of euros in circulation at the end of 2015 was $1.21 trillion, with 20 percent to 25 percent of euro banknotes estimated to be held outside the euro area. Euros and, especially, dollars are widely recognized around the world. They are used as stores of value and sometimes even as mediums of exchange in countries where there is little confidence in the domestic currency. Given their wide acceptability, these two currencies no doubt also feature in illicit activities and black market transactions across the world. However, other than the dollar and the euro, no other major countries' currencies are in great demand outside their national borders.

A reserve currency economy enjoys other benefits as well. Such an economy can more easily sell debt denominated in its domestic currency to foreign investors. Since the government can always print more of its money to pay off the debt to foreigners, this is considerably less risky than owing debt denominated in a foreign currency. Printing all that money could stoke domestic inflation, and this is certainly not something that can be done as a matter of routine, but it is nice to have this option in case the country should face particularly difficult economic circumstances.

Foreigners buying the debt issued by a reserve currency economy can provide cheap financing of government and private consumption. The U.S. has exercised this "exorbitant privilege" to the hilt, with foreign investors now holding about $6 trillion of its federal government debt at low interest rates.

Reserve currency economies also face fewer risks from currency fluctuations. When a country's currency becomes important in international finance, importers and exporters in that country can generally invoice and settle their foreign transactions in the domestic currency. Importers have to sell their goods in domestic markets, so having a stable local currency price for the goods they purchase from abroad reduces the financial risks they face. Similarly, exporters generally prefer being paid a specific amount in the domestic currency for the goods they export, since their production expenses such as wages and interest payments on bank financing are all incurred in the domestic currency. For both importers and exporters, eliminating the need for hedging against exchange rate fluctuations reduces costs.

NOT ALL ROSES

Attaining reserve currency status is not always a sought-after prize. In the late 1970s, after the collapse of the Bretton Woods system of fixed exchange rates, the Deutsche Bundesbank (the German central bank) was increasingly concerned about the deutsche mark becoming a reserve currency and how that would affect German exports, inflation, and control of the exchange rate. In 1979, Bundesbank President Otmar Emminger stated, "Under no circumstance should the Federal Republic become a dumping ground for the unloved dollar which would only expose it to exported inflation." In subsequent years, Bundesbank officials actively sought to dissuade foreign investors from buying up marks; they were worried that the growing circulation of the currency abroad would make it difficult to control its supply as it could lead to volatile flows into and out of Germany. In the 1990s, Bundesbank President Hans Tietmeyer warned that the scale of deutsche mark holdings abroad meant that any loss of faith in the German currency could provoke large-scale selling. This pressured the Bundesbank to maintain high interest rates to avoid sparking a sell-off. The deutsche mark had thus become a burden for Germany as well as a blessing.

This is the flip side of the exorbitant privilege that reserve currency economies enjoy. Reserve currency status increases the demand for financial assets denominated in that currency, creating appreciation pressures that could hurt exports and economic growth. Having a domestic currency with this status can also make it harder to manage monetary policy in a manner that suits domestic economic conditions.

Japan and Switzerland faced acute versions of these problems when the search for safety led many foreign investors to their shores in 2012. The eurozone debt crisis increased demand for safety, but investors also did not want to find themselves locked into holding too many dollars, pushing them to look for assets denominated in currencies such as the Japanese yen and the Swiss franc. The SNB had to take the drastic step of mandating a specific level beyond which it would not allow the franc to appreciate, because the strength of the franc was devastating the country's manufacturing sector. Even tourism was being affected as European and other foreign visitors were dissuaded by the rapidly rising cost, in terms of their domestic currencies, of sojourns to the Swiss Alps. The cap on the franc's value proved difficult to sustain and was eventually abandoned in January 2015.

China faces a similar set of concerns. As the RMB becomes increasingly prominent in international finance, demand for the currency will rise, making it harder to hold down its value relative to other currencies. This will create challenges in controlling the RMB's exchange rate, which could become more volatile.

The Triffin Dilemma

Another important downside to reserve currency status that is often cited is that a reserve currency economy has an obligation to provide the world with liquidity. The logic here is captured in the notion of the Triffin dilemma: to produce the net liquidity the world needs, the country at the center of the global monetary system must run current account deficits. According to this view, a reserve currency economy must perforce run current account deficits (essentially trade deficits) in order to allow the rest of the world to acquire financial assets issued by and denominated in that country's currency (as payment for those current account deficits). This was certainly true in the 1960s, when economist Robert Triffin articulated the proposition that bears his name. Global capital flows were limited at the time and, under the gold standard, the U.S. needed to supply net reserves to the world or, in simpler terms, to provide a sufficient supply of dollars to facilitate expanding international trade, with a commitment to exchange those dollars for gold upon request.

Times have changed (the gold standard was abandoned in 1971), but observers still sometimes mistakenly invoke the Triffin dilemma in discussions of reserve currencies. To be clear, it is not necessary for a country to run a current account deficit—in other words, it does not have to be a net borrower from the rest of the world—to have its currency attain reserve currency status. The Triffin view is manifestly not true in the cases of currencies such as the Japanese yen and the Swiss franc. Both countries have run current account surpluses for much of the past two decades while retaining the privileges of having major reserve currencies. Similarly, even while the euro was gaining prominence in the composition of the global portfolio of reserve currencies, the eurozone was running a roughly balanced current account position with the rest of the world. In fact, the average current account balance as a ratio to GDP during 2000–2007 was positive (or, in the case of the eurozone as a whole, essentially zero) for the major reserve currency economies other than the U.K. and the U.S.

For a longer term perspective, we can look at a country's international investment position. A current account deficit must be financed by borrowing from the rest of the world, which adds to a country's external liabilities. So a country running persistent current account deficits usually has more external liabilities than assets. Similarly, a country running current account surpluses builds up more external assets than liabilities.

The reserve currency economies, it turns out, have diverse net international positions. The U.S. has a particularly large net foreign liability position, amounting to $7.4 trillion at the end of 2015. The U.K. and also the eurozone as a whole have net liabilities. Germany, Japan, and Switzerland have net asset positions. This diversity suggests that it is not essential for a country to run persistent current account deficits, as suggested by the Triffin dilemma, for its currency to attain reserve currency status.

A subtler version of the Triffin dilemma misconception is that the proposition is still relevant, but only for the country that is the major provider of global liquidity because its currency anchors the international monetary system. According to this view, the U.S. has no choice, because of the status of the dollar, but to run current account deficits so it can provide the liquidity the world needs. Based on this logic, China has to be prepared to run current account deficits if its currency is ever going to pose a threat to the dollar's dominance in global finance.

The premise of this argument is questionable even for the anchor global currency, given the high level of integration of global financial markets through cross-border capital flows. Conceptually, in a world with large and free capital flows, a country can provide a range of financial assets to foreign investors and still run a balanced current account if it matches the capital inflows with a similar level of investments abroad. Indeed, the U.S. has provided a vast quantity of financial assets to the rest of the world since the global financial crisis (mostly in the form of U.S. Treasury securities) even as its current account deficit was shrinking. What is far more important for reserve currency status than the home country's current account position is the availability of high-quality, low-risk financial assets—typically government bonds and high-quality corporate bonds—denominated in that currency.

WHAT DOES IT TAKE?

There is no official playbook specifying what it takes to become a reserve currency. The IMF's imprimatur is one determinant, but the IMF is really only a referee. In the global marketplace of currencies, one benchmark that is used as a measure of a reserve currency's importance is the share of global foreign exchange reserves that are held in financial assets denominated in that currency. In the academic literature, there is a set of traditional criteria often invoked in analyzing changes in the composition of global foreign exchange reserves. These criteria provide good guideposts against which to measure the RMB's prospects as a reserve currency. The list includes the openness of the capital account, the existence of a flexible exchange rate, economic size, macroeconomic policies, and the degree of financial market development a country has achieved. The first two criteria have been discussed at length in previous chapters. Let us now consider how China measures up on the remaining ones.

Economic Size

Some economists have argued that China's sheer size and dynamism will lead to its currency becoming a global reserve currency. As discussed earlier, China has clearly become a major economic power, accounting for 15 percent of global GDP in 2015, based on nominal GDP measured at market exchange rates. GDP comparisons across countries can also be done using *purchasing power parity* (PPP) exchange rates, which adjust for differences in the purchasing power of currencies. Based on PPP exchange rates, the Chinese economy is already larger than the U.S. economy and accounts for 17 percent of global GDP (see Table B.1 in Appendix B).

While China's growth over the past three decades is indeed awe-inspiring, it is essential to keep in mind that China has become big and influential before it has become rich and, more importantly, before it has well-developed financial markets or broadly trusted public institutions. After all, if size was the main criterion, it is unlikely that a small country such as Switzerland, which has a GDP less than one-fifteenth that of China, would have one of the main reserve currencies in the world.

Another salient aspect of the size criterion for achieving international or reserve currency status is an economy's share of world trade. Although having large trade flows is neither a necessary nor a sufficient condition for a country to have an international currency, it does boost the potential for the economy's currency to serve as an invoice currency. When a country is large and plays an important role in world trade, its trading partners find that it is more economical to use that country's currency to invoice and settle their trade transactions. Moreover, it also makes sense, then, to hold some foreign exchange reserves in the currency of that country. After all, part of the reason to hold reserves is to continue being able to pay for imports even if international financing were to dry up for some reason.

The value of China's total merchandise (goods) trade now accounts for 12 percent of world merchandise trade, roughly the same share as the U.S. China's share of world trade in goods and services is only slightly lower, at 11 percent. For an economy of its size, China also has a high ratio of total trade to GDP (42 percent), higher than that of economies such as Japan and the U.S. These indicators reflect China's size and rising prominence in world trade.

In addition to trade volumes, another relevant criterion for reserve currency status is the degree to which an economy is interconnected with other economies through trade linkages. This issue has implications for the incentives traders in other countries have to settle their transactions in the home country's currency. Applying a variety of criteria, a recent IMF study found that China was the second most interconnected country in terms of its trade flows. Since China is also ranked second in terms of the size of its trade, it attains the top rank in terms of overall importance in world trade.

Macroeconomic Policies

Sound fiscal and monetary policies that anchor long-run inflation expectations and foster macroeconomic stability are typically important attributes of a reserve currency. China has a low level of explicit public debt relative to the major reserve currency economies. The level of its central government debt was estimated to be about 17 percent of GDP in 2015. This is a positive situation from the perspective of macroeconomic stability, even if it means limited availability of "safe" RMB-denominated assets. Adding in local government debt would boost the level of public debt to 60 percent of GDP, still well below the debt levels of most advanced economies.

China has had a relatively stable inflation rate in the recent past. From 2000 to 2010, the period of the Great Moderation followed by the global financial and economic crisis, inflation was well contained in most major economies. The standard deviations (a measure of volatility) of annual consumer price index inflation in the reserve currency economies were all around 1 percent. During this period, the standard deviations of inflation in emerging markets were in the range of 3 to 4 percent, with China coming in lowest, with a standard deviation of 2 percent. In 2014 and 2015, China's consumer price index inflation has generally come in under 2 percent. China's track record in terms of the level and volatility of inflation should not threaten the RMB's status as a global currency.

Financial Market Development

Financial market development in the home country is one of the essential determinants of a currency's international status. There are three relevant aspects of financial market development. The first is breadth, the availability of a broad range of financial instruments, including markets for hedging risk. To make the currency attractive, foreign central banks and large institutional investors will need access to RMB-denominated securities, including equities and bonds. Foreign central banks and many institutional investors are especially keen to hold government and corporate debt as "safe" assets for their portfolios. The second requisite is depth, which involves offering a large volume of financial instruments in specific markets. To draw in foreign investors, fixed-income markets must have enough depth (i.e., a significant number of participants and tradable securities). Shallow markets tend to be more volatile.

The third essential aspect of financial market development is liquidity, a high level of turnover (trading volume). In addition to having a broad range of deep financial markets, there must be enough trading volume in these markets to assure investors, even large ones, that they can execute trades whenever needed and get into or out of a market without themselves affecting prices dramatically. Thus, breadth, depth, and liquidity are all relevant considerations in assessing the readiness of a country's financial sector to cope with an open capital account and elevate its currency to reserve currency status.

China's financial system remains bank dominated, with the state directly controlling most of the banking system. A large shadow banking system has also expanded rapidly as a way around many of the regulations imposed on the formal banking system.

While the financial system in China is dominated by regular or shadow banks, the more relevant issue for the RMB's role as a reserve currency—beyond financial stability considerations—relates to the availability of high-quality financial assets for foreign investors.

One dimension along which China has made progress is the development of its equity markets. Since 2002, when the QFII scheme (discussed in Chapter 3) was introduced, foreign investors have had access to tradable shares on both the Shanghai and Shenzhen stock exchanges. Until 2005, about two-thirds of the stock market in China was composed of nontradable shares, which were owned directly by the government or state-owned financial institutions. In that year, reforms were introduced to allow nontradable shares in Chinese companies to float freely. These reforms had a dramatic effect. Market capitalization (the total market value of all shares listed on a country's stock exchanges) started to rise after these reforms, surging sharply in 2007 before the financial crisis of 2008–2009 led to a sharp decline. Trading volumes on both exchanges (turnover) also began to rise in the aftermath of the reforms.

Capitalization and turnover in Chinese equity markets now exceed those of most other economies—with the notable exception of the U.S., which remains dominant in terms of its share of global equity market capitalization and turnover. The number of listed firms on the Shanghai and Shenzhen stock exchanges has increased steadily from a total of 1,088 in 2000 to 2,868 as of May 2016 (for comparison, the New York Stock Exchange has 3,215 listed firms and the NASDAQ has 3,142 listed firms, both including foreign ones).

Equity markets do, in principle, provide RMB-denominated instruments that can be held by both domestic and foreign investors and, as noted in Chapter 3, there are an increasing number of channels through which foreign investors can participate even in China's A-share market. The level of foreign investor participation remains limited, however, relative to overall stock market participation because of restrictions on foreign equity investments.

Chinese corporations suffer from weak corporate governance, limited transparency, weak auditing standards, and shoddy accounting practices. In the absence of broad institutional and regulatory reforms necessary to support effective price discovery—allowing buyers and sellers to arrive at a price that reasonably reflects a company's financial conditions and prospects—and the overall efficient functioning of stock markets, these markets could remain unstable. The volatility in the stock market in 2015–2016 and the manner in which the government has addressed it has heightened many of these concerns. I discuss the implications for overall financial stability in Chapter 8. What matters from the perspective of the reserve currency criteria is that, even with greater liberalization of portfolio inflows, international investors are likely to shy away from investing heavily in Chinese equities. Therefore, the country's deep equity markets may be of limited help in promoting the international role of the RMB.

China's fixed-income markets (debt securities), especially for corporate debt, have developed rapidly in recent years. The stock of government bonds stood at $4.3 trillion in March 2016, representing a fivefold increase since 2005. Nonfinancial corporate debt was practically nonexistent in 2005, amounting to less than $100 billion, but the outstanding stock had risen to $2.2 trillion by March 2016. China's overall domestic debt market value of nearly $6.5 trillion is sizable, but lower than that of the top three reserve currency areas: the U.S., Japan, and the eurozone (for more details, see Table B.8 in Appendix B). In the U.S., government debt (including municipal government debt) stood at $18.9 trillion in March 2016, and the stock of corporate debt was $8.2 trillion. Adding in other securities such as federal agency securities and mortgage-related securities pushes the size of the overall fixed-income market to $40 trillion.

Interestingly, China already has a larger market for fixed-income securities than the U.K. and Switzerland, two reserve currency economies. This suggests that the size of the domestic debt market per se does not necessarily impede the RMB's progress as a reserve currency.

The amount of trading activity in Chinese bond markets has also risen over the past decade. The turnover ratio, which refers to the annual trading volume expressed relative to the outstanding stock of tradable bonds, is 0.6 for government bonds and 0.3 for corporate bonds. The corresponding turnover numbers for the U.S. are 6.7 and 0.8, respectively. U.S. government bond markets constitute the most liquid fixed-income markets in the world. The turnover in Japan's government bond markets is 1.2, but corporate bond market turnover, which is only 0.1, is even lower than in China.

China has lifted most restrictions on foreign investors' participation in its bond markets and created channels, including through the QFII scheme, which allows foreign institutional investors to purchase both government and corporate debt securities in China. The level of participation remains modest, however, in view of concerns about the stability and transparency of these markets. The RMB's future trajectory as a reserve currency will depend, to a large extent, on China's success in creating large, liquid, and well-regulated debt securities markets.

SCORECARD

I now summarize where China stands with respect to each of the key criteria for its currency to be regarded as a reserve currency:

- *Economic size*: A country's size and its shares of global trade and finance are important, but not crucial, determinants of the status of its reserve currency. China now accounts for 15 percent of world GDP (17 percent if measured by PPP rather than market exchange rates) and 11 percent of world trade in goods and services. In 2014–2015, it was estimated to have accounted for about one-third of world GDP growth.
- *Open capital account*: Reserves must be acceptable as payments to a country's trade and financial partners, which requires that the currency be easily tradable in global financial markets. China is gradually and selectively easing restrictions on both inflows

and outflows. The capital account has become increasingly open in de facto terms, but there are a number of capital controls still in place.

- *Flexible exchange rate*: Reserve currencies are typically traded freely and their external value is market determined, although this does not preclude occasional bouts of intervention by the country's central bank in foreign exchange markets. China has, over time, increased the flexibility of the exchange rate and, in principle, permitted market forces to play a bigger role in foreign exchange markets. Despite these changes, China still has a closely managed exchange rate, which will become increasingly hard to control as the capital account becomes more open.

- *Macroeconomic policies*: Investors in a country's sovereign assets must have faith in its commitment to low inflation and sustainable levels of public debt, so the value of the currency is not in danger of being eroded. China has a lower ratio of explicit public debt to GDP than most major reserve currency economies and has maintained moderate inflation in recent years.

- *Financial market development*: A country must have broad, deep, and liquid financial markets so that international investors will have access to a wide array of financial assets denominated in its currency. China's financial markets have become large, but they are highly volatile, poorly regulated, and lack a supporting institutional framework.

While China measures up favorably in the first four areas, the last one—financial market development—is likely, ultimately, to determine winners and losers in the global reserve currency sweepstakes. This is where China currently falls short and will need sustained and concerted actions to close the gaps with other reserve currency economies.

Despite its underdeveloped financial markets, however, China is trying to create a new playbook for its currency. Indeed, the RMB has already made its presence felt on the international stage, in part as the result of policy actions undertaken by the Chinese government and in part because of China's sheer size and growing role in international trade and finance.

There is something remarkable about the RMB: even before it met many of the technical criteria considered necessary for a reserve currency, it had already ascended to the status of one in practice.

In principle, only liquid financial assets denominated in convertible currencies can be counted as part of a country's foreign exchange reserves. Yet, despite its lack of convertibility, the RMB had begun to appear in the reserve portfolios of a few central banks earlier in this decade. Chile, Malaysia, and Nigeria are widely believed to have pioneered this trend, starting around 2011. The Chilean central bank, the Banco Central de Chile, started with a relatively modest 0.3 percent of its foreign assets held in RMB-denominated assets in 2011. By the end of 2015, this share had grown to 3 percent. The Malaysian central bank, Bank Negara Malaysia, has never formally declared that it is buying RMB assets, but is widely believed to have done so.

The Central Bank of Nigeria issued a statement on September 5, 2011, announcing that it "has finalized arrangements to diversify its external reserves holdings by including the Chinese renminbi (RMB) to the existing currency mix of United States dollars (USD), the euro (EUR) and the British pound sterling (GBP)." Governor Lamido Sanusi said in reference to buying more RMB assets that "we are looking at anything to start with from 5 to 10 percent of our reserves."

Numerous Asian central banks are looking to RMB assets as an avenue for diversifying their foreign exchange reserves. In 2012, Bank Indonesia announced that it had started buying bonds on China's interbank market to help diversify its reserves. The central banks of Japan, Korea, and Thailand have also declared their intentions to buy RMB securities for their reserve portfolios. A few central banks outside Asia are jumping on the RMB reserves bandwagon as well. In November 2011, Austria's central bank Oesterreichische Nationalbank (OeNB) trumpeted its agreement with the PBC that "enables the OeNB to invest via the PBC in Renminbi-denominated assets." The press release noted proudly that "this is the first agreement of this kind signed by the PBC with a non-Asia central bank, and can be seen as an important step in the good relationship between the PBC and the OeNB." Other central banks in Europe are following the lead of the OeNB. By early 2016, the SNB had allocated 0.7 percent of its foreign exchange reserve portfolio to RMB-denominated assets.

Official statements and other accounts suggest that a number of other central banks also have added or are considering adding RMB assets to their reserve portfolios. In addition to the nine countries mentioned above, the list includes Australia, Pakistan, South Africa, Tanzania, Russia, and the U.K. Foreign central banks that want to buy Chinese bonds for their reserve portfolios must obtain permission from the Chinese government through the QFII scheme. Sovereign wealth funds must do the same.

The IMF estimates that, in 2014, about 1.1 percent of official foreign currency assets were held in RMB, up from 0.7 percent in 2013. This estimation is based on data from about thirty-eight countries (not identified by the IMF), which reported that they held some RMB-denominated assets in their official reserve portfolios (in 2013, the number of reporting countries was twenty-seven). This put the RMB in the seventh spot in terms of the identified composition of official foreign currency assets. The top six are the U.S. dollar (64 percent in 2014, 127 reporting countries), the euro (21 percent), the British pound sterling (4 percent), the Japanese yen (3 percent), the Australian dollar (2 percent), and the Canadian dollar (2 percent). The RMB's share is larger than that of the Swiss franc, which accounts for 0.3 percent, as well as the New Zealand dollar and the Swedish krona, each of which accounts for 0.2 percent.

The shares of the top six currencies, along with that of the Swiss franc, are the only ones identified separately in each of the IMF's quarterly Composition of Foreign Exchange Reserves (COFER) reports. The rest are lumped into the "other" category. The shares of these seven currencies remained roughly the same as the 2014 numbers just noted through the end of 2015. In March 2016, the IMF announced that, starting with the December 2016 reports (to be published in March 2017), the COFER tables would separately show the share of reserves held in RMB as well, reflecting expectations of its rising share and the implication that "IMF member countries will be able to record as official reserves their holdings of RMB-denominated external assets that are readily available for meeting balance of payments financing needs."

It is tempting to read into some of these figures portents of an inexorably surging RMB and, as a corollary, a crumbling dollar. Consider Nigeria. In 2011, its central bank held 0.3 percent of foreign exchange reserves in RMB and 82 percent in dollars. By 2015, the RMB's share rose to 7.5 percent, an increase of 7 percentage points, while the dollar's share fell by the same amount, to 75 percent. To keep this in perspective, though, the foreign exchange reserves managed by Nigeria's central bank amounted to only $28 billion at the end of 2015, and even that number was down from $33 billion in 2011. Recent data suggest that the dollar's share of global foreign exchange reserves has in fact risen marginally from about 62 percent in 2007, just before the financial crisis, to 64 percent in 2015.

Given China's expanding economy and bond markets, a reasonable reserve manager would no doubt be looking to expand holdings of RMB-denominated assets from a pure diversification perspective alone. China has a lower government debt ratio than most advanced economies, and its central government bonds have a relatively good credit rating. As an SNB official put it when discussing the profile of his central banks' reserve allocation: "Over and above the consideration of market size, investments in China are also attractive from the point of view of our security criterion, as they offer additional diversification of market, credit and concentration risks."

In summary, the RMB's progress as a reserve currency is modest so far, but its rise is following an unmistakably upward trajectory. The gains the RMB has made are symbolically important in signaling the shift in perception of the currency's stability and its future role in the international monetary system. At the same time, it is premature to extrapolate the trajectory of the RMB's rise too far into the future. Most of the countries that are acquiring RMB for their reserve portfolios tend to have strong trading relationships with China. Hence, for these countries, access to some RMB liquidity may be useful in facilitating trade transactions in addition to providing the benefit of portfolio diversification.

SWAP LINES

Since 2009, the PBC has moved aggressively to establish bilateral swap arrangements with other central banks in order to facilitate and expand the use of the RMB in international trade and financial transactions. China had, in fact, established swap lines with many Asian central banks even before it started to actively promote the international use of its currency. Most of these were dollar–RMB swaps under which China would provide U.S. dollars in exchange for the local currency of the counterparty economy. In other words, the foreign exchange reserves of economies such as China would often serve as an additional credit line facility if the counterparty economy were to face a liquidity crunch due to a balance of payments or financial crisis.

There is one crucial difference between the earlier swap arrangements and those the PBC has signed since 2009. Every one of the swaps in place now operates in terms of local currencies—that is, the PBC commits to exchanging other central banks' currencies for RMB. As of June 2016, thirty-six central banks had signed such local currency swap arrangements with the PBC. The global reach of these swap agreements is shown in Figure 6.2. Eager to expand its RMB business, and with the goal of making London a major center for RMB-denominated activity, by June 2013 even the Bank of England had signed such a swap line, making it the first G-7 central bank to sign one with the PBC. A number of other advanced economy central banks have since signed swap arrangements with the PBC.

The total amount that could be drawn by the thirty-six participating swap arrangements amounts to the equivalent of half a trillion dollars—clearly, a sizable amount. The largest such arrangement is with the Hong Kong Monetary Authority, for $61 billion. The PBC's arrangements with the Bank of Korea, the Monetary

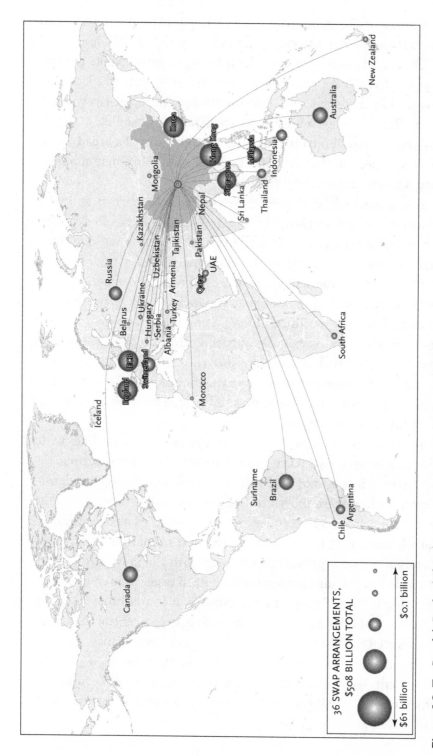

Figure 6.2 The People's Bank of China's currency swap arrangements go global.
Data through June 2016. For more detailed data, see Table B.9 in Appendix B.
Sources: The People's Bank of China and other participating central banks.

Authority of Singapore, the Bank of England, and the European Central Bank are in the range of $46 billion to $55 billion.

China's bilateral swap lines with foreign central banks directly support the RMB's greater international use. But, the amounts involved in these bilateral agreements have been relatively small so far. These modest amounts notwithstanding, the PBC is clearly making an active effort to make the central banks of a broad group of economies comfortable and familiar with RMB-denominated instruments and financial facilities.

The apparent high degree of interest on the part of so many countries—small and large, within and outside Asia—in developing bilateral financial arrangements with China is striking. Like many of the countries that are acquiring RMB for their reserve portfolios, those countries whose central banks have signed bilateral local currency swap arrangements with the PBC view China as a key trading partner. Thus, China's rising importance as a trading power is playing a crucial role in fueling the rise of the RMB. For some countries such as Germany and the U.K., there is the added incentive of creating stronger financial bonds with Beijing, which could prove useful in their efforts to bring more RMB business to their financial centers.

That so many countries are eager to sign currency swap lines with China and even hold its currency as part of their reserve portfolios is not necessarily a sign of the RMB's inevitable march to global dominance. Rather, these moves constitute low-cost bets on the likely outcome of a convertible and more widely accepted global currency. Equally important is the desire on the part of many economies to maintain a good economic relationship with China in anticipation of its rising economic power. Holding RMB reserves may, in effect, be a simple way of trying to buy protection from China, which in turn may be better motivated to provide help to a central bank that has assisted the RMB during its early stages of ascendance.

The magnitudes are small but still the symbolism is hard to miss. Central banks around the world are preparing for a future in which the RMB will play an increasingly prominent role in international finance.

THE IMF ELEVATES THE RMB

The RMB's accession to the IMF's SDR basket puts an exclamation point on the currency's rise to reserve currency status.

The SDR constitutes an international reserve asset created by the IMF in 1969. It is neither a currency nor a claim on the institution, but instead it serves as a potential claim on the freely usable currencies of IMF members. That is, SDRs can, in principle, be exchanged for "freely usable" currencies but cannot be used directly in private transactions. SDRs are distributed among IMF members on the basis of their quotas at the institution. The overall stock of SDRs stood at roughly $285 billion in March 2016, a sizable number but accounting for less than 3 percent of international reserves held by all countries. Foreign exchange reserves, which amounted to $10.9 trillion at the end of 2015, account for nearly 96 percent of total international reserves.

How the RMB Staked Its Claim on SDR Inclusion

In March 2009, PBC Governor Zhou Xiaochuan posted a paper, "Reform the International Monetary System," on the PBC's website. The document laid out the case for SDRs to play a more prominent role in global finance and suggested that the composition of the SDR needed to reflect changing times by incorporating the currencies of the major emerging market economies. The proposal was seen as a signal that China was staking its claim to having the RMB's global importance recognized by its inclusion in the exclusive group of currencies in the SDR basket.

The IMF's position in 2010 was blunt and clear:

> [A]lthough China has become the third-largest exporter of goods and services on a five-year average basis and has taken steps to facilitate international use of its currency, the Chinese RMB does not currently meet the criteria to be a freely usable currency and it would therefore not be included in the SDR basket at this time.

Thus, it appeared that the IMF intended to apply the "freely usable" criterion strictly.

By 2011, the winds had shifted. There was considerable discussion that year of a proposal to include the RMB in the SDR basket. The French government, during its presidency of the G-20 in 2011, promoted this proposal at several venues, viewing it as an important component of international monetary system reform. At a G-20 conference in Nanjing in March 2011, French president Nicolas Sarkozy stated: "Isn't it the time today to reach agreement on the timetable for enlarging the basket of SDRs to include new emerging currencies, such as the yuan? Who could deny the major role the yuan plays in the international monetary system? Tribute is thus paid to the economic power and the political power of China, a major monetary power."

The communiqué issued at the conclusion of the November 2011 G-20 summit in Cannes contained this language:

> We agreed that the SDR basket composition should continue to reflect the role of currencies in the global trading and financial system and be adjusted over time to reflect currencies' changing role and characteristics. . . . A broader SDR basket will be an important determinant of its attractiveness, and in turn influence its role as a global reserve asset.

In other words, including the RMB in the basket would be good for the SDR itself. During his final press conference at the conclusion of that summit, Sarkozy was more direct: "The yuan is a clear candidate [for inclusion in the SDR basket], given China's commitment—which I noted with satisfaction—to gradual convertibility."

China itself had been more circumspect about the prospects of expanding the SDR basket. PBC Deputy Governor Yi Gang urged the IMF to conduct more research into a shadow SDR and argued that "the IMF should consider including currencies of the BRICS [Brazil, Russia, India, China and South Africa—the world's largest and fast-growing emerging economies] countries and other emerging economies when it next reviews its SDR system by 2015." But Yi was also quoted as saying that "China is in no hurry as the SDR has so far been only a symbolic currency basket."

By the beginning of 2015, though, China had made it a policy goal to convince the IMF to include the RMB in the SDR. The PBC viewed this goal as a useful spur to domestic financial sector reforms. In addition, China wanted its place in international finance to be cemented before it took charge of the G-20 presidency in 2016. The presidency would culminate with the September 2016 meeting of G-20 leaders in Hangzhou.

China began an aggressive push early in 2015. At the spring meetings of the IMF in April 2015, Governor Zhou of the PBC committed to a series of reforms to further increase capital account openness. And China did in fact undertake a number of financial market and capital account reforms during 2015. For instance, as discussed in Chapter 3, a number of restrictions on cross-border capital flows were dismantled during the year. The PBC also lifted the longstanding cap on bank deposit rates, the last step toward freeing up banks to set their own rates on deposits and loans. This was an important measure since the IMF had made it clear that a fully market-determined interest rate in its home country was a prerequisite for a currency's claim to reserve currency status.

In August 2015, the IMF released a report summarizing the approach to reviewing the composition and valuation of the SDR. The report noted that the RMB was by then "exhibiting a significant degree of international use and trading," although at a level below those of the other four freely usable currencies that then constituted the SDR basket. The paper also discussed a possible extension of the existing SDR valuation basket until October 2016, whatever the outcome of the review, which would have to be concluded by the end of calendar year 2015. The reason given for such an extension was that introducing a new basket on the first trading day of the new year would expose SDR users to increased risks and costs; a longer lag would make for a smoother adjustment. This proposal was approved by the IMF's executive board on August 11, 2015. The approval was misinterpreted in some media reports as a delay in the deadline for the IMF's review of the composition of the SDR basket.

The report offered a generally positive reading of the RMB's progress toward becoming a widely traded currency. The report noted that a broad range of indicators showed increasing international use of the RMB, albeit from a low base—turnover in foreign exchange markets, official foreign exchange reserves, international banking liabilities, stock and issuance of international debt liabilities, SWIFT cross-border payments, and SWIFT trade finance.

The report noted that deviations between the offshore (CNH) and onshore (CNY) RMB exchange rates raised "potential operational issues." Deviations between the two rates imply that the CNH cannot be a perfect hedge for CNY-based exposures. What this means is that such deviations create complications for the few international institutions, such as the IMF itself, that manage their balance sheets in SDRs. These institutions would find it difficult to manage any volatility arising from their exposure to RMB holdings if the currency traded at different values in various markets.

One important point the report highlighted was that a fully open capital account was not necessary for satisfying the free usability criterion. The report stated that a "currency may be widely used and widely traded even if the issuing member retains some restrictions . . . [but there needs to be] sufficient liberalization within the market in question to ensure that members who may receive financing from the Fund have adequate access to this market." Still, the report made it clear that many of the necessary conditions—convergence of the onshore and offshore exchange rates, availability of hedging instruments, and foreign exchange market liquidity—would all be easier to meet if capital account restrictions were liberalized.

The report concluded with an intriguing paragraph that speaks for itself:

The ultimate assessment by the Board will involve a significant element of judgment. The rapidly changing nature of RMB usage in the world trade and financial system poses challenges for the assessment. Judgment will have to be applied, including on the importance of the various indicators and their proximity to the freely usable concept.

In other words, the decision about whether to include the RMB in the SDR basket would be based not just on purely technical criteria, but would also depend on the outcome of intense political jockeying.

A Step in the Right Direction Turns into a Stumble

In August 2015, a few days after the IMF report was made public, the PBC took a step toward freeing up its exchange rate to allow it be determined by market forces—an important consideration for the RMB's inclusion in the SDR basket. That move, however, did not go as planned (as discussed in Chapter 4), creating more turmoil than either the PBC or IMF had anticipated.

The PBC combined the announcement that it would free up the RMB exchange rate with a 1.9 percent devaluation of the RMB relative to the dollar. This set off expectations that the PBC would seek to push the RMB's value down further in order to boost sagging exports. Immediately after the PBC's action, a significant discrepancy opened up between the CNY (onshore) and CNH (offshore) exchange rates. In currency markets, a tenth of a percentage point difference in the exchange rates between two currencies as quoted on different markets counts as a big gap. For freely traded currencies, such a gap would not last for more than a few moments as currency traders seeking to exploit the differential would quickly close the gap. In mid August, the CNY–CNH discrepancy was, by this standard, a chasm—nearly 1.5 half percent, with the RMB worth much less offshore because currency traders expected it to depreciate further. The PBC's tight control of the onshore market and the lack of completely free movement of capital meant that this wide difference could persist for days.

By October, despite the PBC's aggressive intervention in both onshore and offshore currency markets, the gap was smaller but still sizable. The IMF's assessment that such a discrepancy would pose "operational difficulties"—a gentle phrase for indicating a big problem—meant that this situation, if it persisted, could jeopardize the RMB's inclusion in the SDR basket. A sure thing no longer looked quite as certain.

At the IMF's annual meetings in Lima in October 2015, PBC Deputy Governor Yi Gang gave no ground. His statement to the central bankers and finance ministers from around the world reiterated China's case for the RMB's inclusion in the SDR. He stated, "In addition to actively preparing for reforms that we pledged . . . in April, China has implemented or will soon introduce the following reforms," after which he laid out a series of steps that would take care of any remaining concerns. He added, "We believe that with the completion of these reforms, the RMB can meet the operational requirements for inclusion in the SDR basket."

As the decision drew nearer, China kept the pressure on. Addressing the G-20 leaders in November, President Xi Jinping "welcomed consensus that inclusion [of the RMB in the SDR] would increase the representation and attraction of the SDR, improve the international monetary system and safeguard global financial stability." For all its putative determination to make a decision based purely on technical merits, the IMF was cornered, for Lagarde had no desire to incur the wrath of the Chinese government.

On November 13, 2015, Lagarde issued the following statement:

> The staff of the IMF has today issued a paper to the Executive Board . . . IMF staff assesses that the RMB meets the requirements to be a "freely usable" currency and, accordingly, the staff proposes that the Executive Board determine the RMB to be freely usable and include it in the SDR basket as a fifth currency, along with the British pound, euro, Japanese yen, and the U.S. dollar. The staff also finds that the Chinese authorities have addressed all remaining operational issues identified in an initial staff analysis submitted to the Executive Board in July. I support the staff's findings. The decision, of course, on whether the RMB should be included in the SDR basket rests with the IMF's Executive Board.

The U.S. Treasury signaled its support for the IMF staff's position. On its website it noted that, at a meeting with senior Chinese officials, "Secretary Lew reiterated that the United States intends to support the renminbi's inclusion in the Special Drawing Rights basket provided the currency meets the International Monetary Fund's existing criteria, and the United States is reviewing the IMF's paper in that light."

On November 30, 2015, the IMF executive board announced its decision to incorporate the RMB into the SDR basket with effect from October 1, 2016. There was little opposition to the decision, with most countries falling in line with the recommendation of the IMF staff. Lagarde lauded the outcome:

> The Executive Board's decision to include the RMB in the SDR basket is an important milestone in the integration of the Chinese economy into the global financial system. It is also a recognition of the progress that the Chinese authorities have made in the past years in reforming China's monetary and financial systems. The continuation and deepening of these efforts will bring about a more robust international monetary and financial system, which in turn will support the growth and stability of China and the global economy.

China had won the battle, with neither the U.S. nor any other country willing to stand in its way.

Shifting Weights

The IMF also took the opportunity to change the formula used to calculate the shares of currencies in the SDR basket (the shares have to sum up to one hundred). Previously, the formula essentially involved summing up the country's exports and the stock of global foreign exchange reserves held in assets denominated in its currency. The new formula was meant to reflect the rising importance of cross-border financial flows in addition to trade flows. The new formula assigns equal weight to exports and a financial indicator, reflecting a country's importance in global trade and the currency's importance in global financial markets, respectively. The financial indicator is a composite variable that assigns a 50 percent weight to the share of global foreign exchange reserves denominated in that currency, a 25 percent weight to foreign exchange turnover accounted for by that currency, and a 25 percent weight to the sum of international banking liabilities and international debt securities denominated in that currency.

Under this new formula, the weights of the SDR currencies are as follows: 41.7 percent for the U.S. dollar, 30.9 percent for the euro, 10.9 percent for the RMB, 8.3 percent for the Japanese yen, and 8.1 percent for the pound sterling. Interestingly, the U.S. dollar's share, which was 41.9 percent in the previous SDR basket, was essentially unchanged whereas the shares of the other three currencies fell significantly compared with their shares in the previous basket.

The IMF's decision was an important validation of China's efforts to liberalize financial markets, open up its capital account, and allow the RMB's value to be determined, to a greater extent, by market forces. The decision could modestly strengthen the hands of economic reformers in China and could help sustain momentum toward financial sector liberalization and reforms. However, domestic opposition to further financial sector reforms and market-oriented liberalization measures remains fierce, and this decision by itself seems unlikely to shift the balance substantially.

Not an Immediate Game-Changer

The decision to include the RMB in the SDR basket does not amount to a game-changer in terms of international finance or even from the narrow perspective of generating a surge of capital inflows into China. A handful of international institutions such as the IMF and the BIS manage their balance sheets in SDR terms, so they would have to undertake some portfolio rebalancing. Private financial institutions hardly have any portfolios that are benchmarked against SDRs, so no portfolio-rebalancing effect will follow. But, the symbolic effect could be significant, because the RMB's recognition as an official reserve currency is likely to encourage central banks around the world to begin adding RMB assets to their reserve portfolios. The IMF's imprimatur will help, but ultimately it is the availability of many sufficiently high-quality RMB-denominated financial assets and the ease of moving financial capital into and out of China that will determine the RMB's trajectory as a reserve currency.

The decision could have significant effects on the patterns of global capital flows if it leads to further financial sector reforms, capital account liberalization, and exchange rate flexibility in China. Such changes would open the door for more capital inflows into China and also further tilt the composition of China's outflows away from foreign exchange reserve accumulation by the central bank, as it will spur more foreign investments by China's households, corporations, and institutional investors.

The IMF argued that its decision would be good for both China and the international monetary system:

> Put into a broader context, the inclusion of the [RMB] in the SDR basket could be seen as an important milestone in the process of China's global financial integration. It also recognizes and reinforces China's continuing reform progress. As this integration continues and further deepens, and is paralleled in other emerging market economies, it could bring about a more robust international monetary and financial system, which in turn would support the growth and stability of the global economy. The RMB's inclusion will also enhance the attractiveness of the SDR as an international reserve asset, as it diversifies the basket and makes its composition more representative of the world's major currencies.

The RMB's seemingly inexorable progress toward becoming a viable and perhaps even significant reserve currency has led to the inevitable hand-wringing in some quarters (and, no doubt, a sense of glee in some others) that the RMB will eventually match or even supersede the dollar's dominant role in international finance. This is where the past, or even the present, might prove to be a poor guide to the future. Beyond the hyperbole, which feeds into broader concerns in the U.S. about its domestic decline and the ascendance of China, there is a sobering reality that China must face before it becomes the financial behemoth that many fear.

CHAPTER 7

The Mirage of Safety

The theory of quantum electrodynamics describes Nature as absurd from the point of view of common sense. And it agrees fully with experiment. So I hope you can accept Nature as She is—absurd. I'm going to have fun telling you about this absurdity, because I find it delightful.

QED The Strange Theory of Light and Matter, Richard P. Feynman

The U.S. has been called the safe haven of last—and, sometimes, also the first—resort for investors around the world. The strength of the U.S. dollar during the past few years reinforces the logic of investing in dollar-denominated financial assets. Rock-solid faith that the U.S. federal government will honor its debt obligations has made its Treasury securities the instrument of choice for panicky investors seeking refuge from financial turmoil, even when those securities pay a puny rate of return. This is the heart of the concept of a safe financial asset—an asset that is expected to be safe, at least in terms of maintaining the principal value of an investment. In addition, such an asset must be highly liquid, or easy to trade. Treasury securities certainly have these attributes of safety and liquidity, which has made the dollar the ultimate safe haven currency.

Yet, over the past decade, through the financial crisis, there is one currency that would have given international investors a much better return than investing in U.S. dollar assets. A dollar invested in the S&P 500 at the beginning of 2005 was worth $1.72

in April 2016. Over the same period, a dollar converted into RMB and invested in the Shanghai stock market index would have risen to the equivalent of nearly $3. The Chinese stock market has gone on a wild ride during this period, but the 28 percent increase in the value of the RMB relative to the dollar accounts for a significant portion of the difference.

Despite this huge shift in their relative values, the dollar is still regarded as a safe haven currency whereas the RMB is not. This might seem odd because the RMB has appreciated substantially since 2005—not just against the dollar, but also relative to every major currency that has a similar status, including the euro, the Japanese yen, and the British pound sterling. Moreover, during the past decade, the Chinese economy has done far better than any of these economies. Of course, the RMB is only now acquiring the status of a reserve currency, so perhaps it is just a matter of time before it comes to be seen as a safe haven currency like the other extant reserve currencies.

This issue is of more than just theoretical interest. Although the RMB may eventually become a significant reserve currency, it is unlikely to account for a substantial portion of global foreign exchange reserves if foreign investors, including central banks, look to RMB assets only for diversification rather than for safety. Nearly 64 percent of global foreign exchange reserves are held in dollar-denominated assets, although the U.S. accounts for only about one-fifth of world GDP. The remaining reserves are distributed among other currencies as follows (as of end-2015)—20 percent in euros, about 5 percent each in British pound sterling and Japanese yen, about 2 percent each in Australian and Canadian dollars, and the remaining 3 percent in other currencies.

Whether the RMB becomes an important reserve currency similar to the pound or the yen, or transcends these levels to become a serious competitor to the dollar, depends on whether China is seen as a safe haven rather than just a high-return, high-risk investment destination that provides good portfolio diversification and good returns on average but cannot be counted on for safety. Investor perception will play a crucial role in determining how far the RMB's rise will go, from accounting for nothing earlier in this decade to constituting 1 percent of global foreign exchange reserves in 2014, and whether it will plateau at a low level.

Meanwhile, in the aftermath of the global financial crisis, the concept of a safe financial asset has changed; a safe asset now must offer more than relatively stable value. In the new world of financial fragility, there is a more relevant definition of this concept. It is one that has a negative *beta*—a piece of financial market jargon that means, essentially, that the asset is negatively correlated with the overall market. Or, to put it more simply, the asset's value tends to rise, or at least hold up reasonably well, when the market is performing poorly on average. The flip side of this is often that the value of the asset falls when the market is doing better as a whole, but this is the price to be paid for a degree of protection during bad times. Typically, financial assets that are considered safe also tend to have less volatile returns than others, such as equities.

Investors now prize such safe assets, especially ones that hold their value during times of great danger such as a financial crisis, as insurance against tail risk, the small probability of an extremely large loss. The low risk associated with such an asset is one reason investors may be willing to accept a low rate of return on it. In fact, by early 2016, a number of advanced economy central banks—including those of Denmark, the eurozone, Japan, Sweden, and Switzerland—had negative policy interest rates, which in turn typically means negative interest rates on at least short-maturity government bonds. Governments of these countries were essentially collecting a fee from investors so concerned about safety that they were actually willing to pay this fee to store their money securely in government bonds during turbulent times in financial markets.

This leads to an obvious question: What virtues of a country or its currency cause it to be seen as a safe haven in international finance—a designation that seems to enable its government to borrow money cheaply, or sometimes even for free, from international investors? We can shed light on this issue by returning to the period immediately after the global financial crisis.

The U.S. was the epicenter of the financial crisis that rocked the world economy in 2008, setting off a chain of reactions from which many economies have still not fully recovered. The U.S. economy has since then done far better than those of the eurozone and Japan, whose economies remain mired in low growth and deflationary pressures, in part because the Federal Reserve printed large amounts of money rapidly to keep the economy well lubricated. In addition, the U.S. government used fiscal policy aggressively. Net "privately held" federal debt rose from $4.4 trillion at the end of 2007 to $11.2 trillion in February 2016. This figure excludes the debt purchased by other parts of the U.S. government, such as the Social Security trust funds and the U.S. Federal Reserve (which is technically not part of the government). The corresponding figure for gross debt, including all these items that are ultimately liabilities of the U.S. federal government, is $19 trillion, which is slightly higher than annual GDP ($18 trillion in 2015).

Who has purchased this enormous volume of debt issued by the U.S. federal government? It turns out that foreign investors have purchased more than half (56 percent) of the additional "privately held" federal debt issued by the U.S. since 2007. As of February 2016, foreign investors held about $6.2 trillion in Treasury securities, including foreign central banks' holdings of about $4.1 trillion. That is, foreign investors now hold 55 percent of the $11.2 trillion of "privately held" U.S. federal debt.

The remarkable feature of U.S. Treasuries is they experience a surge in demand every time there is turmoil anywhere in the world, including in the U.S. itself. There are many examples of this latter phenomenon, which is curious because it runs wholly counter to conventional expectations. In August 2011, the rating agency Standard and Poor's cut the rating on U.S. government debt from AAA to AA+ and said the outlook on the long-term rating was "negative." Normally, this would lead to a spike in government bond yields (or, equivalently, a fall in bond prices) as investors reassess the riskiness of the bond and demand a higher yield. The currency of such a country should also weaken as foreign investors pull out money, often accompanied by domestic investors moving money out of the country as well. In fact, the yield on the ten-year Treasury note fell by 50 basis points (half a percentage point) the following month and net foreign capital inflows into U.S. Treasury securities jumped. The other normal outcome—a fall in the value of the dollar, which would have been expected after the rate cut— did not transpire either. In fact, on a trade-weighted basis, the dollar rose in value the next month.

In the fall of 2013, the budget impasse between President Obama and the Republican–controlled U.S. Congress led to a government shutdown and fears of a default—even if only a temporary, technical default—by the U.S. government on some of its debt obligations. Nevertheless, from August to October that year, as the probability of default increased, yields on the ten-year Treasury note stayed in a narrow range, hardly signaling market panic over the possibility of there being even a technical default. Before, during, and after the government shutdown, the dollar remained roughly stable in value relative to other major currencies.

Other safe havens have recently experienced similar phenomena, although not all to the same extent as the U.S. A prominent example in which domestic economic turmoil had little effect on government bond yields is Japan. In December 2014, the rating agency Moody's downgraded Japan's sovereign bond rating from Aa3 to A1, the fifth-highest rating on that agency's scale. Taken literally, this rating implied that Japan's government bonds were at greater risk of default than China's. Yet, the downgrade barely registered a ripple in the yield on Japanese government bonds. During 2015, similar cuts in the ratings were enacted by other agencies, such as Fitch and Standard and Poor's, based on the Japanese economy's growth outlook and the apparent lack of political will to undertake reforms to revive growth. Through it all, yields on Japanese government bonds remained nearly unchanged.

The eurozone debt crisis led to a differentiation between the government bond yields of "core" eurozone economies such as Germany and those of the "periphery" economies including Greece, Italy, Ireland, Portugal, and Spain, which have been volatile. In other words, eurozone members regarded as relatively secure became havens. Switzerland, which is not part of the eurozone but is well integrated into European financial systems and has been seen as a traditional safe haven, became the unwitting recipient of inflows from Europe. Although the euro did decline in value relative to other major currencies as the eurozone debt crisis unfolded, the Swiss franc rose sharply in value, despite the concerted actions of the SNB to prevent this, as these capital inflows flooded in.

The safe havens mentioned here share similar characteristics, but the sheer scale of inflows into U.S. Treasury securities even when the country's financial system was on the verge of imploding suggests that the U.S. is even more special than other safe haven economies. One could argue that the rush into U.S. Treasuries in the presence of global financial turmoil is really more a flight to liquidity and depth than a flight to safety. Given the depth of U.S. financial markets, investments in U.S. government bonds are liquid and easily tradable. Hence, even if the prospect of an eventual dollar depreciation exposes foreign investors to a small loss in principal, they will still come flocking into U.S. Treasuries during stormy times in global financial markets, for they know that they can pull their money back by selling Treasuries without too much trouble.

In fact, foreign holdings of U.S. Treasuries have remained strong for a number of years. There has been little sign, even during periods when the global economy appeared to be getting back on its feet, that investors might be pulling out of Treasuries. Moreover, demand for the dollar and other such safe haven currencies has continued unabated—even as the governments of many of the relevant economies are groaning under high levels of public debt and their central banks are, in effect, printing large sums of money to support economic growth—suggesting that there is more to the story about what it takes for a country and its currency to be regarded as safe havens.

THE ATTRIBUTES OF A SAFE HAVEN

What are the distinguishing characteristics of the safe haven currencies, in addition to their home economies being advanced and rich? The answer, in large part, rests on robust and resilient institutions that, in some respects, seem to trump sheer economic power. Earning the trust of foreign investors, rather than just relying on their avarice, is what separates these economies from others that may be characterized by economic dynamism accompanied by institutional weakness.

The key issue for a foreign investor is the presence of institutions that support private contracting arrangements but also protect property rights and limit the possibility of expropriation by the government or other politically powerful groups. The common characteristics of safe haven currencies, as determined by the behavior of investors rather than by any conceptual criteria, include an open and democratic system of government, an independent judiciary that fosters the rule of law, freedom of the press, and credible public institutions. These institutional factors are the core building blocks of the level of trust that the rest of the world has in the economies that are home to such currencies. Transparency of public institutions, the right to free expression, and an unfettered media are all necessary for building confidence. They do this not by emphasizing strengths, but by making weaknesses and faults in the system obvious, with the democratic process then providing a self-correcting mechanism.

Consider the U.S., whose trump card is an institutionalized system of checks and balances that operates between the executive, legislative, and judicial branches of its government. The system of open and transparent democracy is crucial for explaining the confidence that foreign central banks and other investors have that the U.S. will not default on its debt, either directly or through indirect means such as high inflation. The fact that about $5 trillion in net public debt is owned by U.S. investors, particularly by many groups such as retirees, who form a potent voting block, is a comforting thought for foreign investors. The point here is that the democratic system creates a direct mechanism for ensuring the government's accountability to the citizens it represents and governs, which in turn disciplines its economic policies, at least over the long term.

Moreover, given how broadly the holdings of U.S. Treasury securities are dispersed, the notion of the U.S. targeting a specific country and reneging on its obligations to that country is unrealistic and unlikely to pass legal muster. Indeed, the U.S. legal framework is another bedrock that is not only independent of the executive and legislative branches, but is also seen as a fair and consistent interpreter of the rules. Although one may quarrel with the complexity of U.S. laws and regulations, the fact that they are enforced in a relatively uniform way apparently inspires confidence in domestic and foreign investors.

Many of the U.S. advantages reinforce each other. The strong regulatory and legal frameworks have led many foreign firms to seek listings on U.S. exchanges to "bond" themselves to the U.S. institutional framework. Foreign companies that register with the U.S. Securities and Exchange Commission subject themselves to stronger corporate governance standards and disclosure requirements. In return, they enjoy higher valuations, cheaper funding, and better long-run financial performance than similar companies that do not subject themselves to the discipline and scrutiny of U.S. markets and institutions.

This discussion suggests that a country can influence its currency's role in international finance in ways that go beyond having the characteristics of reserve currency economies. In previous chapters, we saw how China is taking steps to promote the RMB as an international currency and is even making changes to its economic structure that are consistent with eventually making the RMB a viable reserve currency. Let us now consider China's progress in relation to the noneconomic criteria that are relevant to the RMB's prospects of one day ascending to the status of a safe haven currency.

CHINA'S INSTITUTIONAL FRAMEWORK

Notwithstanding its economic strength, China is clearly not regarded as a prime investment destination when the security of financial capital is the primary objective of foreign investors.

Starting in 2014, as economic growth weakened, foreign capital inflows began to dry up and the flow of domestic capital out of the country picked up. No doubt some of the outflows of domestic savings were driven by diversification motives, but capital also started leaking out through unofficial channels. The stock market rout that started in June 2015 exacerbated these trends. These developments in China's capital flows stand in stark contrast to how foreign capital often pours into the government bonds of safe haven economies during times of global financial turmoil, even when those countries' equity markets and other financial markets are themselves under stress.

To earn the faith of international investors, economic might clearly goes only so far. Even if China eventually has a fully open capital account and well-developed financial markets, this element of faith will require broader institutional developments, including changes in the political and legal systems. On this score, there has been little progress in recent years, even as the economy has forged ahead to become one of the most powerful in the world.

China has had one-party rule since the People's Republic was established in 1949. The country has neither an open political system nor an independent judiciary, which appear to be necessary features for a country to have its currency attain safe haven status. Another lesson from history is that economic liberalization and free markets tend to go hand in hand with more democratic governments, either as a matter of government policy or because of the desire for more political freedoms as a country's population grows richer. Is there a prospect for reforms to go beyond the economic sphere in China?

POLITICAL REFORMS

In June 1949, Mao Zedong gave a speech to commemorate the twenty-eighth anniversary of the CPC. In the speech, titled "On the People's Democratic Dictatorship," Mao set out his vision of democracy. The essay approvingly cited a manifesto adopted by the Nationalist Kuomintang's First National Congress in 1924 led by Sun Yat-sen, which stated: "The so-called democratic system in modern states is usually monopolized by the bourgeoisie and has become simply an instrument for oppressing the common people. On the other hand, the Kuomintang's Principle of Democracy means a democratic system shared by all the common people and not privately owned by the few." Building on Sun's ideas, Mao then went on to define his own vision as follows: "A state system which is shared only by the common people and which the bourgeoisie is not allowed to own privately—add to this the leadership of the working class, and we have the state system of the people's democratic dictatorship."

Sun Yat-sen was well liked and respected by the Communists. However, under Chiang Kai-shek, who led the Kuomintang after Sun's death in 1925, the Communists and Nationalists had a bitter falling out. This culminated in hostilities that started in 1927, continued until a truce was negotiated when Japan invaded China in 1937, and then erupted into a civil war in 1946 as the truce between the two sides broke down a year after Japan's surrender to the Allied forces. Revealing the bitterness he felt toward Chiang, in his essay Mao wrote, "Chiang Kai-shek betrayed Sun Yat-sen and used the dictatorship of the bureaucrat–bourgeoisie and the landlord class as an instrument for oppressing the common people of China. This counter-revolutionary dictatorship was enforced for 22 years and has only now been overthrown by the common people of China under our leadership."

Mao then went on to clarify what he meant by the seemingly contradictory juxtaposition of democracy and dictatorship, after making a distinction between two groups:

Who are the people? At the present stage in China, they are the working class, the peasantry, the urban petty bourgeoisie and the national bourgeoisie. These classes, led by the working class and the Communist Party, unite to form their own state and elect their own government; they enforce their dictatorship over the running dogs of imperialism— the landlord class and bureaucrat–bourgeoisie, as well as the representatives of those classes, the Kuomintang reactionaries and their accomplices—suppress them, allow them only to behave themselves and not to be unruly in word or deed. If they speak or act in an unruly way, they will be promptly stopped and punished. Democracy is practiced within the ranks of the people, who enjoy the rights of freedom of speech, assembly, association and so on. The right to vote belongs only to the people, not to the reactionaries. The combination of these two aspects, democracy for the people and dictatorship over the reactionaries, is the people's democratic dictatorship.

President Xi Jinping (Figure 7.1) is known to have been influenced by Maoist ideology and his conception of democratic government appears to hew closely to Mao's conception of the form of government suitable for China. In one of his speeches after becoming President, he argued that China ought not to ape the political system or development model of other countries "because it would not fit us and it might even lead to catastrophic consequences. The fruit may look the same, but the taste is quite different." He added that the Chinese people had "experimented with constitutional

Figure 7.1 The Politburo Standing Committee, 2012–2017.
Members of this committee, which constitutes China's top decision-making body, are: (center) President Xi Jinping; (left, from top to bottom) Zhang Dejiang, Liu Yunshan, Zhang Gaoli; (right, from top to bottom) Premier Li Keqiang, Yu Zhengsheng, and Wang Qishan.
Credit: Kyodo via AP Images

monarchy, imperial restoration, parliamentarianism, multi-party system and presidential government, yet nothing really worked. Finally, China took on the path of socialism." He admitted that China had made mistakes and suffered serious setbacks during the process of building socialism, but ultimately this was the best form of government to meet the Chinese peoples' needs and aspirations.

In fall 2013, just a few months after Xi had taken over as president from Hu Jintao, reports started to appear in both domestic and international media about a circular issued by the General Office of the CPC Central Committee. Such documents are usually not made public, but this one seemed to have been allowed into the public domain to send a clear message that government statements about market-oriented reforms and economic liberalization were not to be interpreted as presaging reforms in any other spheres. Document Number 9, as it came to be known (the name refers to the circular number assigned to it), did not identify any authors, as is the norm for such party circulars, but it was clear that such a sweeping document must have had the approval of top leaders. Beijing political circles had little doubt that the document bore President Xi's imprimatur and was to be interpreted as an official statement from the highest echelons of the party.

The circular, dated April 2013, was titled "Communiqué on the Current State of the Ideological Sphere." The document identified a set of "noteworthy problems," which could be traced to the intense ideological struggle in which China was engaged with the West. Seven perils to social stability, the economic system, and the Party's leadership were listed, including promoting Western constitutional democracy, universal values, civil society, neoliberalism, freedom of the press, historical nihilism, and questioning of the nature of socialism with Chinese characteristics. The document warned, "These mistaken views and ideas exist in great numbers in overseas media and reactionary publications. If we allow any of these ideas to spread, they will disturb people's existing consensus on important issues . . . and this will disrupt our nation's stable progress on reform and development."

The document exhorted Party leaders to strengthen their resolve to prevail in ideological struggles with the West and to guide

Party members in distinguishing between true and false theories. There was a call to maintain "unwavering adherence to the principle of the Party's control of media" and "strengthen management of the ideological battlefield" to counter the threat posed by Western anti-China forces and internal "dissidents" trying to infiltrate China's ideological sphere and challenge mainstream ideology. The document called for "management of all types and levels of propaganda on the cultural front . . . strengthen guidance of public opinion on the Internet [sic] . . . and allow absolutely no opportunity or outlets for incorrect thinking or viewpoints to spread."

In early 2015, there were reports about a sequel to Document Number 9. The new Party circular, Document Number 30, was not available to the public but reportedly called for cleansing Western–inspired liberal ideas from universities and other educational and cultural institutions. In comments published on official websites that reinforced the message, Xi urged universities to "enhance guidance over thinking and keep a tight grip on leading ideological work in higher education." He also wrote, "Never allow singing to a tune contrary to the party center. Never allow eating the Communist Party's food and then smashing the Communist Party's cooking pots."

THE PARTY AND THE CONSTITUTION

All indications since he took office are that Xi has adopted a hard-line stance against political liberties and freedom of expression, focusing on reducing dissension within the Party and enhancing Party discipline. Although there were some potentially promising signs early on in his regime of a greater willingness to consider political and institutional reforms, such expectations were dashed fairly soon.

In December 2012, two months after he had been appointed general secretary of the CPC—a step that, by convention, preceded his appointment as president—Xi made a speech in Beijing to commemorate the thirtieth anniversary of the adoption by the National People's Congress (NPC) of China's Constitution. In the speech, he made a statement that attracted wide attention within and outside China: "Rule of the nation by law means, first and foremost, ruling the nation in accord with the Constitution; the crux in governing by laws is to govern in accord with the Constitution." He then went on to say "No organization or individual has the privilege to overstep the Constitution and the law, and any violation of the Constitution and the law must be investigated. We must establish mechanisms to restrain and supervise power. Power must be made responsible and must be supervised."

This speech was interpreted as potentially signaling a departure from the tepid and rote statements made by his predecessors about the importance of the Constitution, which had not been as forceful about its primacy. Because the Constitution indicates that people exercise their power through the State or, more precisely, through the NPC—the legislative body whose composition is largely determined by the CPC—Xi's pronouncements were hardly dramatic statements on their own. Still, in a system in which even small changes in slogans can portend significant shifts in direction, the phrases used by Xi attracted attention since they were in a high-profile speech in the midst of the political transition from the previous leadership. But any hope that Xi's statement marked the dawn of political reform was quickly erased.

Since then, China has taken a strident tone against aspirations to a constitutional democracy, viewing it as part of an insidious plot by the West to weaken the Party's control. Various statements by officials and official news media have criticized the very concept of constitutionalism, which is seen as seeking to unacceptably elevate the rule of law above the Party. A propaganda official remarked, "Promotion of Western constitutional democracy is an attempt to negate the party's leadership." A commentary in the official newspaper *People's Daily* echoed this view, arguing "Constitutionalism belongs only to capitalism. . . . [It] is a weapon for information and psychological warfare used by the magnates of American monopoly capitalism and their proxies in China to subvert China's socialist system."

The subject remains a touchy one for the government. In mid October 2015, shortly before President Xi's visit to the U.K., the British government had planned to display a copy of the Magna Carta at Renmin University of China in Beijing. The Magna Carta—the "Great Charter" agreed to by King John of England in the year 1215 and seen as underpinning the concept of constitutional democracy and enshrining individual rights—was on tour around the world in celebration of its eight hundredth anniversary. At the last moment, Beijing scotched the U.K.'s plan. No official explanation was given; Renmin University simply did not receive the necessary permission. The document had to be displayed, instead, in the British ambassador's residence.

Soon thereafter, a prominent Chinese academic's book about the "dream" of constitutional democracy was banned, just a few days before China's annual Constitution Day. The book, *Zouchu Dizhi* [*Moving Away from the Imperial Regime*] by Qin Hui, suddenly became "out of stock" on account of its having "quality problems." Interestingly, even Xi's December 2012 speech about the primacy of the Constitution, which had been regarded as highly significant at the time, was downplayed subsequently. The CPC's Central Propaganda Office did not include that speech or any mention of it in an edited compilation of "main ideas and arguments" from Xi's speeches that it put together in 2014: *A Primer of Important Speeches by General Secretary Xi Jinping.*

Official rhetoric and actions leave little to the imagination about the government's intentions regarding political reform and freedom of expression. The notion of a more open, representative democracy and a free press, or at least the freedom for private citizens to express their views without fear, are anathema to China's current leaders. Their calculation that delivering good economic growth would tamp down pressures for dramatic societal or political changes appears to have been correct so far.

Whether financial and other markets can function efficiently without the free flow of information is an open question. But, certain reforms remain necessary if a market-oriented system is to work smoothly, especially a legal framework that protects contractual arrangements and property rights adequately. As is typical, China is attempting to have it both ways.

CHINA'S APPROACH TO LEGAL REFORMS

The U.S. is not the only country where law degrees seem to be a useful qualification for the presidency (President Barack Obama was once a law professor). A few years after earning a degree in chemical engineering from the prestigious Tsinghua University in Beijing, Xi Jinping returned to Tsinghua for further studies and received a Doctor of Law degree in 2002. Premier Li Keqiang has an undergraduate law degree from Peking University (and a PhD in economics from the same university) and Vice President Li Yuanchao has a Doctor of Law degree from the Central Party School of the CPC. Both President Xi and Vice President Li appear to have earned their law degrees on a part-time basis, building on their study of Marxist philosophy and ideological education. Still, since this is an area where, at least on paper, China's leadership has expertise, there were expectations that some legal reforms would be in the offing after the leadership transition in 2013.

The Third Plenum of the eighteenth CPC Central Committee, a meeting of key government leaders and officials, was held in November 2013. The meeting concluded with agreement on an extensive set of economic reform proposals, along with a few other reforms including measures to fight government corruption. The communiqué from this plenum contained a brief mention of legal reforms, which evoked little interest because few details were provided and the phrasing seemed to echo long-standing slogans. However, it became clear from President Xi's speeches and remarks in the following months that, as part of a campaign against corruption and to serve as a foundation for a more market-oriented economy, he viewed legal reforms as a key building block for strengthening China's domestic economy.

These ideas matured over the next year, with detailed plans for legal reforms being drawn up, creating excitement that significant changes were afoot that would start shifting China toward becoming a society governed truly by the rule of law. The main theme of the Fourth Plenum of the eighteenth CPC Central Committee, held in October 2014, was "Ruling the Country through Law." The communiqué laid out the goals of legal reform as follows: "Our overall objective in comprehensively advancing the law-based governance of the country is the establishment of a socialist rule of law system with Chinese characteristics and the building of a socialist rule of law country."

Such statements about socialist principles and Chinese characteristics are seen as slogans that are par for the course for CPC documents and are often regarded as innocuous. The communiqué went on to describe how the legal system needed to be modernized, with justice administered impartially, and noted that governance, the exercise of state power, and administration of government needed to be law based. After calling for greater efficiency and transparency in the legal process, the document also highlighted the need to "ensure that citizens' personal rights, property rights, basic political rights and other forms of rights are inviolable; and ensure that citizens' economic, cultural, and social rights are respected." Such language was no doubt music to the ears of proponents of legal reforms in China, who are eager to see the judiciary become more independent from, or at least less subservient to, the CPC.

However, the communiqué soon quashed all hopes of more fundamental reforms. The subsequent text in the document left no ambiguity about the role of the CPC and whether the Party itself would be subservient to the rule of law:

> The Party's leadership is the most essential feature of socialism with Chinese characteristics and the most fundamental guarantee for socialist rule of law in China. The need to exercise the Party's leadership throughout the whole process and in every aspect of the law-based governance of the country is a basic lesson we have learned in developing socialist rule of law in China.
>
> The position of leadership of the CPC is written into China's Constitution. Upholding the Party's leadership is fundamental to socialist rule of law; it is the foundation and lifeblood of both the Party and

the country, affects the interests and well-being of people of all China's ethnic groups, and is an integral part of our efforts to comprehensively advance the law-based governance of the country. The Party's leadership is consistent with socialist rule of law: socialist rule of law must uphold the Party's leadership, while the Party's leadership must rely upon socialist rule of law.

On February 26, 2015, shortly before the annual meeting of the NPC, the Supreme People's Court (SPC), the nation's highest court, formally released the legal reform plan. The plan, titled "Opinion of the SPC on Deepening Reform of the People's Courts Comprehensively," was to underpin the fourth five-year reform of the legal system over the period 2014 to 2018. The document makes a promising start, stating the need to "guarantee the independent and fair exercise of the courts' judicial powers." After reiterating the objectives identified by the NPC communiqué, the document lays out the basic principles for reforms. The first principle reiterates what the reforms entail and also makes clear, from the perspective of those hoping for a shift toward the true rule of law, what the reforms would not change:

> Persist in the Party's leadership, ensuring a correct political orientation. People's courts deepening judicial reform shall adhere to the Party's leadership throughout, fully bring into play the Party's core function of viewing the overall situation and coordinating leadership in all areas; truly realize the organic unity of the Party's leadership, the people as the masters, and governance in accordance with law; to ensure that judicial reforms maintain the correct political orientation throughout.

The document also noted that "deepening of reform of the people's courts will be carried out start to finish under the leadership of the party." The President of the SPC, Zhou Qiang, was quoted as saying in a speech to the Party Congress that the SPC would "resolutely resist the influence of mistaken Western concepts and ways of thinking." He is said to have specifically highlighted judicial independence and separation of powers as odious Western concepts that were not suitable for China. In a similar vein, President

Xi was quoted as saying that questions such as whether the Party or the Constitution was more powerful constituted a false choice and a political trap. He noted that the CPC's leadership was a fundamental element of the socialist legal system.

By the summer of 2015, there was a broad crackdown on "rights lawyers," who were representing dissidents in court cases or bringing cases against the state based on claims of individual rights. The *People's Daily* attacked a group of such lawyers, who had been seized by the authorities, for "colluding with petitioners, sensationalizing grievance cases on the Internet, seeking personal fame and status, and participating in a 'criminal syndicate.'"

The upshot of this collision between "rule of law" rhetoric and practice is that it has become clear that the government intends to establish stronger property rights, streamline laws that govern commercial transactions, and improve the efficiency of the legal system in adjudicating disputes among private entities. These reforms are no doubt necessary to allow a market economy to function more effectively. The transparency of laws, rules, and regulations and the settling of disputes in a fair and quick manner are essential for commercial enterprise to thrive, as the CPC leaders clearly recognize.

However, China's leaders have no intention of allowing *themselves* to be constrained by the legal system. Hence, the proposed reforms, even if carried out fully, will not change the balance of power between the government and the judiciary. The legal system will remain subservient to the CPC and will not in any way provide checks and balances on the government.

CENTRAL BANK INDEPENDENCE

An important characteristic of safe haven economies is that their central banks are independent. Of course, no central bank is truly independent because it must be accountable to the public and the government it serves. Even in economies where the central bank is independent by law and has the sole objective of keeping inflation low and stable, which are the key characteristics of an inflation-targeting framework, the central bank usually decides on the level of inflation to target not just by itself, but in consultation with the government.

A central bank would soon lose its legitimacy if it undertook policies that were not seen as being in the general interest of the economy. The key aspect of independence, however, is that the central bank not be subject to the whims of politicians, who may favor growth over keeping inflation under control, which could be detrimental to the long-term health of the economy if it resulted in runaway inflation. Another consideration is that the government should not have the ability to use the central bank's money-printing presses to finance its deficit spending, which could erode the value of the currency and set off spiraling inflation and currency depreciation. This is a temptation to which many emerging market governments have fallen prey, usually culminating in high and unstable inflation.

An even more salient characteristic for a central bank is that of operational independence. Even if the institution does not have the ability to choose its objectives, such as whether it should give higher priority to keeping inflation low or keeping the exchange rate stable, it must have the freedom to use the monetary policy instruments at its disposal to accomplish these objectives without further government interference.

These characteristics are seen as essential to give investors, both domestic and foreign, confidence that the central bank will protect the value of its currency. The major central banks such as the U.S. Federal Reserve, the European Central Bank, the BOJ, the Bank of England, and the SNB all have statutory independence, which includes operational independence for implementing monetary policy. These central banks have the independence to use the tools at their disposal, such as interest rates and the share of deposits that banks are required to hold as reserves at the central bank, to achieve their objectives. Since the financial crisis, many of these central banks have taken more drastic measures—even purchasing government bonds and other financial assets such as stocks to influence the entire spectrum of interest rates and asset prices. The key point, however, is that these central banks have undertaken such unconventional operations of their own accord, without their national governments prompting them to print money to finance budget deficits. Such operational independence is seen as critical to maintaining financial stability and the confidence of investors in the value of the currency.

In China, the notion that any government agency is independent is dubious. In the case of the PBC, however, there are some important subtleties in its relationship with the Party. For the first thirty-five years after its inception in 1948, the PBC was a subordinate department of the Ministry of Finance. In 1983, the State Council formally designated the PBC as a central bank. It was only in 1995 that the NPC legally confirmed the PBC's status by adopting the central banking law. This law put the PBC on par with other ministries such as the Ministry of Finance, a salient consideration in a system in which an agency's position in the government hierarchy matters for being able to make independent decisions and influence high-level leadership and policymaking within the CPC.

Indeed, the PBC has independence from the government in some respects, as noted in the central banking law (which was amended in 2003): "The [PBC] shall, under the guidance of the State Council, independently implement monetary policies, perform its functions and carry out its operations according to law free from any intervention of local governments, departments of governments at all levels, public organizations or individuals."

This statement is positive insofar as it indicates that the PBC will not, in principle, be subject to pressures to finance government budget deficits directly—a key concern in many emerging market economies that lack fiscal discipline. However, as with many other matters regarding the Chinese government, caveats apply to this optimistic characterization. A memorandum issued by the CPC Central Committee in 1993 states: "As the central bank, the People's Bank of China shall conduct monetary policy independently." But, the same document then makes it clear that "the People's Bank of China shall be under the leadership of the State Council."

In practical terms, this has come to mean that interest rate policy and exchange rate policy decisions have to be approved by the State Council. The State Council also sets targets for the growth of monetary and credit aggregates. The PBC has limited operational independence in terms of tactics—such as the exact timing of specific policy changes—but not in the broader sense of the term.

The true picture is somewhat more complex. With its reasonably deft management of monetary policy over the years, despite being constrained by the country's policy of having to tightly manage the value of the RMB exchange rate, the PBC has garnered some level of credibility and de facto independence within the Party hierarchy. Its reasonable track record of fighting inflation, along with the high level of expertise and professionalism of its staff relative to those of certain other government agencies, appears to have earned the PBC the confidence of the top leadership.

Governor Zhou Xiaochuan and other senior staff such as Deputy Governor Yi Gang are articulate and move comfortably in the highest level international policy circles. On the other hand, the opacity of its policymaking and weak communication of its policy strategy has not won the PBC any plaudits. Still, relative to other government agencies, the PBC has attained at least a modicum of confidence and respect even among international investors, who tend to be instinctively dismissive of Chinese officialdom.

Notwithstanding its track record and the respect its senior personnel command within and outside China, however, the PBC's lack of even operational independence, let alone statutory independence, implies that it does not meet the characteristics of an independent central bank. Concerns that this could one day affect the PBC's ability to function effectively and subject it to the CPC's whims are likely to deter international investors from perceiving the RMB as a safe haven currency.

MIND THE INSTITUTIONAL GAP

The CPC has clearly done a skillful job of managing the economy, at least when considering GDP growth as the measure of success.

China stands out as an anomaly in the context of the voluminous academic literature that a well-developed institutional framework—typically characterized by independent legal institutions, the rule of law, an open and transparent democratic system of government, and good public and corporate governance—are important determinants of growth. But, when it comes to earning the trust of foreign investors, a key characteristic of a safe haven economy, strong institutions are indispensable.

Many foreign investors may decide the risks of expropriation or a weak legal framework to protect their rights are compensated for by the high growth potential of the Chinese economy. This may explain the high levels of FDI into China, but it also suggests why foreign investors are unlikely to view it as a predictable, low-risk destination for investment when safety matters more than yield.

China's government remains opaque and the political machinations and decision-making processes at top levels are shrouded in secrecy. It is certainly not the case that the CPC is a monolithic institution that speaks and acts fully in concert, brooking no internal dissent. There are multiple rival factions constantly jockeying for power, often acting as a check on the unconstrained power of any particular faction. Powerful provincial governments also often act as a check on the power of the central government. These countervailing forces that wax and wane are no substitute, however, for the sort of durable and institutionalized checks and balances that characterize the U.S. and other advanced economies. Thus, even setting aside the issue of its low level of financial development, it is difficult to envision China being seen as a safe haven given the current form of its political and legal frameworks.

CHAPTER 8

House of Cards?

> The reconstructed Burgess fauna, interpreted by the theme of replaying life's tape, offers powerful support for this different view of life: any replay of the tape would lead evolution down a pathway radically different from the road actually taken ... the diversity of possible itineraries does demonstrate that eventual results cannot be predicted at the outset. Each step proceeds for cause, but no finale can be specified at the start, and none would even occur a second time in the same way, because any pathway proceeds through thousands of improbable stages. Alter any early event, ever so slightly and without apparent importance at the time, and evolution cascades into a radically different channel.
>
> *Wonderful Life*, Stephen Jay Gould

Doomsday warnings about the Chinese economy run rampant in the Western media. That an economy not run on market principles could generate consistently high growth for such a long period is unprecedented in recent history. China does not conform to conventional wisdom that factors such as a well-developed financial system, rule of law, and democracy are necessary for sustained high growth. Hence, the notion that its economy is a house of cards, apt to crumble at the slightest ill wind, may well be comforting to those on the outside, even as China has become large and powerful.

China's growth model has certainly created enormous risks, the likes of which have spelled doom for other economies in the past. Over the past decade and a half, growth has been driven to a large extent by massive and, to a significant degree, inefficient investment and an associated buildup of debt. This debt was financed by a banking system that has not been effective at allocating resources to the most productive opportunities. And even a generous interpretation of China's growth success has to acknowledge the inefficiencies and costs associated with a growth model that has delivered spectacularly in terms of GDP but has led to environmental degradation and a massive waste of resources.

Although it is not the objective of this book to evaluate China's growth outlook or the risks of a major crisis, it is hard to avoid these issues in discussing the prospects for the RMB. After all, a shaky economy with a floundering financial system, one in which domestic and foreign investors lack confidence, cannot serve as the foundation for a currency that is trying to establish a prominent role in international finance.

The Chinese economy faces risks in several categories. The first is related to capital account liberalization and the possibility of a surge of capital outflows, which could destabilize the financial system as well as the overall economy. The second is a set of concerns specifically about China's financial system, including the stability of the banking system, wild swings in the stock market, and the size of the shadow banking system. The third set of risks is related to more fundamental aspects of China's economy, political structure, and policymaking. These include the possibility of a dramatic growth slowdown, political instability fed by the government's desire to further tighten its control, and policy missteps. Each of these risks could imperil or, at a minimum, delay the RMB's rise.

These risks do not fall into neat silos, of course, and feedback loops between them could create even greater uncertainty. For instance, a slowdown in economic growth could lead to a surge in corporate bankruptcies and worsen the problem of nonperforming loans in the banking system, which in turn could trigger more capital outflows. China also faces a difficult and risky transition from a largely command-driven economy to a more market-oriented one. Indeed, many of the reforms and measures taken to promote the RMB's international role have created their own risks for the economy.

THE CAPITAL ACCOUNT

Allowing for the free flow of financial capital has been an important element of the plan for increasing the RMB's international stature. The prestige that having a globally recognized currency brings is certainly a relevant consideration. This still leaves one key question unanswered: Why has the Chinese government given such a high priority to capital account liberalization in light of the many domestic challenges the economy faces? After all, China still needs to strengthen its financial system, restructure its state-owned enterprises (SOEs), and deal with a looming demographic problem as its population ages. Even prominent reform-minded Chinese economists, many of them trained in the West, have argued that the risks of capital account liberalization far outweigh the benefits.

In a 2013 speech, the influential economist Justin Yifu Lin, who has a PhD from the University of Chicago and was the first World Bank chief economist from an emerging market economy, laid out his reasons for opposing capital account opening: "A financial structure featuring large amounts of capital flows will result in excessive economic volatility in developing countries which still have twisted financial structures and lower levels of financial deepening." He did empathize with the PBC, noting:

> I do understand the embarrassing international position China's central bank has been put in as the U.S. sets the rules and the IMF seemingly echoes its policies. If China does not open its capital account, the central bank will have to shoulder the great pressures of a reality in which the U.S. dollar is the anchor currency and the U.S. itself has a huge international capital flow.

He then went on to excoriate scholars who had argued that China would benefit from a more open capital account: "Of course we cannot blindly copy and follow Western theories as, for example, the new theories raised by U.S. banking academics lack structural conceptions and do not meet the practical needs of developing countries."

Yu Yongding, another well-respected and reform-minded economist who had long argued that China should have a free-floating exchange rate, was more measured. In a piece written in 2013, he made the case that "with China's financial system too fragile to withstand external shocks, and the global economy mired in turmoil, the [PBC] would be unwise to gamble on the ability of rapid capital-account liberalization to generate a healthier and more robust financial system." After laying out the risks of capital account opening in the absence of a floating exchange rate, a better financial system, and legal reforms to ensure property rights, he concluded, "Given China's extensive reform agenda, further opening of the capital account can wait; and, in view of liberalization's ambiguous benefits and significant risks, it should."

A Matter of Sequence

Another way of framing this issue is to consider how China determines the order in which it will undertake capital account liberalization relative to other policy changes and how that affects the benefit–risk tradeoff from capital account opening. This has implications for China's growth and financial stability, and therefore for the RMB's international role.

Many a developing economy has learned the harsh lesson that opening up its capital account without having a market-determined exchange rate and a well-functioning financial system is risky. A fixed or tightly managed nominal exchange rate makes it harder to cope with capital flow volatility because the exchange rate cannot act as a shock absorber. Large imbalances can build up if capital floods into or out of the economy while the central bank is trying to protect a particular exchange rate. Similarly, an underdeveloped and poorly regulated financial system can raise economic risks as foreign capital inflows can be misallocated to weak projects, lead to a run-up in external debt, and have little positive impact on long-term productivity and growth.

China has turned the academic wisdom about the right order of reforms on its head—moving forward more aggressively on opening the capital account relative to fixing the financial system and increasing the flexibility of the exchange rate. How well can the economy weather the risks created by violating the textbook approach to reforms? An analysis of China's external balance sheet (i.e., its international investment position), suggests that the economy faces only modest direct risks from a more open capital account. As noted in Chapter 3, FDI and portfolio equity together account for 75 percent of China's external liabilities. This structure of liabilities is safer than one dominated by external debt, especially foreign currency external debt, which has felled many emerging market economies in the past because debt puts the entire burden of risk on the borrower. In the case of FDI and portfolio equity investment, foreign investors share in the capital as well as currency risk—meaning that they take part of the hit if the investments do not perform well or the domestic currency falls in value. In contrast, interest payments and the obligation to repay external debt at face value remain the same irrespective of whether the domestic economy does well or not.

Another source of risk is that an open capital account often encourages an accumulation of external debt. Short-term external debt denominated in foreign currency has been the scourge of emerging markets and was a major source of vulnerability for Latin American and Asian economies during the 1980s and 1990s. Large volumes of such debt exposed these economies to crises when foreign capital dried up, so the loans could not be rolled over and currency depreciation drove up the domestic currency value of such debt, making repayment of the debt harder.

China has traditionally had a low level of foreign currency external debt, amounting to about $760 billion or 6 percent of GDP at the end of 2015, a lower ratio than virtually any other major emerging market (total external debt, including debt denominated in RMB, was $1.4 trillion). The stock of foreign exchange reserves, which was $3.2 trillion in May 2016, is sufficient to meet all these debt obligations. Moreover, China's net foreign assets amounted to $1.6 trillion at the end of 2015, implying it has enough foreign assets to more than cover all of its foreign liabilities. In short,

China is not subject to the traditional risks associated with opening up the capital account in advance of increasing exchange rate flexibility.

Reinforcing this view, China's approach to capital account liberalization has allowed it to retain some control over capital flows. The QDII approach gives the government much greater control over when and how much money can be moved offshore as domestic financial institutions participating in the scheme are allocated specific investment quotas that can be modified over time. Similarly, the QFII scheme for inflows, along with the FTZs and Mutual Fund Connect and Stock Connect programs that allow for flows in both directions, are all part of the controlled approach to capital account liberalization. These programs allow the government to control the volume of flows in both directions and, to a significant extent, the composition of flows as well.

There are limits to this gradualist strategy, however, as the Chinese government has discovered. Trying to maintain a gradual approach to freeing up the exchange rate while opening up the capital account can create tensions that show up in large and volatile movements of capital.

Capital Outflows

Even as the Chinese economy continued to post relatively robust growth rates in the aftermath of the financial crisis and became the main driver of world growth, political uncertainty related to the leadership transition during the summer and fall of 2012 led to concerns about capital flowing out of China. Some of the increase in capital outflows from China has been consistent with the government's steps to liberalize outflows. Private-sector outflows are likely to increase further as Chinese corporations look for investment opportunities abroad and as financial market development allows households to take advantage of avenues for diversifying their savings into foreign investments.

However, the scale of outflows during 2015 indicates how quickly sentiments about economic and financial market conditions can shift. These capital flow surges in one direction or another can be exacerbated if the exchange rate is not allowed to adjust freely, and speculative pressures on the currency start building up.

The downward pressures on the RMB–dollar exchange rate after the PBC announced a shift to a more market-determined exchange rate on August 11, 2015, exemplify this phenomenon. In the immediate aftermath of this shift, which was accompanied by a nearly 2 percent devaluation of the RMB relative to the dollar, financial market participants appeared to interpret the move as signaling Chinese policymakers' concerns about the state of the economy. This move, in tandem with the sharp fall in Mainland stock markets since July 2015, led to a surge in outflows. The prospect of further currency depreciation also prompted many corporations to start paying down their foreign currency external debts as those debts would grow in RMB terms if the currency were to depreciate further. During 2015, China's foreign currency external debt shrank by about $140 billion. In balance of payments accounting, paying off external debt amounts to a capital outflow.

Foreign exchange market intervention undertaken by the PBC to keep the RMB's value from falling sharply then led to a significant reduction in reserves. Foreign exchange reserves had hit their peak of $3.993 trillion, a whisker short of the $4 trillion mark, in June 2014. China then began to hemorrhage reserves, which were down to $3.2 trillion by February 2016, a 20 percent decline in a year and a half.

As noted in Chapter 3, part of this decline represents currency valuation effects. Since the level of reserves is expressed in terms of dollars, depreciation of currencies such as the euro and the Japanese yen relative to the dollar over this period would imply a lower value of reserve assets denominated in those currencies. China does not report the currency composition of its foreign exchange reserves (although in 2015 it started reporting the composition of a portion of its reserve stocks to the IMF on a confidential basis). Hence, one can estimate currency valuation effects based only on particular assumptions about the currency composition of China's reserves. Another valuation effect is the result of marking to market the reserve portfolio. That is, if the market prices of the foreign bond and stock holdings in China's foreign exchange reserve portfolio were to change, then using those prices could result in an apparent increase or decrease in the value of the portfolio even with no purchases or sales of the assets in that portfolio. The PBC does not publicize the asset composition of its reserve portfolio.

Estimates of the valuation effects on China's reserve portfolio differ across official sources and private-sector analysts. In any case, it appears that valuation effects can account for at most about one-third of China's reserve losses during 2015 and early 2016. Hence, capital outflows during this period clearly put pressure on the PBC to expend some of its stock of reserves to keep the RMB's external value stable.

Many emerging market economies have faced balance of payments crises following a rapid rundown of foreign exchange reserves. In China's case, as noted earlier, the stock of reserves still remains high by traditional metrics. The stock is more than sufficient to repay China's external debts many times over and to pay for more than a year and a half's worth of imports. But, as a ratio of bank deposits, the amount of reserves is less comforting. If Chinese households and corporations were to withdraw deposits on a massive scale and cart the money abroad, reserves would cover only about 15 percent of total bank deposits. This is, of course, an excessively dire scenario. But, to take account of such factors, the IMF calculates a composite metric of reserve adequacy that takes account of potential capital flow volatility. By this measure, China had one and a half times the adequate level of reserves at the end of 2014. Even with the fall in reserves since then, reserves are well above this metric.

Still, further freeing-up of capital outflows could cause households and corporations to shift at least a portion of their deposits out of the banking system for purposes of portfolio diversification. Substantial deposit withdrawals that occur for that and other reasons, including concerns about the stability of the banking system, can damage banks and strain the entire domestic financial system. However, it is reassuring that, even with large capital outflows in 2015, Chinese bank deposits still grew by 13 percent. In other words, capital outflows do not, so far, seem to pose an imminent threat to the banking system.

Capital Flight

A more worrisome aspect of capital outflows is related to capital flight through both illegitimate and legitimate channels. Capital flight is quite different from more conventional outflows that are driven by a desire for portfolio diversification or macroeconomic factors such as higher interest rates in other countries. One possibility—which for obvious reasons is difficult to verify—is that President Xi's much-heralded anticorruption drive caused some ill-gotten wealth to leave the country to avoid expropriation during the crackdown process. On the other hand, these flows could also represent outward invest-ment flows reflecting the same concerns about macroeconomic and financial stability laid out earlier. These factors are difficult to disen-tangle, but the correlation between these two types of flows, which may rise in tandem when an economic slowdown and factors such as the corruption crackdown coincide, raises concerns about surges of capital outflows that in turn could threaten financial stability.

Illicit capital flows are a particular concern for financial stabil-ity because they bypass traditional channels that the government can control. By definition, these flows are difficult to measure with much precision. One widely used proxy measure based on official data is net errors and omissions (NEOs), which is the residual in the balance of payments accounting and reflects unrecorded capi-tal account or current account transactions.

The balance of payments covers both trade in goods and ser-vices (the current account) and cross-border financial flows (the capital account). By definition, the two must sum up to zero. If a country imports more goods and services than it exports (a cur-rent account deficit), then it must receive net financing from the rest of the world (a capital account surplus) to finance that differ-ence. Although a capital account surplus sounds like a good thing, it actually means that a country is borrowing from the rest of the world. The reverse holds as well. A current account surplus is balanced by a capital account deficit, an outflow of capital from the home country to the rest of the world.

Changes in international reserves are one way to balance the overall account if the current account and capital account do not add up to zero. During the early 2000s, China was running both current account and capital account surpluses. In other words, it had a positive trade balance (exports less imports) and was also getting net inflows of foreign capital (more inflows than outflows). The difference was accounted for by China's accumulation of reserves, which in effect amounts to official capital outflows because it represents PBC purchases of foreign assets.

In some cases, the balance doesn't add up, even when accounting for the increase or decrease in official international reserves. To make the balance of payments actually balance out to zero, the residual is attributed to NEOs. A residual could arise because of incorrect measurement or weak data collection procedures. When the residual is large and persistent, however, it is likely that NEOs reflect intentionally inaccurate reporting of trade and financial transactions or evasion of capital controls.

Positive NEOs reflect money coming into the country in a manner that circumvents controls on inflows. Correspondingly, negative NEOs typically reflect money leaving the country through unofficial channels. During the early to mid 2000s, China regularly recorded positive NEOs, as foreign investors were trying to acquire RMB-denominated assets to take advantage of RMB appreciation. However, China's NEOs have been persistently negative since 2009 (Figure 8.1). During 2014, such outflows amounted to $108 billion, and in 2015 they rose to $188 billion. These large negative NEOs are strongly suggestive of substantial illegitimate capital outflows.

It is important to understand why NEOs are so large in China and to identify the channels through which these unofficial capital flows take place. This phenomenon provides some hints about how China's capital account has become quite open in de facto terms despite the many controls and administrative regulations still in place. It also contains signals about how financial market participants view the future prospects for the Chinese economy.

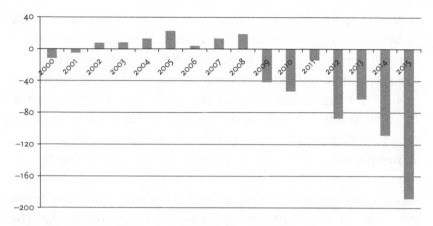

Figure 8.1 Net errors and omissions (in billions of U.S. dollars).
Source: The State Administration of Foreign Exchange.

Trade Misinvoicing

Trade misinvoicing is a well-recognized and time-honored means of circumventing capital controls. The operation is simple. Consider the hypothetical example of a Chinese importer who buys computer chips worth $5 million from an exporter in Malaysia but agrees with the Malaysian exporter that the bill would show a higher amount—say, $6 million. The importer then has an apparently legitimate reason to buy the extra $1 million worth of U.S. dollars. She could then keep the dollars in an offshore account and wait for the RMB to depreciate. If the RMB did indeed depreciate, the $1 million would be worth more in RMB. The foreign exporter who obligingly provides an inflated invoice may receive some compensation for enabling this transaction. So everyone is happy—except for the Chinese government statistician who would not be able to reconcile the flow of money related to this transaction with the data on the value of the computer chips imported, since those data are collected by another agency, the China Customs Agency, which monitors international trade transactions (and assuming the chips were, in fact, valued correctly by that agency). The $1 million difference would go into the errors and omissions category of the balance of payments.

During the mid 2000s, when there was considerable incentive to bet on RMB appreciation, China faced the opposite problem of imports being underinvoiced and exports being overinvoiced. In this case, for instance, Chinese exporters would send foreign importers invoices for larger amounts than the value of goods being traded. Consider another hypothetical case: one in which a U.S. importer buys $5 million worth of textiles from China but requests an invoice showing a total of the RMB equivalent of $6 million. The foreign importer then takes the additional $1 million worth of RMB— seemingly purchased for a legitimate trade transaction—and keeps it in an account in China through a proxy, making a profit when the RMB appreciates relative to the dollar. For his trouble in providing an inflated invoice, the Chinese exporter would enjoy a small cut of the profits from such a transaction. Again, the $1 million difference would go into the errors and omissions category.

Such transactions are of course much easier to conduct when an exporter or importer has associates and relatives in nearby economies such as Hong Kong and Taiwan, or when companies have subsidiaries or branches in other countries. Compared with merchandise trade (goods), services trade makes misinvoicing even easier since it is harder to match financial flows with actual trade transactions when there are no tangible goods involved.

Rather than using trade misinvoicing, it is possible to bet on whether a currency is going to increase or decrease in value directly through the use of financial derivatives. This is why trade misinvoicing is not much of an issue among the advanced economies, where it is easy to access foreign exchange derivatives markets and there are few restrictions on capital flows. These derivatives can be used to hedge foreign exchange transactions, reduce currency risk in import and export transactions, or even conduct pure currency speculation.

In the case of China, onshore foreign exchange derivatives markets were sanctioned officially only in recent years. The offshore markets for trading currency options in RMB, including in Hong Kong, still remain thin. The onshore markets are subject to government control, either directly or indirectly, on account of the fact that many of the major participants, such as the large domestic commercial banks, are state owned. Through the major state-owned banks, such as the Bank of China, that have a large presence in financial markets outside the Mainland, the government can also exercise some control over offshore RMB derivatives trading. It is for this reason that trade misinvoicing is still a significant factor in illicit capital flows across China's borders.

Macanese Roulette

Money laundering and capital flight also go hand in hand. Casino operations in Macau have long been regarded as a major conduit for money laundering and illicit capital flows from the Mainland. Anecdotal evidence indicates the widespread use of this channel for moving funds of illicit origin, whether coming from corruption, embezzlement of public or private entities, or other illegal activities. A variety of techniques is used to launder money through casinos and carry out cross-border monetary transfers for individual customers, sometimes without any actual transfer of funds involved.

Jorge Gordinho, a professor at the University of Macau, summarizes the types of transactions involved:

> [M]oney laundering through casinos generally has two types of objectives. The main objective is to pass the funds through the casino, typically taking as an entry point the buying of gambling chips, followed by the placing of bets, usually of reduced values or bets that in most cases cancel each other out (black and red on roulette, both teams in sports betting, etc.) in order to avoid significant amounts of losses. The gaming session ends with the redemption of the chips through the issuance of a casino check. A secondary objective may be to ensure that these transactions (buying chips, placing of bets, redeeming chips) are split or divided so that each does not exceed the value that triggers the automatic recording of operations, a practice known in the jargon as "smurfing."

Gordinho also hints at the complicity of gambling promoters, who assist in the transfer of funds to the casinos of Macau. He notes that, in "the case of VIP Baccarat, the amounts involved can be very significant. Moreover, in many cases, there will be no actual transfer of funds, but rather a simple balancing of accounts between credits in Mainland China and debits in Macau. This is one of the reasons why the gaming promoter sector [in Macau] is rather developed."

Regulatory authorities on the Mainland have long been aware of this conduit and have taken aggressive steps to combat these operations as capital flight has picked up. In late 2015, the PBC and the Monetary Authority of Macau jointly launched onsite inspections and tightened up implementation of anti-money-laundering regulations.

Banking Dens

An alternative channel for capital flight that has been identified by the SAFE is also difficult to measure but is regarded as widely prevalent. This channel is related to informal financial institutions that act as conduits for cross-border transfers. The system works as follows: at agreed-to exchange rates, underground banks transfer foreign currency funds to the offshore banking accounts of wealthy individuals while receiving local currency funds using anonymous domestic accounts, with no actual capital moving across the border. The accounting is balanced through shell companies, false invoices, and other instruments. According to a statement made by a SAFE official at a press conference:

> [The PBC], the Ministry of Public Security, the Supreme People's Court, the Supreme People's Procuratorate and the SAFE took a nationwide special action against transfer of illegal income through offshore companies and underground banks in mid-to-late April, and have solved some major underground bank cases, thus strongly intimidating lawbreakers.

In 2015, China's Ministry of Public Security is reported to have cracked down on an illegal foreign exchange network that it said handled up to $64 billion in transactions. In early September 2015, authorities discovered thirty-seven underground banking dens, accounting for deals totaling more than $38 billion, according to a statement on the ministry's website.

Capital Outflows in Search of Soft and Hard Assets

There are a number of other motives for capital flows from China to the U.S. and other advanced economies, through both legitimate and illegitimate channels. One is related to real estate purchases, which might have been boosted by safe haven inflows into countries such as Canada, the U.K., and the U.S. during the anticorruption drive in China. These purchases could also reflect a desire on the part of Chinese investors to diversify their portfolios into hard assets at a time of low worldwide yields from fixed-income assets and volatile returns on equities. The U.S. National Association of Realtors reports that sales of residential real estate to Chinese clients (including those from Hong Kong and Taiwan) now exceed sales to clients from any other country. For the 12-month period ending in March 2015, the estimated value of sales to Chinese clients was about $28 billion, more than double the level of $13 billion in 2013, and more than double the sales to clients from any other country. Flows into other housing markets, such as those in Hong Kong, have also been large and volatile in recent years.

Another factor that could be boosting inflows into the U.S. and other Western economies is related to the large number of tuition-paying Chinese students enrolled in institutions of higher education. The Institute of International Education estimates that about 305,000 Chinese students were enrolled in U.S. universities in the academic year 2014/2015, representing 31 percent of the total foreign student enrollments in U.S. universities. China's government does not bar the transfer of funds abroad for educational purposes, which could be fueling financial flows to other countries such as the U.K. as well.

A third category is related to procurement of visas that are (or, in the case of Canada, were) offered by certain countries to investors who can bring in large sums of money and create jobs. In the

U.S., EB-5 immigrant visas provide a path for obtaining permanent residency (green cards) for foreigners who invest a minimum of $500,000 and create at least ten jobs in the country. The program, which caps the annual number of visas issued at 10,000, hit that limit for the first time in August 2014. Chinese nationals accounted for nearly 90 percent of EB-5 visas issued during 2014, compared with just 13 percent in 2004. This translated to 8,308 EB-5 visas for Chinese nationals in 2014, a huge surge over the number issued a decade ago, when only a handful of visas were granted to Chinese.

Although a full-blown capital flight crisis seems unlikely, particularly given China's relatively strong external balance sheet characterized by a low level of external debt and a large stock of foreign exchange reserves, the government has certainly been concerned about illegitimate outflows and the fact that they may exacerbate overall capital outflows, adding to the financial and macroeconomic stresses the economy is already facing. These stresses pose risks to the stability of the financial system, which could act as the proverbial canary in the coalmine.

THE FINANCIAL SYSTEM

Given how important the home country's financial markets are for a reserve currency's prominence, even perceptions of instability regarding China's financial markets can have significant effects on the RMB's trajectory in international finance. In China, the financial system has traditionally played multiple roles. Rather than merely intermediating domestic and foreign savings into domestic investment, it has functioned as an instrument of social and fiscal policy. State-owned banks, which dominate the financial system, were directed to provide credit to favored sectors and industries. Until recently, the cap on bank deposit rates meant that households and corporations received very low returns on their savings. When adjusted for inflation, these rates were generally close to or below zero. This allowed the banks to finance debt accumulation at low interest rates by SOEs, provincial governments (through shell companies), and other borrowers, in effect transferring wealth from savers to borrowers (mostly state owned or state affiliated). By financing SOEs that in turn provided housing, education, and health care to their employees, banks also became a part of the social transfer mechanism.

In a rapidly expanding economy, the inefficiencies of the financial system were papered over by rising incomes and a high domestic savings rate. With the economy slowing and capital account liberalization giving savers opportunities to shift away from domestic bank deposits, there are now multiple points of stress on the Chinese financial system. Indeed, foreign investors considering investing in RMB-denominated assets view the volatility of and risks inherent in China's financial markets as a major deterrent. Hence, it is worth reviewing each of the potential risks and assessing how substantive concerns about them are.

Growing Mountain of Debt

China's overall level of debt has raised considerable concerns about a looming crisis. Prominent academics such as Carmen Reinhart and Kenneth Rogoff of Harvard University have warned of the dangers of high levels of debt, especially public debt. In their book *This Time Is Different: Eight Centuries of Financial Folly*, which provides a sweeping account of financial crises, they document how high debt levels in an economy can increase the risks of crises or, at a minimum, affect growth adversely. China has a low level of explicit public debt relative to the major reserve currency economies. The level of central government debt was estimated to be 17 percent of GDP in 2015, which is far lower than in most other emerging market or even advanced economies. In the U.S., for instance, gross federal government debt, which includes the holdings of that debt by the Federal Reserve and by other arms of the U.S. government such as the Social Security Trust Funds, is more than 100 percent of GDP. Publicly traded federal debt in the U.S. is about 74 percent of GDP.

The low level of central government debt is, however, hardly the full picture for China. Provincial governments had, for a long time, used a charade to get around the constraint (imposed by the central government) against issuing their own debt. They set up shell companies that borrowed from banks and other sources, then turned around and financed pet projects of local governments. The IMF has calculated a measure of augmented debt, which includes various types of local government borrowing, including off-budget borrowing by such local government financing vehicles via bank loans, bonds, trust loans, and other funding sources. By this measure, China's public debt-to-GDP ratio was estimated to be 60 percent in 2015, which would still be less than the public debt-to-GDP ratios of major advanced economies.

China's general government budget deficit has been quite small in recent years; it was less than 3 percent of GDP in 2015. This implies a fairly manageable state of public finances. Unfortunately, the picture is again not quite as soothing if one takes a broader view of public deficits in China. For instance, the IMF measure includes local government spending financed by land sales whereas the official deficit figures do not. By the IMF's definition, the "augmented fiscal deficit" in 2015 was 10 percent of GDP.

According to a recent McKinsey report, the level of gross debt in 2014 was 282 percent of GDP. This includes government debt (55 percent of GDP, similar to the IMF's estimate) and debt owed by financial institutions (65 percent of GDP), nonfinancial corporations (125 percent of GDP), and households (38 percent of GDP). For comparison, according to this report, U.S. gross debt in 2014 was 269 percent of GDP, accounted for mostly by government debt (89 percent of GDP) and household debt (77 percent of GDP).

The level of Chinese corporate debt, which rose to nearly 150 percent of GDP in the first quarter of 2016, is a major concern, especially since a substantial portion of outstanding bank loans has gone to large SOEs. Many SOEs in China are profitable because they have monopoly power in certain sectors, access to cheap energy and land, and can obtain low-cost financing from capital markets because of the implicit guarantee that the government will not let them go bankrupt. Such profit-making enterprises do not rely on bank loans as they make enough money to finance their working capital requirements and even to make new investments. In contrast, it is the weak, loss-making SOEs that have relied more on bank loans.

With cheap financing available and with prospects of continued strong growth, including in infrastructure and residential investment, SOEs in industries such as steel, aluminum, cement, and hard glass expanded their capacity rapidly during the boom times of the previous decade and the first half of this decade. Now that investment growth is slowing, it has become clear that there is considerable excess capacity in these industries. This augurs falling prices (especially given weak demand in the rest of the world), mounting losses, and the inability to pay off bank loans in full.

The notion that such high debt levels heighten the risks of a financial meltdown is, however, overblown. One benign view is that, in an economy that saves nearly half of its annual GDP and relies largely on its banking system to intermediate these savings into physical investments, it is no surprise that bank credit and overall debt are so high. One should not take too much comfort from this view, of course, as the quality of intermediation (i.e., the allocation of that credit) by China's state-owned banking system leaves much to be desired.

One factor worth keeping in mind when evaluating the probability of a crisis is that most of the major borrowers and creditors are owned by the state, so it is unlikely there will be a cascading financial panic triggered by banks calling in debts. Financial crises in other countries have been set off by liquidity problems—when even solvent companies have to shut down for want of short-term financing to carry on their day-to-day operations. In China's case, the PBC and the banks can easily generate the liquidity needed to keep even insolvent corporations, not to mention solvent ones, afloat for a while.

The balance sheet of the government as a whole is healthier than an examination of just the gross debt figures would suggest. There are undoubtedly corporations that have borrowed too much and will suffer considerable financial stress, which could result in bankruptcy or painful restructuring. The government, on the other hand, has a large trove of assets, including its foreign exchange reserves, ownership stakes in the state enterprises, and foreign investments through the sovereign wealth fund. A legitimate concern, however, is that many of the problems with debt in China will ultimately come home to roost in the banking system, which has financed much of the debt accumulation.

Banking System

By some measures, China's banking system, which is owned almost entirely by the government at various levels, is one of the best in the world. But, on closer inspection, this turns out to be a chimera.

Banks still dominate the financial landscape in China and are quite profitable. The average ratio of nonperforming assets (NPAs)—loans that are unlikely to be paid back—to total loans outstanding was around 2 percent in early 2016, a healthy level of the NPA ratio by any standard. This number, while impressive given the amount of credit the Chinese banking system has pumped out in recent years, is an understatement—to put it mildly—of the true extent of the problem. This inaccuracy partly reflects the banks' use of risk assessment tables—which evaluate probabilities of default for various types of loans—that were created based on historical data when the economy was expanding rapidly. Now that growth is slowing, many of the loans made in the past to large enterprises in the manufacturing sector are likely to prove less safe than suggested by those data.

There is also one avenue through which banks can avoid having NPAs show up on their books: keeping companies afloat by "evergreening" their loans (i.e., giving even weak and unprofitable companies new loans to pay off their old loans). However, it becomes increasingly difficult to roll over an ever-larger stock of underperforming loans, especially when economic growth is slowing. Adding in the category of "special mention" loans, those that are not yet in default but have a high probability of becoming so, even the official data put the NPA ratio at about 5 percent at the end of 2015, about 1 percentage point higher than the corresponding ratio at the end of 2014.

Private analyst estimates of the actual ratio of NPAs range from 6 to 7 percent (e.g., BNP Paribas, CLSA, JP Morgan) to as much as 20 percent (e.g., Autonomous Research), with even higher ratios of around 25 percent for the smaller banks. Despite the overhang of potentially bad loans, Chinese banks do not face the potentially catastrophic problems that many Western banks faced during the financial crisis. This is, in part, because most of their funding comes from bank deposits, which tend to be stable, rather than from debt. Nor are these banks holding large amounts of exotic derivatives on their asset portfolios. Moreover, banks have about 17 percent of required reserves at the PBC. That is, they have to hold 17 percent of their deposits at the PBC as a safety margin. Reducing that safety margin by even 1 to 2 percentage points can free up a significant amount of cash for banks, which makes a liquidity crisis—a shortage of short-term funding—unlikely.

Even if a banking crisis can be avoided, however, a big bill will eventually come due to cover losses from loans made to companies that become insolvent or go bankrupt. Ultimately, banks must have the capacity to make new loans to support economic growth and the wherewithal to repay their depositors, so they will need to be given new resources. In the past, the government has taken two types of measures: sweeping NPAs into asset management companies, which have the sole task of disposing of those loans even if at a loss, and infusing new capital into the banks. Whatever combination of these two approaches is taken to dealing with banks' loan losses, taxpayers will eventually be stuck with the bill in one form or another.

Even assuming an ominous scenario—that as much as 20 percent of the overall loans made by the banking system will go into default—the actual cost of making up the losses will be smaller. First, some of the nonperforming and special mention loans will be paid back at least partially. Second, the banking regulator requires banks to hold provisions of at least one and a half times (150 percent of) potential bad loans to cover losses from such loans. Third, the assets used as collateral for some loans can be sold off, even if at a discounted price.

If one were to take the dire view that as much as one-fifth of the loans made by Chinese banks will turn out to be bad loans, the final bill will be on the order of about 10 to 15 percent of GDP and will come due over a few years. This estimate is based on an overall stock of loans that is about twice the amount of annual GDP and assumes that, after making the adjustments discussed earlier, bank recapitalization needs will be, at most, half the value of the stock of nonperforming loans. This is not a disastrous scenario, although it would certainly cause a great deal of economic pain. The IMF estimates that, even under a grim scenario (15 percent default rate on corporate loans) and using conservative assumptions about the state of bank balance sheets and potential recoveries from asset sales, total bank losses on their loan portfolios would amount to 7 percent of GDP. Again, this is a sizable but manageable cost.

A bigger issue the Chinese economy faces is whether the financial system, especially the banks, are being freed up from government directives and allowed to operate on a commercial basis to a greater extent. In recent years, there has in fact been some progress on banking reforms. The government has eliminated controlled interest rates on bank deposits and loans, so banks can now determine these rates freely based on market conditions, and with suitable differentiation across different types of loans and based on the repayment capacity and riskiness of borrowers. The implicit backing of all bank deposits by the government has been replaced with an explicit deposit insurance system, in principle exposing even state-owned banks to market discipline since depositors are now more likely to pay attention to the financial condition of banks in which they keep their savings. But in practice it is far from clear that banks, especially the large state-owned ones, have really changed their modus operandi.

While there has been modest progress on banking reforms, at a minimum, addressing the legacy problems created by past state-directed lending to state-owned enterprises and distorted incentives in the banking system will incur significant costs. Meanwhile, concerns have been rising about another, less transparent part of the financial system.

Shadow Banking

Shadow banking refers to financial activities that take place outside the normal banking system. That is, it involves intermediation of credit through entities and activities that are not subject to regulations that apply to the regular banking system. This definition implies that banks can also engage in shadow banking activities that are outside their traditional roles of deposit-taking and loan creation.

China's shadow banking sector has expanded rapidly, then, as a way of avoiding many of the regulations imposed on the formal banking system, including (until recently) controlled interest rates, a high level of reserve requirements on bank deposits, and rising demand for financial intermediation services that are not satisfied by traditional institutions or conventional banking products (both for savings and credit).

Definitions of the shadow banking system vary, but the types of credit that fall under its rubric include three main categories: first, *entrusted loans*, which involve nonfinancial corporations as borrowers and lenders, with banks acting as intermediaries but bearing none of the credit risks; second, *trust loans*, which are financial transactions undertaken by trust companies that are regulated separately from banks and have some characteristics of banks and fund managers; and third, *bank acceptances*, which are instruments issued by banks that commit to pay a fixed amount in a given period and are backed by deposits of the party seeking these certificates. These certificates can in turn be used to back commercial transactions. Other credit instruments counted as part of the shadow banking sector include peer-to-peer lending, financial leasing, and also credit provided by pawnshops and other unofficial lenders.

There is a range of other instruments that is also often included in definitions of the shadow banking system, including wealth management products (WMPs). WMPs are saving instruments that offer higher returns than traditional bank deposits and can even be offered by banks themselves. WMPs had become quite popular as a way of circumventing the low deposit interest rates that banks offered because of the officially imposed caps on those rates. In fact, despite the inherent risks of these products, the government tacitly encouraged WMPs as a means of indirect liberalization of deposit rates. This helped the government avoid the big banks' strong opposition to deposit rate liberalization, as those banks did not want to have to compete with smaller banks for deposits. With a deposit rate ceiling, depositors naturally preferred to put their money in larger banks that were seen as safer, and smaller banks had no way to entice depositors to come to them instead. WMPs gave small banks a tool with which to compete with large ones and provided a transition to fully liberalized deposit rates.

With the deposit rate cap having been eliminated, WMPs have become less relevant as an instrument for getting around that cap. However, banks still like using WMPs since the funding they raise through these instruments is not subject to the same strict regulatory oversight as regular deposits.

By the IMF's conservative definition, which comprises the three main items noted here (entrusted loans, trust loans, and bank acceptances), China's level of "social financing," the amount of credit provided by the shadow banking system, was about 35 percent of GDP in 2015. Broader definitions of shadow banking that encompass other items—even, on occasion, including corporate bond markets—can lead to substantially higher estimates of the size of China's shadow banking system. Even by these broader estimates, the shadow banking system is not large relative to that in many advanced economies, although its growth rate in China in recent years is certainly among the highest in the major economies. Data from the rating agency Moody's, based on a broad definition of shadow banking, indicate that shadow banking assets amount to 65 percent of GDP in China, compared with 150 percent in the U.S. and a world average, weighted by country size, of about 120 percent.

The concept of total social financing (TSF) provides a useful measure of overall credit in the economy that includes bank loans, shadow banking, corporate bond financing, and other forms of credit. TSF measures broader developments in credit creation in the Chinese economy as the relative importance of bank loans in overall credit has declined in recent years. At the end of 2015, the stock of TSF in China amounted to 200 percent of annual GDP—a remarkably high number by international standards.

Worries about the financial stability risks posed by the growth of shadow banking have prompted the government to impose stricter regulation on shadow banking activities, both by banks and nonbank financial entities. Off-balance-sheet activities of commercial banks could affect their risk profiles in ways that are not picked up by the reporting required under traditional bank regulation. Although the Chinese government does not back trust companies and other nonbank financial entities explicitly, their liabilities pose broader risks because they could become liabilities of the state. These institutions are seen as having the implicit backing of the government, since the failure of any such institution could undermine confidence in the overall financial system, which would force the government to step in. This implicit backing allows these institutions to expand their balance sheets with limited regulatory oversight.

With rising concerns about the implications of the shadow banking sector for financial stability, Chinese regulatory agencies stepped up their oversight of this sector in 2015. Much of this attention has been focused on WMPs. Commercial banks are now required to establish a separate department for WMPs, to set up a specific accounting system for these products, and to report all their WMP operations to the China Banking Regulatory Commission (CBRC). Restrictions on the operation of trust companies have been tightened. These companies are now required to reduce lending when their capital levels fall as a result of losses and also to establish a mechanism for managing crises, including delaying executives' incentive compensation, restricting dividend payouts, and disposing of some businesses. Trust companies are required to pay in to an insurance pool in an amount equal to

1 percent of their assets under management. Commercial banks have been barred from bearing credit risks for entrusted loans. Entrusted loan investments in securities, futures, stocks, and financial derivatives have been prohibited. As a result of such measures, shadow banking activity in China declined during 2015.

Although it is seen as a dangerous part of the financial system, the shadow banking system does have the potential to play a useful role in improving the allocation of resources in the economy. Many private corporations, including small and medium-size enterprises, rely on this system for credit, which they are unable to procure from traditional banks. A better regulated shadow banking system could complement the activities of the traditional banking sector and also catalyze changes and efficiency improvements in that sector.

But, shadow banking is nontransparent and has no formal safety backstops, such as the support of a deposit insurance mechanism. The lack of tight regulation of many shadow banking activities, in tandem with the assumption on the part of many market participants that there is an implicit government guarantee backing these activities, could be a dangerous combination. The government has endeavored to disabuse market participants of this notion, although its unwillingness to allow trust companies and other institutions to fail has made this task harder.

In its present form and at current levels, it is unlikely that the shadow banking system by itself poses significant threats to overall financial stability. Nevertheless, the risks in this sector could translate into vulnerabilities in the formal banking system, especially given the connections between the two sectors through products such as WMPs.

Stock Market Swings

Chinese stock markets have been in the limelight for much of the past two years. The gyrations in China's stock market since 2014 have left investors around the world gasping for breath, with declines in China's stock indexes since mid 2015 setting off stock market tumbles around the world. China's stock market hardly seems big enough to cause such dramatic waves. The value of all traded stocks in China amounts to just about half the country's GDP, a far smaller share than in most advanced economies. While some investors who entered the party late might have gambled away their life savings, the reality is that bank deposits and housing wealth, rather than stock market investments, account for most of the wealth of a majority of Chinese households. And foreign investors play, at best, a bit part in China's stock market drama; their holdings amount to barely 2 percent of the value of all traded stocks.

Cheerleading the Stock Market

Starting in early 2014, both stock market indexes in China (Shanghai, Shenzhen) began to rise sharply and more than doubled in just over a year (Figure 8.2). With the economy sputtering in 2014, the rising stock market became a convenient tool for propping up both investment and household consumption. The government did nothing to dissuade the frothiness, leading stock prices to rise by about 150 percent from July 2014 to the peak in early June 2015, even as

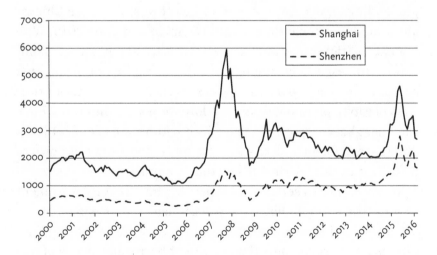

Figure 8.2 Shanghai and Shenzhen stock market indices.
Data shown in this figure are for the end of each month.
Sources: Shanghai Stock Exchange and Shenzhen Stock Exchange via CEIC.

economic growth was slowing. Over this period, the Shanghai composite stock index rose from 2,000 to more than 5,000 points.

In fact, the government seemed to be cheerleading for the stock market. In an October 2014 interview with *Xinhua*, a CSRC spokesman argued there were good reasons for the stock market to boom: "[T]he macroeconomy has been good, liquidity is ample and other factors such as reforms have been put into effect, all of which are boosting the market confidence and laying a solid foundation for future reforms … financing costs are expected to go down further. The stock market is only reflecting all these positive developments." In April 2015, by which time the Shanghai index had doubled in less than a year, the *People's Daily* proclaimed that "4000 is merely the start of the bull market." Dismissing the idea that such a sharp and rapid increase could be a sign of a stock market bubble, the newspaper observed: "What is a bubble? Tulips and bitcoins are bubbles. The stock market will enjoy full support from China's development strategy and economic reforms."

The Tumble

Despite some regulatory measures taken in early 2015 to limit margin lending (loans that are used to invest in stocks), the Chinese stock market run continued until the middle of June 2015. With regulatory tightening and rising concerns about an economic slowdown, especially among manufacturing sector firms that account for a large portion of stock market activity, stock prices then began to plummet from their lofty peaks. By the end of June, the Shanghai composite index, which had hit a peak of 5,166 on June 12, had fallen back to 4,277. By July 8, the index was down to 3,500, a one-third decline in less than a month.

This prompted a series of measures by the Chinese government to limit the turmoil. First, the government took steps to curtail the downward pressure on stock prices. It began by placing limitations on short selling—the practice of borrowing shares of one or more listed firms and essentially making a bet that the price of those shares will fall. If stock prices were indeed to fall, the short-selling investor could net a profit by buying the shares at a cheaper price than the contracted selling price. Such short selling is part of the normal functioning of stock markets, but the CSRC threatened to arrest those engaged in "malicious short selling," which it blamed for the stock market decline. The CSRC then banned initial public offerings by companies for a few months, thereby limiting the supply of new shares coming on to the market. The CSRC also suspended trading in the shares of more than 1,000 firms and imposed a six-month ban on stock sales by shareholders with a 5 percent or higher equity stake in a given company.

Second, the Chinese government took measures to increase demand for stocks and prop up their prices. New rules were promulgated allowing pension funds to invest up to 30 percent of their net assets in equities. Previously, pension funds had not been allowed to invest in equities because of the risky nature of these investments. Banks were given permission to allow investors to borrow more easily to finance stock purchases and were also given permission to make loans to corporations using equity as collateral. State-owned funds and institutions were encouraged to buy stocks, and the PBC pledged to lend RMB 250 billion ($40 billion) to major brokerage firms through the China Securities Finance Corporation to help them cope with liquidity shortages.

The measures were backed up by propaganda that included news articles in official media blaming "foreign forces" for the stock market turbulence. In addition, nearly 200 people were arrested for allegedly spreading false information that caused the market crash. Those arrested included financial practitioners, regulatory officials, and journalists. Such actions served only to fuel concerns about whether the government would take more substantive measures to boost confidence in the stock market or limit itself to a witch hunt to root out "evil speculators." These heavy-handed interventionist measures hurt the credibility of the government and created doubts about its attitude toward market-oriented reforms.

Time-out Measure Intended to Calm, Instead Stokes Panic

The government's other actions to stabilize the market did not inspire confidence, either. By the end of 2015, the CSRC decided it had to limit volatility in China's stock markets. On January 1, 2016, it introduced a "circuit breaker" mechanism, intended to give markets a break and cool things off when there was a wave of investor panic resulting in a sharp fall in major stock price indexes. The index chosen for the purpose of calibrating the circuit breaker was the CSI 300. This index, maintained by the China Securities Index Company, tracks three hundred major companies' stocks traded on the Shanghai and Shenzhen stock exchanges. It is roughly the counterpart of the S&P 500 index in the U.S. or the FTSE 100 (referred to as the "footsie") in the U.K. The circuit breaker had two elements: (1) a 5-percent decline in the CSI 300 index would halt trading for 15 minutes and (2) a 7-percent decline in the index would shut down trading activity for the remainder of that business day.

Other countries have stock market circuit breakers, but they tend to have larger tolerances for volatility. In the U.S., for instance, a 7-percent decline in the S&P 500 index triggers a 15-minute halt to trading, and it takes a 20-percent decline in the index to close markets for the entire trading day. In India, a 10-percent decline in one of the major stock indexes (National Stock Exchange or Bombay Stock Exchange) triggers a temporary halt in trading whereas a 20-percent decline closes markets for the day.

One reason for introducing circuit breakers even in advanced-economy stock markets is that a significant amount of stock trading activity is now determined by computerized algorithms rather than by human traders acting on their judgment and instincts. A time-out can limit extreme volatility when such computer-driven algorithmic trading activity pushes stock prices rapidly and dramatically in one direction or another. For instance, since most trading algorithms use largely the same market information and may have similar stop-loss provisions, a fall in a stock's price could set off a wave of selling pressure that could trigger an even steeper fall in prices if, for no matter how short a period, there are few buyers even at lower prices.

How did markets react to this safety device in China? The initial test came on Monday, January 4, 2016, which was the first trading day of the first full week of the new year. In the preceding few days, there had been a spate of negative news about the state of the Chinese economy. The stock markets got off to a rough start that Monday. By 1:13 p.m., the CSI 300 index had fallen 5 percent from its opening level, triggering the 15-minute time-out. When trading resumed, many investors decided to sell their holdings before the second element of the circuit breaker kicked in, driving prices down further. Seven minutes after trading resumed, the day's losses on the CSI 300 index had mounted to 7 percent, shutting off trading for the remainder of the day.

Later that week, a fresh bout of fear hit the stock markets. On Thursday, January 7, 2016, the first element of the circuit breaker kicked in at 9:42 a.m., about 12 minutes after trading had started. Trading resumed at 9:57 p.m. More panic ensued and, two minutes later, the second element of the circuit breaker was set off and markets shut down for the day. On both days, the circuit breaker worsened panic-driven stock sell-offs rather than comforting market participants.

Recognizing that the circuit breaker had backfired, creating even more volatility in the Chinese markets, the CSRC backed off. One week after its introduction, the circuit breaker was deactivated. Xiao Gang, the head of the CSRC, was blunt in evaluating the challenges his agency faced, noting that the "abnormal stock markets' volatility has revealed an immature market, inexperienced investors, an imperfect trading system and inappropriate supervision mechanisms." Six weeks later, Xiao lost his job.

Fortunately, because of China's underdeveloped credit markets, the stock market boom was not built on a base of cheap credit. While parts of the financial system are exposed to sharp corrections in equity prices, there are unlikely to be systemic consequences that infect the rest of the financial system and create a major adverse feedback loop. In short, despite its characterization as being akin to the untamed and tempestuous Wild West, China's stock market by itself is unlikely to trigger an unraveling of the country's financial system or its economy.

Indeed, despite all its volatility, interest in the stock market remains strong. According to the official news agency *Xinhua*, in January 2016, the number of investors in China's stock market climbed above the 100 million mark, with about one-fifth of those investors active in some form or another of trading at least once a week.

Although there are many reasons to be concerned about financial stability, China has, for a number of years, adopted a strategy that resulted in problems such as nonperforming loans, but with rapid growth generating resources that have helped to keep those problems at bay. Slowing growth could pull the rug out from under this strategy that depends on China's growing out of its problems.

MORE FUNDAMENTAL CONCERNS ABOUT ECONOMIC AND POLITICAL STABILITY

There is a set of basic issues regarding the Chinese economy's growth potential and the government's commitment to economic reforms that could affect foreign investors' interest in the RMB and the extent of the currency's acceptance in international finance. I now examine three of the most pressing issues.

Growth Prospects

In January 2010, an article in *Foreign Policy* magazine caused a stir. The author, economist Robert Fogel of the University of Chicago, made this bold prediction:

> In 2040, the Chinese economy will reach $123 trillion ... China's per capita income will hit $85,000, more than double the forecast for the European Union, and also much higher than that of India and Japan ... the average Chinese megacity dweller will be living twice as well as the average Frenchman when China goes from a poor country in 2000 to a superrich country in 2040. Although it will not have overtaken the United States in per capita wealth, according to my forecasts, China's share of global GDP—40 percent—will dwarf that of the United States (14 percent) and the European Union (5 percent) 30 years from now. This is what economic hegemony will look like.

Fogel argued that China's education system, dynamism in the rural sector, a strong services sector, and a merit-oriented political system would all keep productivity growth strong, enabling the country to grow at 8 percent a year over the following three decades. Those wishing to dismiss Fogel, and there were many scholars who considered his predictions wildly optimistic, could not do so lightly. After all, Fogel had won the Nobel Prize in Economics for his pioneering quantitative work on economic history, including explaining historical growth in the U.S.

By 2016, however, Fogel's grand predictions about China's growth appeared to have been repudiated decisively, with the factors he mentioned as its strengths largely discredited. Even the Chinese government seemed to have accepted the notion of a "new normal," with growth in the range of 6 to 7 percent.

On a more subdued note, in 2005, Dwight Perkins of Harvard University and Thomas Rawski of the University of Pittsburgh had forecast that China would register real GDP growth in the range of 6 to 8 percent from 2005 to 2015 and 5 to 7 percent over the following decade. They, too, argued that China could generate sufficient productivity growth to make this a feasible outcome, but only if it undertook a number of economic reforms. In fact, China registered average annual GDP growth of 9.7 percent from 2005 to 2015, so growth in the range of 5 to 7 percent over the next decade, while still remarkable for such a large economy, would represent a significant drop.

China's slowing growth after 2013 has fueled even greater pessimism about the country's growth prospects. Crystallizing this view, Lant Pritchett and Lawrence Summers of Harvard University make a strong case, based on empirical analysis of historical growth patterns of a large sample of countries, that no economy can escape "regression to the mean." Fast-growing economies will eventually slow down, for one reason or another, especially if they have weak public institutions, high levels of corruption, and are not democratic, all of which are true of China. They conclude: "China's experience from 1977 to 2010 already holds the distinction of being the *only instance* [emphasis in original], quite possibly in the history of mankind, but certainly in the data, with a sustained episode of super-rapid growth [more than 6 percent per annum] for more than 32 years." They argue that the most likely scenario is that China's growth is likely to slow to around 4 percent.

Most growth forecasts for China tend to be conditioned on certain assumptions about policies, with more optimistic forecasts being predicated on continued reforms. Pessimists about China's growth prospects make an even stronger argument that the rebalancing and economic transformation desired by the government will *necessitate* a slowdown in growth. Michael Pettis of Peking University and I debated this through an exchange of open letters organized by *Bloomberg News* in March 2015. Pettis took the view that fixing the debt overhang and shifting away from credit-financed, investment-led growth would require growth to drop to 3 to 4 percent per year. In his view, growth of more than 7 percent could be achieved only by further reckless credit expansion.

While acknowledging the problems caused by the debt overhang, I argued that, with the right reforms, the government could maintain growth in the 6- to 7-percent-per-annum range at least over the next 2–3 years. My case rested on the following factors, which should enable China to grow without necessarily creating even greater debt problems. First, although its labor force is no longer growing, China still has a pool of underutilized labor that could be moved to more productive employment, which underlies the government's urbanization strategy. Second, development of corporate bond markets and other financial markets that could allocate capital more efficiently—given that China still has investment needs—would benefit economic growth; despite high levels of investment, China still has a much lower capital-to-labor ratio than advanced economies (about one-sixth that of the U.S.). Third, an improved financial system could also do better at allocating capital and, in particular, financing growth in the services sector, which tends to generate better employment growth than heavy manufacturing. Fourth, the low level of explicit public debt leaves China room to use fiscal policy to boost growth while promoting higher consumption; this can be achieved through suitably targeted tax cuts and higher expenditure on the social safety net. I summarized the argument as follows: "There is substantial misallocation of resources in China, so economic and financial sector reforms that result in improved resource allocation can help China maintain growth in the government's target range while promoting rebalancing."

Whether China can escape the deleterious effects of the debt overhang and execute the far-reaching reforms needed to fix the economy remains to be seen. A complex and unpredictable political environment heightens the challenge.

Political and Social Instability

The possibility of political instability is a perennial wildcard, especially given the opacity of Chinese politics. Belying the notion of a centrally run apparatus with a linear and well-defined power structure, the CPC is more like a seething cauldron. Old and new leaders, along with their minions, constantly jockey for power while provincial leaders have their own fiefdoms that they work fiercely to protect. Much of the skullduggery and shifting of alliances in the upper reaches of the CPC takes place behind the scenes, while public events such as the Communist Party congresses generally amount to little more than carefully orchestrated ratifications of agreed-upon changes in policies and personnel.

Soon after he took office in March 2013, President Xi Jinping proclaimed an ambitious anticorruption campaign. The pronouncement was met with skepticism both inside and outside China, with corruption seen as a widespread problem that pervaded all levels of the CPC, right to the top, and that would therefore be difficult to root out. But, in this case, actions spoke louder than words.

Many prominent CPC leaders have been ensnared by this campaign, including powerful officials once regarded as immune to any such actions. In September 2013, Bo Xilai, the high-flying Secretary of the CPC for Chongqing, was found guilty of corruption, stripped of his wealth, and sentenced to life imprisonment. In December 2014, Zhou Yongkang, a former chief of domestic security, was arrested for abuse of power, accepting bribes, and revealing state secrets. He, too, was given a life sentence and expelled from the CPC. Many other well-connected officials have fallen prey as well. The anticorruption campaign appears, by all accounts, to have popular support as rising income and wealth inequality is seen as partly reflecting corruption among the political elites.

The anticorruption campaign has also, however, taken on aspects of a selective purge by President Xi to consolidate his power and cleanse the CPC of potential challengers to his position and influence within the party. Cheng Li of the Brookings Institution has argued that President Xi has strengthened his personal power and his administration's authority over the military. He has done so through "political and tactical moves, including the purges of the two highest-ranking generals under the previous administration on corruption and other charges; the arrest of over 40 senior military officers on various charges of wrongdoing . . . and, most importantly, the rapid promotion of 'young guards.'"

There seems to be near unanimity among China scholars who agree that, barely halfway through his first term in office, President Xi had already accreted power on a scale not seen in recent times, making him the most powerful leader since Mao Zedong, who founded the People's Republic in 1949. This concentration of power has generated a strong pushback from party elites, including some who have the blessings of retired leaders such as Jiang Zemin, a former CPC general secretary who remains involved and influential in political circles.

In the summer of 2015, leading official news outlets acknowledged the existence of such high-level opposition to President Xi's initiatives, including the anticorruption campaign. After noting that the reforms had reached a critical stage, one article used unusually strong language to characterize the level of resistance: "The in-depth reform touches the basic issue of reconfiguring the lifeblood of this enormous economy and is aimed at making it healthier. The scale of the resistance is beyond what could have been imagined." Similar strong sentiments were expressed in other official media sources: "The stubbornness, ferocity, complexity and weirdness of those who haven't adapted to reform or are even opposed to reform may go beyond what people imagine."

A scholar at the Chinese Academy of Governance identified three disaffected and powerful groups that were leading the resistance—cadres whose power had been weakened by the reforms, civil servants unhappy with austerity rules, and retired leaders who were trying to fight off threats to their influence. An official media article aimed at the third group cautioned that former officials ought to "cool off" like a cup of tea after guests have departed, and that leaders who did not go quietly into the night when their time had passed posed a "quandary for new leaders, fettering their hands from doing bold work . . . undermining party cohesion and fighting strength." Another newspaper pointedly remarked that, "after retirement, when one no longer holds a position, one shouldn't plot any politics."

In March 2015, a *Wall Street Journal* essay by David Shambaugh of George Washington University, a noted scholar and observer of Chinese politics, attracted considerable attention by warning of the imminent collapse of the CPC. In previous work, Shambaugh had written about how the CPC was able to adapt to shifting circumstances. But, in his essay entitled "The Coming Chinese Crackup," he wrote: "The endgame of communist rule in China has begun, and Xi Jinping's ruthless measures are only bringing the country closer to a breaking point." Justifying his change in views about the stability of the system, he noted that "times change in China, and so must our analyses." The essay went on to argue that Xi was precipitating the final phase of the CPC by overplaying a weak hand and severely provoking key party, state, military, and commercial constituencies with his aggressive anticorruption campaign. Another scholar, Roderick MacFarquhar of Harvard University, said that "for all of Mr. Xi's personal power, his campaign against corruption is fraught with danger, putting at risk the future of the Communist party he is determined to save."

The jury is still out on whether the foundations of President Xi's and the CPC's hold on power are fragile. Indeed, through the summer of 2016, there was no sign of a diminution of Mr. Xi's power or control by the Party apparatus. However, there is little doubt that economic growth is an important determinant of social and political stability in China. Indeed, this may explain why President Xi has prioritized market-oriented economic reforms even while decisively shutting down legal, political, and broader institutional reforms.

Having pinned his government's authority and power on delivering good economic outcomes, the social and political risks that come with economic mismanagement, either actual or perceived, make this a high-stakes game. And this is precisely where a dangerous flashpoint lurks, as President Xi and the CPC try to manage the balancing act between their knowledge that market-oriented reforms are essential and their instinct that stability and control matter above all else.

Policy Instability: One Step Forward, Two Steps Sideways

There are two reasons to be concerned about the path that China is taking toward market-oriented reforms. The first is the unbalanced nature of the reforms. The second is the government's ambivalent approach toward economic liberalization and the operation of free markets.

Reforms on the real side of the economy have not kept pace with financial liberalization. The former include further restructuring of state enterprises, liberalization of the services sector so new firms can enter this sector more easily and operate with fewer restrictions, streamlining of the tax and public expenditure systems, and easing of restrictions on labor mobility within and across provinces. China's economy and the RMB's rise have also been impeded by the lack of a robust institutional framework—including transparency in the policymaking process, sound corporate governance and accounting standards, and operational independence for the central bank and regulatory authorities—that ought to supplement financial and other market-oriented reforms.

The turmoil in equity and currency markets during 2015 and 2016 appears to have shaken confidence in the economic management skills of the leadership. For all the concerns about economic mismanagement, the reality is that the government is moving ahead—gradually and perhaps somewhat maladroitly—with financial sector reforms that are essential for China to sustain strong growth. Freeing up interest rates and exchange rates to be determined by markets are by no means small steps for China, although they have been a long time coming and are not yet fully in place. China has taken major steps down the path of capital account liberalization that will be difficult to reverse. The real risk is that volatility of the sort witnessed recently could erode political support and economic space even for the reforms to which the technocrats are committed.

A more fundamental concern is that the government seems to be caught in a deep internal conflict between its stated objective of letting markets operate freely and its desire to maintain stability and control above all else. This conflict pervades the entire reform process. After three days of volatility following the August 11, 2015 move to free up the exchange rate, the government reverted to intervening in the foreign exchange market to keep the currency's value stable. Other reforms, while well-intentioned, have followed a similar one-step forward, two-steps sideways trajectory.

Such ambivalence about the functioning of markets colors the thinking of government officials. At the press conference held on August 13, 2015, to soothe market concerns about the PBC's true intentions regarding the exchange rate, PBC Deputy Governor Yi Gang reiterated his faith in the market, saying, "Trust the market, respect the market, fear the market, and follow the market." But, he added that the PBC would act "when the market's volatility is excessive, when the market begins behaving like a herd of sheep."

During the stock market turmoil, an official CSRC statement pointedly declared, "The stock market is required to serve the people and the party and the party alone represents the people. So if the market goes the wrong way or 'misbehaves,' it is unpatriotic and should be corrected. Anyone who drives or helps the market 'misbehave' is a traitor."

In January 2016, George Soros, the famed financier who "broke" the Bank of England in 1992 by forcing it to devalue the British pound sterling and leave the European Exchange Rate Mechanism, declared that he was shorting the RMB. That is, he was making a financial bet—no doubt a large one—that the RMB would decline in value. Many other hedge funds were reportedly making similar bets; they would make a considerable amount of money if the RMB were, in fact, to depreciate significantly.

The government's response was mainly rhetorical and orchestrated through official news media. A researcher for China's

Ministry of Commerce wrote a front-page opinion piece in one of the leading newspapers under the headline, "Declaring War on China's Currency? Ha Ha." That article, along with other articles in Chinese official media, warned such speculators that waging a "war on the renminbi" or betting on the "ultimate failure" of the Chinese economy would fail and threatened that "reckless speculations and vicious shorting will face higher trading costs and possibly severe legal consequences." Such strong rhetorical responses may strike a chord with Chinese citizens, but the reactions in markets suggest that they are hardly adequate substitutes for more substantive measures to rebuild confidence that the government is committed to free markets.

There are legitimate reasons to be concerned about the brittleness of China's economy. Moreover, its political structure appears to have become even more rigid under Xi Jinping, raising the risk that political and social stability might unravel suddenly and dramatically if adverse shocks to the economy or other events were to break the Party's tight control of society and the state. Indeed, one could make a plausible argument that a relatively modest trigger could set off a destabilizing chain of events. On the other hand, Western prognostications of the likelihood of such disastrous outcomes are overstated and it is quite likely that the government will, in fact, be able to manage the economic, social, and political tensions it faces—although the lack of flexibility in China's economic and institutional frameworks means that there are likely to be many missteps and stumbles along the way.

International perceptions about China's economic and political stability are, however, as important as reality on the ground in terms of the RMB's widespread acceptance as an international currency. These perceptions will be affected by progress on the reforms that are necessary to support the currency's international use. While domestic reforms have been uneven and poorly executed, China's leadership has been far more effective in using the country's financial clout to expand its sphere of economic and geopolitical influence. In the next chapter, I explore the prominent role the RMB plays in this drive to expand China's global influence.

CHAPTER 9
Rising Global Influence

There is a perennial classical question that asks which part of the motorcycle, which grain of sand in which pile, is the Buddha. Obviously to ask that question is to look in the wrong direction, for the Buddha is everywhere. But just as obviously to ask that question is to look in the right direction, for the Buddha is everywhere.

Zen and the Art of Motorcycle Maintenance, Robert M. Pirsig

On October 5, 2015, twelve countries from Asia, Latin America, and North America reached an agreement on the Trans-Pacific Partnership (TPP). The deal, covering countries that account for about $28 trillion in GDP, or about 40 percent of global GDP, and one-third of world trade, was one of the largest trade deals in more than two decades. The countries covered by the agreement were Australia, Brunei, Canada, Chile, Japan, Malaysia, Mexico, New Zealand, Peru, Singapore, the U.S., and Vietnam. As you scan the list, one Asian country not included on the list no doubt stands out: China.

The deal was concluded after marathon negotiations over many years that culminated in a long weekend meeting in Atlanta, Georgia, in the U.S. that finally broke through the remaining obstacles. When the deal was done, President Obama triumphantly noted:

When more than 95 percent of our potential customers live outside our borders, we can't let countries like China write the rules of the global economy. We should write those rules, opening new markets to American products while setting high standards for protecting workers and preserving our environment. That's what the agreement reached today in Atlanta will do. Trade ministers from the 12 nations that make up the Trans-Pacific Partnership finished negotiations on an agreement that reflects America's values and gives our workers the fair shot at success they deserve.

Although it was not primarily intended to exclude China, the subtext of the agreement was clear. With China's rising economic and political clout in the Asian region and beyond, this was a way for the U.S. and its allies to circle the wagons. If the TPP were to be ratified by national legislatures in all the member countries, which was far from assured at the time, it would represent an important achievement for the U.S. and Japan in creating a modest although perhaps mainly symbolic counterweight to China's expanding influence. For these big economies, the TPP would not produce game-changing economic effects, but it would halt, at least temporarily, the seemingly inexorable waning of U.S. and Japanese influence and the corresponding rise of Chinese influence in the Asian region.

An article in *The Wall Street Journal* summarized the prevailing wisdom about how this agreement could reshape the balance of power in the Asian region:

> A sweeping trade deal concluded on Monday marks a victory for Japan and other U.S. allies in the battle with China over shaping the future of global commerce. The 12-member Trans-Pacific Partnership, which doesn't include China, highlights the price that Beijing is paying for delaying overhauls as other countries write a new rule book for trade across 40% of the global economy.... Japan's leadership views the agreement as key to its economic and security goals as China expands its influence in the region, especially in Southeast Asia, where Japan has long been a major investor and aid donor.

Within China, opinions about the TPP ranged from measured to strident. An influential Communist Party paper called the *Study Times*, published by the CPC's Central Party School that trains aspiring officials, acknowledged there were those in China who viewed the

TPP as a "plot" to isolate and restrain the country's global ambitions. Still, the newspaper editorial recommended that China seek to join the TPP because the treaty's broad aims were in line with China's own economic reform agenda. "The rules of the TPP and the direction of China's reforms and opening up are in line," the article noted. "China should keep paying close attention and at an appropriate time, in accordance with progress on domestic reform, join the TPP, while limiting the costs associated to the greatest degree," it added.

Among Chinese officials, the views were mixed as well. China's trade minister said the country did not feel "targeted" by the TPP, but would carefully evaluate its likely impact. Reform-minded officials in Beijing took a positive attitude, recognizing that outside pressure often helps to overcome domestic opposition to reforms. PBC chief economist Ma Jun wrote that China could benefit from the TPP's "higher standard" requirements in the areas of competition, free enterprise, environmental protection, and labor rights. He noted that "the pressure of these reforms is good for China and TPP member-countries' competitiveness. . . . [Such reforms] would substantially enhance China's own economic growth potential."

Just as China used outside pressure—the conditions for joining the WTO in 2001—as a spur for domestic reforms, an aspiration to become a member of the TPP could help dislodge some of the opposition to state enterprise reforms. The environmental provisions in the TPP could generate momentum toward coaxing China to move away from polluting industries, take measures to reduce carbon emissions, and shift from environmentally destructive production techniques. Protection of intellectual property rights, another TPP condition, will become important for China itself as it tries to encourage domestic innovation and changes in its industrial structure that promote higher value-added and more advanced high-tech industries rather than its traditional low-wage manufacturing and heavy industries.

The debate took on a sharper edge, however, when another PBC economist estimated that lost trading opportunities could initially knock half a percentage point off the country's annual economic growth. Reacting to this estimate, Sheng Laiyun, a spokesman for China's National Bureau of Statistics, said that China could take "countermeasures" to offset the negative economic impact of the country's exclusion from the TPP. These included bilateral and regional free trade agreements.

Beijing has, for instance, been pushing its own trade pact, the Regional Comprehensive Economic Partnership (RCEP), a proposed sixteen-nation free trade area that would be the world's biggest such bloc, encompassing 3.4 billion people. The RCEP would comprise the ten nations that constitute the Association of Southeast Asian Nations club plus six others: China, India, Japan, South Korea, Australia, and New Zealand. This framework, backed strongly by Beijing, was seen as a prominent alternative to U.S. plans, but it lost some of its momentum when the TPP agreement was completed.

China clearly remains concerned that initiatives such as the TPP could result in excessive U.S. influence and sidelining of China's views in the process of rewriting the rules governing global trade. Statements by U.S. officials that the trade pact will be open to other countries such as China and Russia—as long as they are willing to commit to the rules negotiated under the TPP—have not given them much reassurance. Noting the potential for conflicts between regional trade deals and global trade rules, President Xi said in a speech that "We need to encourage equal footing participation and extensive consultation and make free trade arrangements open and inclusive to the extent possible."

While pushing to increase its economic reach through trade, China had begun to realize that international finance would be the new and more important battleground for wielding geopolitical influence. Recognizing that the RMB did not yet have the potential to be a global contender, China adopted a complementary strategy—using its financial firepower to increase its international economic influence, with the RMB riding on the back of these efforts.

FLEXING ECONOMIC MUSCLES

In the 2000s, as China's financial clout and foreign exchange reserves grew, it began using those resources to increase its sphere of economic and political influence, offering investments, aid, and various forms of financial support to other economies. The recipients of much of this largesse were its neighbors in Asia as well as a number of economies in Africa and Latin America that had large stocks of natural resources that China craved for its manufacturing machine. This led to concerns that, with its money, China was simply exploiting the countries to which it was giving aid or loans and, even worse, that the money was propping up corrupt regimes, enriching venal officials, and creating a debt burden that would come to haunt those countries.

According to American Enterprise Institute estimates, over the past decade China has accounted for a cumulative investment of $220 billion in sub-Saharan Africa alone and $120 billion in South America (compared with about $60 billion in the U.S.). China has been open to giving money to countries that have been shut out from borrowing in international financial markets and are loath to turn to Western institutions or countries. In Ecuador, whose President Rafael Correa aligned himself with the socialist government in Venezuela, Chinese money has financed dams, roads, highways, bridges, and hospitals. In return China has, by some estimates, locked in nearly 90 percent of Ecuador's oil exports, revenues from which go largely toward paying off those loans. Ecuador's former energy minister said, "The problem is we are trying to replace American imperialism with Chinese imperialism."

China has maintained that it adheres strictly to a principle of noninterference in other countries' internal affairs, especially when it comes to political matters, and that its aid and investment are provided with "no political strings attached, and never offering blank promises." These statements were made by a spokesperson for China's foreign ministry at a combative press conference with Western media in December 2015 when she was asked why China's aid to African countries had not helped in improving democracy or human rights in the region. She added later that "China has helped Africa build 5,675 kilometers of railway, 4,507 kilometers of highway, 18 bridges, 12 ports, 14 airports and terminals, 64 power stations, 76 sports facilities, 68 hospitals, over 200 schools." The implication of that and similar statements was that China's assistance was targeted toward Africa's economic development, without the sort of interference in ancillary matters that was a typical and unwelcome concomitant of financial assistance from the West.

There is a vibrant and far-from-settled debate about whether Chinese money has been a net benefit for recipient countries. Both sides in the debate have used strong words. For instance, Moisés Naím, a Latin American intellectual who was Venezuela's minister of trade and industry in the early 1990s, has characterized China's activist aid program as "rogue aid . . . that is nondemocratic in origin and nontransparent in practice; its effect is typically to stifle real progress while hurting average citizens."

Backing up this view, a recent, provocative study by researchers at the University of Sussex argues that receiving high levels of Chinese aid has a harmful effect on human rights and on economic and political competition across Africa. Chinese aid to African states increases the risk of civilian abuse by giving state leaders and politicians access to funds with which to carry out violence against political opponents and dissidents, thereby perpetuating existing leaders' and regimes' hold on power. These results are not just a consequence of China funding countries that were already violent, typically have high rates of repression, or have abundant natural resources. Rather, according to this study, China's political agenda influences its aid flows. For instance, African states that recognize Taiwan as an independent entity receive no aid from China.

On the other hand a study by AidData, a research organization that monitors development finance around the world, offers a more positive tone. The study concludes that aid from China is, in fact, oriented toward poorer countries, including ones that have provided foreign policy support to China at international forums. Still, even this study finds that commercially oriented forms of Chinese state financing are directed mainly to countries rich in natural resources and with higher levels of corruption. Research by scholars at the Brookings Institution confirms that China's overseas direct investment is driven mainly by profit motives and is concentrated in resource-rich economies, although Chinese investors do seem more willing than Western countries to take chances investing in politically unstable countries. Deborah Brautigam of

Johns Hopkins University, an expert on the China–Africa relationship, arrives at a similar mixed evaluation that Chinese money has in some ways played a positive role in Africa's economic development but with significant risks and costs to some sectors.

While the academic debate rages, China has moved to strengthen its economic relationships in Africa, including with some countries that are pariah regimes in the eyes of the West. In December 2015, soon after President Xi's visit to Harare, the capital of Zimbabwe, that country's government announced that the RMB would become legal tender within the southern African nation. The government also announced proudly that this was part of a deal in which China would cancel about $40 million in debt owed by Zimbabwe. But, in an economy ravaged by hyperinflation and economic mismanagement, the government's sanctioning of the RMB's status as an official currency is likely to have limited impact, let alone any international implications. Earlier in 2015, the government had essentially euthanized the ailing domestic currency, allowing Zimbabweans to exchange bank balances of up to 175,000 trillion Zimbabwean dollars (that is indeed trillion with a *t*) for 5 U.S. dollars.

An amusing digression illustrates the farcical nature of the situation. Zimbabwe's longtime President, Robert Mugabe has, for decades, been seen as a loyal friend of China. To reward his loyalty, a group of Chinese citizens based in Hong Kong awarded him the Confucius Peace Prize in October 2015. The prize was set up to "promote world peace from an Eastern perspective" and to offer an alternative to the Nobel Peace Prize, which the Chinese government has often criticized for reflecting purely Western values. For instance, when the Dalai Lama was awarded the Nobel Peace Prize in 1989, a government spokesman lashed out, saying that "it is interference in China's internal affairs. It has hurt the Chinese people's feelings. ... The Dalai Lama is not simply a religious leader but also a political figure [who is seeking to] divide the mother country and undermine national unity." The Confucius Prize citation for Mugabe praised his long and devoted service to his people, the commitment he had shown to his nation's "political and economic order," and his support of pan-Africanism. But apparently even ruthless despots have certain standards. Mugabe turned down the award when he learned that it was not awarded by a Chinese government agency. How unfortunate; it would have put him in the illustrious company of previous winners Fidel Castro and Vladimir Putin.

President Xi's visit to Africa in December 2015 culminated with a grand declaration at a summit in Johannesburg that China and Africa were "good friends, good partners, good brothers." Striking a lofty note, the communiqué issued at the end of the summit stated that the relationship would be characterized by "one upgrade, five pillars, and ten plans." The upgrade was to establish a new China–Africa strategic partnership featuring the following five pillars: political equality and mutual trust, win–win economic cooperation, mutually enriching cultural exchanges, mutual assistance in security, and solidarity and coordination in international affairs. The ten major cooperation plans were to be in the areas of industrialization, agricultural modernization, infrastructure construction, financial services, green development, trade and investment facilitation, poverty reduction and public welfare, public health, people-to-people exchanges, and peace and security.

To say that African leaders welcomed all of this warmly would be an understatement. China offered not just soaring rhetoric but cold cash as well—$60 billion of funding support in grants, loans, and capital for various development funds. Not only that, China also wrote off a number of loans it had made to poorer countries in Africa. To top things off with a more human touch, President Xi announced that China would provide scholarships to thousands of African students, train 1,000 media professionals, and launch 200 "Happy Life" projects and special programs focusing on women and children. And all of this without bringing up topics such as economic reforms, corruption, and political repression that could make the African leaders uncomfortable. In words that were no doubt music to the ears of the leaders, President Xi made China's policy of noninterference crystal clear: "China supports the settlement of African issues by Africans in the African way."

China's initiatives in Africa have not directly elevated the RMB, and China's government has not pushed hard for these countries to use RMB in their transactions. Nevertheless, the stronger trade and financial relationships that many countries in the region have with China are generating greater interest in using RMB to diversify foreign exchange reserve portfolios and for trade settlement.

A NEW APPROACH

Clearly, China's investments in and aid to Africa and Latin America, which have ramped up over the past decade, were strengthening its economic and political linkages with countries in those two continents. In other quarters of the international community, however, such commercial and charitable endeavors were not viewed as favorably. China's foreign investments and aid were facing pushback and, what is worse, failing to turn the country into a respected and constructive member of the global financial community. At the other end of the spectrum of foreign investments, China's foreign exchange reserves were giving it little leverage and exposing it to the policies of foreign central banks that determine the value of the government bonds that are in the PBC's reserve portfolio.

A reset in the nature of its economic relationships would clearly help China realize its economic and geopolitical ambitions, eventually paving the way for broader adoption of the RMB. The Chinese are quick learners, taking a pragmatic approach and adjusting strategy when circumstances demand it. They have grown more savvy and disciplined in their approach to international engagement, using a wide range of tools.

China is now employing a multipronged approach to setting the global agenda. First, it is gradually increasing its influence in international institutions and at least establishing a toehold even in ones where it does not have a direct and immediate interest. This allows it to change the rules of the game from the inside. Second, it is setting up multilateral institutions where it gets to call the shots. This allows it to control the rules of the game, which also serves to subtly catalyze changes in the existing institutions. Third, it is partnering with other like-minded countries to set up institutions that are meant to build trust and stronger economic linkages with countries that it sees as partners as well as potential competitors. Fourth, it is using other arms of the state, including state-owned banks, SOEs, and development agencies, to increase its global financial reach and power.

CHANGING EXISTING INSTITUTIONS

The first element of China's global strategy involves increasing its influence in existing multilateral institutions. At the IMF, the granddaddy of international financial institutions (IFIs), China's capital contribution of $42 billion gives it a 6 percent share of the overall capital pool of about $650 billion and a corresponding voting share. The U.S. has a 16 percent voting share while Japan's, like China's, is 6 percent. At the World Bank, another major IFI, China has a voting share of 5 percent, compared with 16 percent for the U.S. and 7 percent for Japan.

The major IFI in Asia is the Asian Development Bank (ADB), which has a capital stock of about $150 billion. Japan and China have been jostling for influence at this institution for a long time. Japan has a voting share of 12.8 percent, making it the dominant shareholder. The share of the U.S. is also almost 12.8 percent, a figure that, by design, is a smidgen less than that of Japan to emphasize the Asian leadership of the institution. China's share is 5.5 percent, making it the second largest shareholder from the Asian region, while India's share is 5.4 percent, ranking it just below China and emphasizing how even decimal-place differences in voting power are freighted with symbolism at such institutions. As the largest shareholder, Japan has had the privilege of appointing the president of the ADB. China now has a much larger economy than Japan's, so this situation no doubt rankles the Chinese, who have bristled at their low status in the largest multilateral institution in the region.

The irony of Japan's still maintaining a larger voting share in existing international institutions has certainly not gone unnoticed by China. Even at the IMF, where recent reforms increased the voting shares of China and other emerging market economies, Japan remains ahead symbolically, with a voting share of 6.18 percent compared to China's 6.12 percent.

While it is making progress in the major IFIs, China has also been gradually marking its presence in other, less prominent IFIs around the world. China has established a beachhead in institutions such as the African Development Bank, the Caribbean Development Bank, and the Inter-American Development Bank, although, as a non-regional member, its direct contributions to these institutions sum up to only about $1 billion. Africa has more trade with the European Union as a whole, but China is the single country that accounts for the largest share of Africa's trade. For many Latin American countries, China has become the largest export market. So China's presence in these regional institutions allows it to start playing a role—modest at first, but easily scalable—in the economic governance of these regions.

How far is China willing to go to engage the existing IFIs on their own terms, rather than seeking changes in those institutions when it is signing up for entry? Consider China's accession to the WTO in 2001. After a long and difficult series of negotiations, China agreed to most of the standard conditions for WTO membership, which gave it much greater access to foreign export markets, but also came with a commitment to open up its own markets to foreign companies and investors. During its push to increase exports during the 2000s, China benefited greatly from this improved market access. But, foreign firms and investors found themselves stymied at every turn by rules that limited their operations, forced them to share technology with local firms, and allowed them to enter certain areas of business only if they partnered with domestic firms. And now that China is a large and powerful member of the WTO, it can play a greater role in influencing how the organization defines and applies rules for international trading.

There is an even starker and more interesting example illustrating how China is willing to seem accommodative and open to compromise when it joins existing institutions.

In January 2016, China became a member of the European Bank for Reconstruction and Development (EBRD) with a small capital contribution of $400 million, amounting to less than 1 percent of the total capital base. The EBRD was set up in 1991 to promote free enterprise and entrepreneurial activities in the countries of the former Soviet bloc. With its experience advising countries making the transition from communist or socialist to market economies, the institution has expanded its reach to other regions as well. It now has outstanding loans and investments in 30 countries from central Europe to central Asia and the southern and eastern Mediterranean regions.

China is the sixty-fifth member of the EBRD. What is particularly interesting about EBRD membership is that China was willing to sign on to the institution's mandate, which reads as follows: "Uniquely for a development bank, the EBRD has a political mandate in that it assists only those countries 'committed to and applying the principles of multi-party democracy [and] pluralism.'" This is not an afterthought among many other EBRD mandates. The very first article in the institution's charter states that its members are "committed to the fundamental principles of multiparty democracy, the rule of law, respect for human rights and market economics."

The EBRD sets out a list of standards or values that govern its work. The first item is again about democracy, with the statement making a clear connection between economic and political reforms:

> Supporting reforms that strengthen democracy is an important aspect of the EBRD's mandate. . . . One of the EBRD's founding principles is that democratic and market reforms go hand in hand, and after more than 20 years of working in the transition region, this has been borne out: the most advanced economic reformers in the region, according to the EBRD transition indicators, have also gone the furthest in building democratic institutions.

It is quite striking that China was willing to sign up for membership in the EBRD although the mandate is inconsistent with the tenets of the CPC and despite qualifying for only a marginal voting share at the institution. One interpretation for this willingness is that China's version of democracy differs from what the West thinks of as free and open democracy. Consider the following sentiments expressed in a February 2015 editorial in *Xinhua* "Why Should China Say No to Wrong Western Values." The article neatly encapsulates China's own interpretations of concepts such as human rights, liberty, and democracy, indicating its position that its interpretations are as valid as Western interpretations:

> China does not oppose the ideas of liberty, democracy, equality and human rights, which are among the core values of Western culture. In fact, these concepts are included in the Constitution. However, China's understanding of these concepts may differ to the West....
>
> China has always stressed the protection of human rights, which are the basic goals of countries seeking for good governance. However, it holds different values from the Western thought that human rights are natural born. China holds that the concept of human rights depends on objective conditions, like history, traditions, and economic and social development, thus, there is no universal concept of human rights....
>
> Liberty is cherished the world over, including in China. In the political spectrum, liberty is a symbol of Western political thought that is based mainly on the individual. Chinese traditions and Marxist ideology, however, is based on collective liberalism....
>
> China's people's congress system emphasizes the legislative body's support for and supervision over the government to achieve effective decision making. It rejected a multi-party system; the west-style [sic] 'separation of powers.' ... History has told the Chinese that denying the leadership of the CPC and socialism leads to chaos and stagnation.

Another interpretation, which is equally plausible, is that China is willing to appear reasonable and open to compromise when it seeks membership in existing institutions. Over time, it then strives to subtly influence existing international institutions from the inside rather than through brute economic or political force from the outside.

So far, China has made the majority of its capital contributions to the IFIs in hard currencies such as the dollar, the euro, and the yen. Now that the IMF has designated the RMB as an official reserve currency, China will no doubt be able to legitimately make further capital contributions in its own currency. As China's economy grows and its role in existing IFIs becomes more prominent, the RMB will play a bigger role in the capital bases and financial operations of these institutions.

THE ASIAN INFRASTRUCTURE INVESTMENT BANK

While it was signing up for membership in multilateral institutions around the world, China was frustrated that in the most important international and regional organizations that it cared about, it still had second-class status. Its bid to gain greater influence at the IMF had been stymied for a long time by U.S. Congressional intransigence. While all countries, including the U.S., had agreed in 2010 to a reworking of IMF voting shares to give China and other emerging markets more voting power, the agreement had to be ratified by national legislatures. Virtually all major countries but the U.S. had done so by 2014, but in the U.S. this issue became entangled in the political deadlock between the Obama administration and the Republican–controlled Congress. It was only in January 2016, one month after the deadlock in the U.S. was broken, that the agreed-on changes came into effect. By that time, the new voting shares were already lagging behind economic reality as they had been based on GDP and other economic variables from a few years prior. But, it seemed unlikely that China could further increase its voting share in proportion with its economic might anytime soon. Even in its own backyard, China was not attaining the status it felt it deserved. At the ADB, the major multilateral institution in Asia, China had been unable to dislodge Japan from that country's position of prominence.

China decided it needed to take a more active role in asserting its presence in international finance, which could best be done by bankrolling its own institutions. Its leaders recognized that China could put its money to good use by financing infrastructure projects in Asia—a crying need for countries in the region that lacked the funds to undertake large investments. It would be logical for other countries in the region to sign up for such an institution, where they would have a more prominent role than in other international institutions and could also obtain financing for much-needed infrastructure projects. Thus was born the idea for an Asian Infrastructure Investment Bank (AIIB). President Xi Jinping and Premier Li Keqiang mooted the initiative during their travels in Asia in fall 2013. The bank's stated goal was to finance infrastructure projects such as roads, railways, and airports in the Asia–Pacific Region.

The U.S. was wary of China's attempts to create alternatives to the existing multilateral institutions. With a proposed initial capital amount of $50 billion that could be increased to $100 billion, the AIIB would clearly be a significant competitor to the ADB and the World Bank. These latter two institutions are in a similar line of business of lending for development projects and together have a capital base of about $400 billion. Recognizing that it could not stop other countries in the Asian region, most of which are either small or not advanced, from signing up with the AIIB, the U.S. decided its best strategy was to undermine the legitimacy of the institution by questioning whether the governance of a China–led institution and its lending practices would mirror China's weak legal and institutional framework. A key element of this strategy was making sure that its advanced-economy allies would not sign up to the AIIB.

The U.S. mounted a fierce, largely behind-the-scenes, drive to delegitimize the AIIB. A U.S. official was quoted as asking, "How would the new institution add value? How would the Asian Infrastructure Investment Bank be structured so that it doesn't undercut the standards with a race to the bottom?" The U.S. was keen to corral not just the major advanced economies such as the eurozone, Japan, and the U.K., but also other advanced countries such as Australia and South Korea, hoping to convince them not to sign up to join the AIIB.

China had a secret weapon in its arsenal—Jin Liqun, an internationally respected Chinese official (Figure 9.1). Jin is well known as a master strategist, an articulate speaker who does not mince words, and a forceful advocate for China's positions. Jin, who has extensive international experience working in multilateral

Figure 9.1 Jin Liqun, President of the AIIB.
Credit: Imaginechina via AP Images

institutions such as the ADB and the World Bank, was assigned to lead the charge in setting up the AIIB. As the covert diplomatic battle between China and the U.S. was heating up, he wrote that "the U.S. risks forfeiting its international relevance while stuck in its domestic political quagmire. . . . History has never set any precedent that an empire is capable of governing the world forever."

Despite Jin's lobbying efforts, it appeared that the U.S. was winning the diplomatic battle. In October 2014, when a ceremony was held in Beijing to sign a memorandum of understanding to launch the AIIB, twenty-one countries—mostly from Asia—had signed up. The countries present at the signing ceremony were Bangladesh, Brunei, Cambodia, China, India, Kazakhstan, Kuwait, Laos, Malaysia, Mongolia, Myanmar, Nepal, Oman, Pakistan, the Philippines, Qatar, Singapore, Sri Lanka, Thailand, Uzbekistan, and Vietnam. Other than China and India, none of these was a large economy and no major advanced economies were on the list.

Indonesia signed the memorandum of understanding a month later, in November 2014.

The deadline for signing up as a founding member was March 31, 2015. Until at least late February 2015, the U.S. strategy appeared to be working, with the major advanced economies maintaining a united front.

The Grand Kowtow

Then, in early March, to the stunned surprise of the U.S. administration and with barely a day's advance notice, Britain broke ranks. For the U.K., a strong relationship with China was crucial to giving itself an edge in the race to persuade Beijing to direct as much RMB business as possible toward London rather than Frankfurt and other competing financial centers. Britain's Chancellor of the Exchequer (finance minister) George Osborne could not hide his delight at having edged ahead of his European counterparts in the race to be in China's good graces while also preserving his country's economic interests. He declared, with evident glee:

> I am delighted to announce today that the U.K. will be the first major Western country to become a prospective founder member of the Asian Infrastructure Bank . . . [giving] our companies the best opportunity to work and invest in the world's fastest growing markets is a key part of our long term economic plan. Joining the AIIB at the founding stage will create an unrivalled opportunity for the U.K. and Asia to invest and grow together.

U.S. administration officials were apoplectic in private but somewhat more restrained in public. The White House issued a statement noting that this "is the U.K.'s sovereign decision. We hope and expect that the U.K. will use its voice for adoption of high standards." The U.S. couched most of its displeasure in terms of concerns about whether the AIIB would meet the "high standards" of existing multilateral institutions such as the World Bank when it came to governance, not to mention environmental and social safeguards. But eventually, a U.S. official could not hold back and, within the bounds of diplomacy with one of its closest international allies, hit out at the U.K.: "We are wary about a trend toward constant accommodation of China, which is not the best way to engage a rising power." The U.K. did not back down, with a spokesman saying, "There will be times when we take a different approach [to the United States]. We think that it's in the U.K.'s national interest."

The U.K. was only the first of many dominoes to fall. Soon after the U.K. signed up, France, Germany, and Italy released a joint statement to the effect that they were keen, in close collaboration with their international and European partners, to "join the founding members of the AIIB in order to work on establishing an institution that will adhere to best practices in the areas of governance, security, loans, and public procurement."

Recognizing that it could not stop more of its allies from jumping ship, the U.S. switched its position from high dudgeon to high principle. A senior U.S. official had this to say:

> Our messaging to the Chinese consistently has been to welcome investment in infrastructure but to seek unmistakable evidence that this bank ... takes as its starting point the high watermark of what other multilateral development banks have done in terms of governance. Every government can make its own decision about whether the way to achieve that goal is by joining before the articles of agreement are clarified or by waiting to see what the evidence looks like as the bank starts to operate.

There was one U.S. ally that weighed the costs and benefits of signing up to be a founding member of the AIIB and decided that, despite its strong economic relationship with China, bowing to Beijing in this instance might not serve its interests best. Japan's finance minister Taro Aso stated that his country would not contemplate joining the AIIB until it had demonstrated strict lending standards, including assessments of the environmental and social impacts of development projects.

Local news reports quoted Prime Minister Shinzo Abe as saying that it was important for strategic reasons that Japan stick with the U.S. despite their European allies' signing up to the AIIB. Abe was quoted as saying at a meeting of his party that "the United States now knows that Japan is trustworthy."

By April 2015, when the charter of the AIIB was being agreed on, fifty-seven countries from Asia, Africa, Europe, Latin America, and Oceania had signed up as founding members. With so many countries falling over each other to join the institution, its initial authorized capital was pushed to $100 billion, with the total contribution of members from outside the Asian region capped at $25 billion. China contributed $30 billion, the largest amount by far of all the members. China has 26 percent of the total voting share and India 7 percent. Russia has the third largest stake with 6 percent. To leave no ambiguity about who will be calling the shots at the institution, the headquarters is located in Beijing.

By September 2015, when President Xi visited Washington, the U.S. and China decided to call a truce on the AIIB. In an elegantly crafted sentence—elegant less in its linguistic than in its bureaucratic flourishes (to which, as a former bureaucrat, I tip my hat)—the two countries expressed agreement on a set of lofty and sufficiently vague principles:

> Both sides acknowledge that for new and future institutions to be significant contributors to the international financial architecture, these institutions, like the existing international financial institutions, are to be properly structured and operated in line with the principles of professionalism, transparency, efficiency, and effectiveness, and with the existing high environmental and governance standards, recognizing that these standards continuously evolve and improve.

China has not been willing to concede the moralistic high ground on the governance issue either. At the China Development Forum conference in Beijing in March 2015, ADB President Takehiko Nakao (Figure 9.2) was asked if his institution and the AIIB would have a cooperative or competitive relationship. He acknowledged that the ADB itself could benefit from some reforms and went on to say that the two banks could work together, as long as the AIIB followed "best practices" in terms of its governance and lending operations.

Figure 9.2 ADB President Takehiko Nakao and China's Finance Minister Lou Jiwei.
Credit: Asian Development Bank

This provoked a stern response from Chinese Finance Minister Lou Jiwei, who was speaking on the same panel. Lou said, "I disagree with the notion of best practice. Who is the best? As Nakao just said, ADB needs further reform. If the practice is the best, why are reforms still needed." He dismissed many of the procedures of the existing multilateral institutions as being unnecessarily bureaucratic and complicated, noting that the AIIB would put a greater emphasis on a lean bureaucracy and swift decision making.

Lou also pointed out that the AIIB was dominated by developing countries, so their wishes would have to be taken into consideration in devising rules and procedures. But his view was clear; the AIIB would strive not so much to depart from rules set by Western countries as to improve upon them: "some rules that were put forward by the West are not always the best. If we discuss, it's possible that we can develop practice even better than the Western one."

China has not been shy when it comes to making the point that the AIIB will not only demonstrate governance that is as effective as that of existing multilateral institutions, but will do even better. Using the advantage of starting with a blank slate, the AIIB is in fact creating a governance structure that removes many of the problems present in existing multilateral institutions. At least on paper, the AIIB's governance structure has many positive elements: a simple and transparent formula for setting country voting shares, the absence of any single country's veto power over major decisions, and a nonresident executive board that supervises but does not interfere with the management of the institution.

These are all improvements over the rigid governance structures to be found in existing multilateral institutions. For instance, the IMF has a full-time resident executive board that costs a lot of money to maintain and ends up interfering in the regular operations of the institution, rather than providing oversight and leaving executive decisions to management. Efforts to change this structure have failed—in no small part because the very same executive board would have to approve the change in its role.

China has declared that, while it has the largest voting share at the AIIB, it will not have veto power over majority decisions. Although the veracity of this statement remains to be tested, this would mark a clear distinction from the IMF, where major policy decisions require a supermajority of 85 percent approval. The U.S., with a voting share of 16 percent, thus effectively has veto power over major decisions, something that many other countries have, on occasion, found galling.

At a speech in Beijing in January 2016 to formally inaugurate the AIIB, Jin Liqun, who had by then been elected as the first president of the institution, stated that it would be "lean, clean and green." With his customary eloquence, he added that the AIIB would be "an institution built on transparency, openness, accountability and independence. An agile and innovative institution that learns from the past and recognizes the promise and opportunities of the future."

The AIIB stands as a perfect example of China's impatience with marginal changes in the rules of global governance. It is now grabbing the reins and seeking to rewrite the rules but in a way that ostensibly improves on the existing order, which China and other emerging markets see as having been defined by and mainly serving the interests of the major advanced economies. And there is no dearth of interest in the AIIB, showing that there is little hesitation among both emerging market and advanced economies in joining a Chinese-led institution. In May 2016, Jin Liqun confidently asserted that the institution's membership would expand to 100 countries before the end of the year. He noted that, while Japan and the U.S. had declined to join the institution, the door would always remain open to them and that, in any event, Japanese and U.S. companies would be treated fairly in the bidding process for any AIIB-financed projects. He added, pointedly, that the bank was recruiting top talent from around the world, including from the U.S., and was even in the process of appointing a Japanese national to a senior-level position.

Although the AIIB does not directly advance the RMB's role, there is little doubt that over time such institutions will create financial beachheads in other countries that China can use to promote the use of RMB in trade and finance. Meanwhile, even as it was setting up the AIIB, where it will be the dominant power, China has also been engaging its emerging market allies on other fronts.

BONDING AMONG THE BRICS

China has taken a leadership role in a group of the major emerging market economies called the *BRICS*, comprising Brazil, Russia, India, China, and South Africa (Figure 9.3). Together, these economies account for about one-quarter of world GDP and a population of three billion, roughly two-fifths of the world population.

Brazil, Russia, India, and China held their first formal BRIC summit in Yekaterinburg, Russia, in June 2009 (South Africa had not yet been invited to join the club). The countries were bound together by not much more than an acronym, coined by Jim O'Neill of Goldman Sachs, and a desire to exert greater influence in the international monetary system. This was spurred in part by the functioning of the G-20, a group comprising most of the major economies in the world. The G-20, in which emerging markets have roughly equal numerical representation with the advanced

Figure 9.3 Leaders of the BRICS nations, from left, Russia's President Vladimir Putin, India's Prime Minister Narendra Modi, Brazil's President Dilma Rousseff, China's President Xi Jinping, and South Africa's President Jacob Zuma at the BRICS summit in Fortaleza, Brazil, July 2014.
Credit: AP Photo/Silvia Izquierdo

economies, had taken on the mantle of coordinating international policy during the depths of the global financial crisis in 2008. However, by the middle of the next year, the emerging markets were beginning to feel that the advanced economies, which had precipitated the crisis to begin with, were running the show, both directly and through their control of the reins at the IMF and other major international institutions that assisted the G-20 in its work.

The four BRIC countries demanded a greater say in the running of major institutions and also in helping to design any changes in the rules and procedures governing international finance. They wanted to send a clear signal that they would no longer accept old arrangements whereby leadership of the major institutions would be carved up among the advanced economies—the IMF for Europe and the World Bank for the U.S.—through an implicit deal. The declaration at the end of their first summit read:

> We are committed to advance the reform of international financial institutions, so as to reflect changes in the world economy. The emerging

and developing economies must have greater voice and representation in international financial institutions, and their heads and senior leadership should be appointed through an open, transparent, and merit-based selection process. We also believe that there is a strong need for a stable, predictable and more diversified international monetary system.

There was considerable skepticism about whether the BRIC economies had enough shared interests to be more than just a talking shop. These countries may all have common complaints about advanced economies, but they are also geopolitical rivals. For instance, China and India have a long history of border tensions, and China's claims to some portions of land in the northeast corner of India have created simmering tensions between the two countries. It was hard to imagine that a shared set of grievances directed at advanced economies would be enough for this group to coalesce in more constructive actions. This skepticism was, if anything, heightened when South Africa was invited to join the group in 2010. Clearly, the BRICS would have to put some money on the table to be taken seriously.

China, the largest economy in the group with a vast stock of foreign exchange reserves, saw its opportunity to lead. And it seized the opportunity by the horns.

First, the Chinese teamed up with others in the group to set up the BRICS New Development Bank. Established in July 2015, its main goal is to promote sustainable development in the five countries. Fearful of being sidelined, India lobbied aggressively to locate the headquarters in New Delhi. India lost the battle but, as a compromise, was allowed to appoint the first president of the institution. China insisted that the institution be based in Shanghai but, recognizing that further aggressive moves to take charge of the institution could create bad blood, compromised on other elements of control. The initial $50 billion of subscribed capital is derived from equal contributions by the five members, who also have equal voting shares and no veto power over decisions made by a majority of the members. Each of the founding members contributes at least one vice president to the organization.

In July 2015, a reserve-pooling arrangement among the BRICS, called the *Contingent Reserve Arrangement*, also came into being. It is described in the official documents as follows: "a self-managed contingent reserve arrangement to forestall short-term balance of payments pressures, provide mutual support and further strengthen financial stability. The [Contingent Reserve Arrangement] is a framework for the provision of support through liquidity and precautionary instruments in response to actual or potential short-term balance of payments pressures." The overall volume of the arrangement is $100 billion, with China notionally contributing $41 billion; Brazil, India and Russia, $18 billion each; and South Africa, $5 billion. The five countries do not actually put this money into a pool, but simply commit to providing the agreed-on amounts if any one of them were to need the money to respond to a currency crisis. The loan would provide hard currencies to pay off debts or maintain stable imports in the face of a sudden stop of capital inflows. The country in need would obviously not be one of those putting up the money.

The amounts that can be drawn by Brazil, India, and Russia equal their notional contributions. For China, the access amount is half its contribution while for South Africa, it is two times its contribution. Thirty percent of a country's maximum access amount would be released as long as the other signatories agreed. The remaining 70 percent would be available if the country in question had negotiated a loan program with the IMF, which usually involves a commitment to sound economic policies, including disciplined fiscal and monetary policies.

Through these two new institutions, the BRICS have earned the right to be taken seriously as an economic group. They have done this by showing that they can put money on the table in a coordinated way, thereby easing concerns about how the lack of fully congruent—and often conflicting—economic and geopolitical interests could hamper their economic cooperation on the world stage. With its vast financial resources, China has become the first among equals in this group.

As is the case with China's growing presence at the IFIs, the BRICS initiatives do not directly elevate the RMB's role. Still, by fostering stronger financial linkages between the key emerging market economies and creating alternatives to the existing global financial architecture, this is another way of chipping away at the present configuration of global reserve currencies. China is not stopping at such initiatives, recognizing that its wealth could also be used to simultaneously promote its own development and those of its neighbors.

SILKEN GIFT OR NOOSE?

The Silk Road has long fascinated historians and other scholars investigating the many ways in which the continents of Asia and Europe were connected in historical times. In fact, it was only in the late nineteenth century that German geographer Baron Ferdinand von Richthofen coined the phrase *Silk Road* to refer to a specific route of East–West trade that existed about two millennia ago. The phrase came to be used more widely in the twentieth century to refer to the historic routes of economic and cultural exchange across Eurasia. Rather than being a single, clearly designated route, the Silk Road was in fact a patchwork of roads, trails, and paths.

The name is also a misnomer in some ways because trade in silk from China accounted for only a small portion of the trade conducted along these routes. Still, at least in the popular imagination, it was silk that was the most prominent element of trade between China and the West. This impression was fed by the accounts of various travelers, including the chronicles of the famous itinerant Ibn Battuta who, in the fourteenth century, traversed much of the area along what has come to be known as the Silk Road. He was struck by the prodigious amount of silk produced in China. Reflecting on his brief time in the country, he wrote, "Silk is most plentiful among them, for the silkworm is found sticking and feeding upon the trees in all their districts; and hence they make their silk, which is the clothing of the poorest among them. Were it not for the merchants, it would bring no price whatever, and still, a cotton dress will purchase many silken ones."

Despite the general notion that the Silk Road was a major conduit of commerce, some authors have argued that the importance of the routes in economic exchanges was far overshadowed by its prominence in cultural and religious exchanges. Yale University historian Valerie Hansen writes: "the Silk Road was one of the least traveled routes in human history and possibly not worth studying—if tonnage carried, traffic, or the number of travelers at any time were the sole measures of a given route's significance." Yet, she argues, the Silk Road had a profound impact on history because travelers along the various routes "planted their cultures like seeds of exotic species carried to distant lands. . . . While not much of a commercial route . . . this network of routes became the planet's most famous cultural artery for the exchange between east and west of religions, art, languages, and new technologies." These routes facilitated the spread of Buddhism from India and of Islamic culture and religion from Arabia and Persia into Central Asia and China.

China's government likes emphasizing linkages to history in forging stronger connections to countries in Asia and Europe, but the focus is now clearly on commercial interests rather than exchanges of culture or religion. In the fall of 2013, President Xi Jinping proposed two major economic initiatives—the Silk Road Economic Belt and the 21st-Century Maritime Silk Road. The two have come to be referred to jointly, and rather clunkily, as the *Belt and Road Initiative*.

The initiative covers, but is not limited to, the area along the ancient Silk Road. The Belt and Road (Figure 9.4) is envisioned as

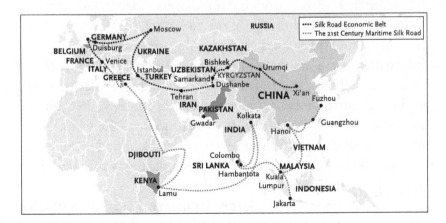

Figure 9.4 The new Silk Road.
Sources: Adapted from *Reuters and Xinhua*

covering the continents of Asia, Europe, and Africa, connecting a large and disparate group of economies, from the economically vibrant and rich to those that are poor and have a huge potential for economic development. The Silk Road Economic Belt focuses on tying together China, Central Asia, Russia, and the Baltics; linking China with the Persian Gulf and the Mediterranean Sea through Central Asia and West Asia; and connecting China with Southeast Asia, South Asia, and the Indian Ocean. The 21st-Century Maritime Silk Road, which is actually a set of maritime routes rather than a road, is designed to go from China's coast to Europe through the South China Sea and the Indian Ocean on one route, and from China's coast through the South China Sea to the South Pacific on the other.

On land, the initiative will focus on jointly building a new Eurasian Land Bridge and developing a few specific economic corridors: China–Mongolia–Russia, China–Central Asia–West Asia, and China–Indochina Peninsula. The initiative will encompass existing plans for a China–Pakistan Economic Corridor and a Bangladesh–China–India–Myanmar Economic Corridor.

In November 2014, President Xi announced that the Silk Road Fund would begin operation the following month, with an initial commitment of $40 billion. The stated objective was "to promote connectivity, and contribute to the realization of the master blueprint and bright future of the Belt and Road Initiative in accordance with a principle of market-orientation, international standards and professional excellence." The notion of following market principles and meeting or exceeding the best international standards of governance permeates many of the documents. This is no doubt meant to emphasize that the Belt and Road initiative is not merely a device to strengthen control of China's or other countries' state enterprises. Moreover, China wants to make it clear that projects undertaken under the initiative will not foster or tolerate low technical, environmental, or governance standards.

It is easy to see how, despite concerns held by developing countries in the Asian region about hitching their economic and political fortunes too closely to China, the initiative is tempting for these countries, which desperately need more extensive and better infrastructure, but lack the funding to build it and are keen to develop closer economic relationships with China.

During President Xi's visit to Pakistan in April 2015, he announced $46 billion worth of financial support for energy and infrastructure projects. This figure would eclipse all the economic- and security-related financial assistance given by the U.S. to Pakistan since 2002, amounting to roughly $31 billion. Pakistani Prime Minister Nawaz Sharif thanked China for "its commitment to help us resolve the energy crisis and make Pakistan self-sufficient in energy." Pakistani officials and newspaper editorials referred to stronger economic ties with China as "a game-changer for Pakistan's economics" and as demonstrating "the direction of foreign policy for the future and [suggesting] a possible shift away from traditional allies, including the U.S." One editorial said that the economic cooperation agreement marked "China taking on the role of Pakistan's most important ally from either west or east." Mr. Sharif could barely contain his enthusiasm: "Mountains and rivers join our territories; and our hearts and minds unite our nations. . . . We are good neighbors, close friends, dear brothers, and trusted partners. We have an all-weather, time-tested cooperative strategic partnership. We are truly iron brothers."

The Belt and Road Initiative also conveniently ties in the international expansion of China's influence with the goal of improving the economic prospects of the country's underdeveloped western and southern provinces, many of which are landlocked. This would improve the regional balance of China's growth and the level of internal integration of the economy. It would also provide a boost to growth, at least temporarily helping to address considerable overcapacity in the manufacturing sector and opening up more markets for Chinese exports.

The Chinese government has not been reticent about the broader economic objectives of the initiative, including using it to promote financial integration and the international role of the RMB. While China has not emphasized such objectives conspicuously, there are plenty of hints about them in various official documents, as captured by statements such as the following:

> We should deepen financial cooperation, and make more efforts in building a currency stability system, investment and financing system and

credit information system in Asia. We should expand the scope and scale of bilateral currency swap and settlement with other countries along the Belt and Road.... We will support the efforts of governments of the countries along the Belt and Road and their companies and financial institutions with good credit-rating to issue Renminbi bonds in China. Qualified Chinese financial institutions and companies are encouraged to issue bonds in both Renminbi and foreign currencies outside China, and use the funds thus collected in countries along the Belt and Road.

Despite being open about the scope of the initiative, Beijing is sensitive to concerns that its initiative is meant mainly to further its own economic interests, serving as a tool for the political subjugation of neighboring countries. The political aspect is one about which China is particularly sensitive, as it has long held that the U.S. and other Western countries have no business interfering in its internal affairs, such as in the governance of its autonomous regions including Hong Kong and Tibet, based on Western notions of democracy, free speech, and human rights. A government document notes the Belt and Road Initiative upholds the five principles of peaceful coexistence: mutual respect for each other's sovereignty and territorial integrity, mutual nonaggression, mutual noninterference in each other's internal affairs, equality and mutual benefit, and peaceful coexistence.

China has also been careful to deflect any notion that the Belt and Road Initiative is the equivalent of the Marshall Plan. This initiative of the U.S. government ran from 1947 to 1951, channeling a large sum of money (roughly $13 billion) from the U.S. to help the countries of Western Europe rebuild their economies, which had been ravaged by World War II. Some historians have argued that the Marshall Plan was as much a product of America's desire to protect its economic and geopolitical interests as it was an act of altruism. Walter LeFeber, a revisionist historian from Cornell University, has argued that the plan was designed to serve the economic needs of the U.S., while also being good for Europe and the world. In a co-authored book he notes that "the impetus for a European recovery plan was political as well. [U.S. President] Truman and [U.S. Secretary of State] Marshall saw the plan as a means of defending

American interests in Europe against Soviet encroachment, shoring up Western European economies so that the region would not be susceptible to Moscow-directed subversion."

One item in a Q&A posted on the Silk Road Fund's website tackles the comparison with the Marshall Plan head on and dismisses any notion of similarity between the two initiatives:

> The Marshall Plan was a product born of America's unique postwar position. Average per capita GDP of China is currently about US$7,000, making it a middle-income country, very different from America's position in the world at that time. . . . A major part of the Fund's work is to make good use of China's foreign reserves. Therefore, the Fund and the Marshall Plan are different in their essence.

As with other initiatives, China finds it useful to start with a set of slogans. For China's new periphery diplomacy, the catchwords are *Qin, Cheng, Hui*, and *Rong*. Qin (closeness) refers to developing closer bilateral relationships through high-level official visits. Cheng (earnestness) is showing sincerity when solving problems and resolving conflicts. Hui (benefit) involves seeking mutual benefits through cooperation. Rong (inclusiveness) means taking a broad enough view of the Asia and Pacific region that it can include other countries that share similar goals.

OTHER ARMS OF THE OCTOPUS

Some of China's financial institutions also play a subtle but important role in expanding the country's role in international finance, with the RMB's rise being fueled—but only in a backdoor way—through them. The China Development Bank (CDB), for instance, makes overseas loans to Chinese corporations operating abroad, as well as foreign corporations. At the end of 2014, overseas loans amounted to $163 billion, about 13 percent of the CDB's overall loan portfolio of $1.3 trillion. By the end of 2015, the CDB's overseas loan portfolio had risen to nearly $330 billion (out of an overall loan portfolio of about $1.9 trillion).

The Export–Import Bank of China is another institution that allows the country to expand its influence abroad, in this case largely through financing related to trade deals. This institution does not publish data on its overseas loans. Using data on export credit provided to buyers of China's exports and on-lending of loans from foreign governments and IFIs, one can estimate that in 2014 there was about $53 billion of overseas lending outstanding, amounting to 19 percent of the overall loan portfolio.

China is clearly determined to exercise its role as a major global economic power through both direct and subtle means, influencing the existing world order but also trying to reshape the global monetary system to its own liking. The AIIB helps Beijing put a stamp of legitimacy on China's operations to extend its spheres of economic and political influence, even while subtly redefining the rules of the game.

The AIIB is a textbook example of China's increasingly savvy and disciplined approach to international economic engagement, an approach that emphasizes constructive engagement rather than brute financial force. Beijing is using the AIIB as a tool of international economic diplomacy that supplants China's earlier roughshod bilateral approach, which sparked resentment even among some countries that were recipients of Chinese financing.

China is becoming a leading member of the international community—not, as the West prefers, by being co-opted into existing institutions under the current rules of the game, but on its own terms and by co-opting other countries into the system of rules it wants to dictate. This goal subsumes another objective, which is to eventually alter the rules of global finance that China sees as conveying undue privilege to the existing reserve currencies. Among other ends that the Chinese government hopes to achieve through this process, it will allow the RMB to fairly stake a claim to being one of the world's dominant reserve currencies.

CHAPTER 10
Conclusion

> I should have liked to have closed these lectures by leading up to some great climax. But perhaps it is more in accordance with the true conditions of scientific progress that they should fizzle out with a glimpse of the obscurity which marks the frontiers of present knowledge. I do not apologize for the lameness of the conclusion, for it is not a conclusion. I wish I could feel confident that it is even a beginning.
>
> *Stars and Atoms*, Sir Arthur S. Eddington

The RMB has come a long way in a short time. The currency is making an impressively rapid ascent into the upper echelons of international finance. The RMB's growing prominence as an international currency could, over time, conceivably diminish the roles of the major currencies—even that of the dollar—as units of account and media of exchange in intermediating international trade and finance transactions. However, the RMB is now hitting constraints that result from the structure of its domestic economy and will limit its progress as a reserve currency (i.e., a store of value). Moreover, given the nature of its political system, it is unlikely the RMB will attain the status of a safe haven currency. Thus, although it is likely to continue its ascent, the notion that the RMB will become a dominant global reserve currency that rivals the dollar is far-fetched.

China has adopted a unique approach to the RMB's role in the global monetary system. As with virtually all other major reforms, China is striking out on its own path toward a more open capital account, using a controlled approach to liberalization of financial flows. The government is likely to continue dismantling explicit controls even while attempting to exercise "soft" control over inflows and outflows through administrative and other measures. Nevertheless, on its current trajectory, China will have a nearly open capital account by 2020, enhancing the RMB's role in global trade and finance.

Given China's size and financial clout, the government's measures to promote the international use of the currency are gaining traction, although some of the results are still modest in scale. About 30 percent of China's cross-border trade transactions are now denominated and settled in RMB. The RMB is the fifth most important payment currency but still accounts for less than 3 percent of worldwide payments for cross-border trade and financial transactions. The RMB also accounts for less than 2 percent of turnover in global foreign exchange markets. In themselves these may seem unimpressive numbers, but considering that the starting point for each was essentially zero just a few years ago, they merit attention. Linear extrapolations of this rate of progress are, however, likely to prove unduly optimistic.

The RMB's inclusion in the IMF's SDR basket is an important symbol of the currency's ascendancy in global finance for it now has the IMF's imprimatur as an official reserve currency. The RMB is also beginning to appear in the foreign exchange reserve portfolios of a number of central banks around the world. These shifts, some of which are, at this point, more symbolic than substantive, will develop critical mass over time and have the potential to start transforming the global monetary system. At the same time, the RMB's inclusion in the SDR basket could be seen as a way for the IMF—and the international community that it represents—to exercise leverage over China in internalizing the global repercussions of its domestic policies, which have increased in tandem with China's weight in the world economy and the opening up of its economy.

The Chinese leadership's stated commitment to financial sector and other market-oriented reforms—if implemented effectively and with careful management of transitional risks—sets the RMB on a clear course to becoming a significant reserve currency.

All is not well, however, with the reform process. Liberalization of the financial sector and capital markets has been carried out unevenly and without a clearly articulated strategy, which, in addition to imbalances across several areas of needed reforms, has created its own set of risks. Reforms on the real side of the economy have not kept pace with financial liberalization. China's economy and the RMB's rise have also been impeded by the lack of a robust institutional framework—including good public and corporate governance, a transparent policymaking process, and effective regulatory institutions—that ought to supplement financial and other market-oriented reforms.

China's leaders will eventually have to go beyond modest financial sector and economic reforms to more fundamental ones without which a market-oriented system cannot work well. Under the right circumstances, losing some stability and control might be well worth it for a better-functioning market economy, which in turn is a necessary foundation for a currency that can function on the same level as those of its advanced economy counterparts.

The Chinese leadership's endorsement of financial sector and capital account liberalization—coupled with unambiguous repudiation of fundamental political, legal, and institutional reforms—sets the RMB on a clear course. Despite becoming a reserve currency, the RMB has essentially given up its claim of being seen as a safe haven currency, one that investors turn to for safety. In the absence of these fundamental reforms, especially the rule of law and a democratic system of government, the rise of the RMB will erode but not seriously challenge the dollar's status as the dominant global reserve currency.

Even if the RMB fails to become a safe haven currency, however, China's positioning on the global stage will allow it to exercise considerable influence on the global monetary system. The economy's rapidly growing size and dynamism will help promote the international use of its currency, especially within Asia. The AIIB, the Belt and Road Initiative, and joint initiatives with other

BRICS economies will allow China to diversify its foreign investment allocations beyond traditional investments, yielding better economic returns and also an intangible but substantial payoff in terms of increased influence in Asia and beyond. These channels will also help promote the international use of the RMB.

Other major shifts in global finance are in the offing as well. The structure of capital outflows from China to the U.S. and other advanced economies is already shifting from official purchases of government bonds to other channels—including FDI and equity investments abroad—as international portfolio diversification by Chinese households, corporations, and institutional investors begins dominating China's capital outflows.

The RMB's prospects as a global currency will ultimately be shaped by broader domestic policies, especially those related to financial market development, exchange rate flexibility, and capital account liberalization. Thus, the various policy reforms that are needed to support the international role of the RMB could also create significant changes in China's economy and the patterns of its capital inflows and outflows.

The RMB's rising prominence as a reserve currency could improve the stability of regional and international financial systems by creating more competition among existing reserve currencies, in principle providing an incentive for the home economies of those currencies to institute better economic policies. This, in turn, requires that China's macroeconomic policies as well as its financial market development and regulation contribute to its own macroeconomic and financial stability. How China navigates these challenges matters not just to China itself, but also to the rest of the world.

The story of the Chinese currency began two millennia ago. There have been many twists and turns, and also much intrigue, in the lead-up to the creation of the RMB and now its role as a global currency. The most interesting chapters of the story are yet to be written.

Implications of the RMB's Rise for the U.S.

CAPITAL FLOWS

China's capital account liberalization could have significant effects on the volume and, more importantly, the composition of its investments in the U.S. For nearly two decades, the major channel for capital flows to the U.S. has been the official accumulation of foreign exchange reserves. A more flexible exchange rate and a broader financial system that facilitates hedging against currency risk would reduce China's reserve accumulation while simultaneously reducing the "fear of floating" (i.e., concerns about currency volatility). For instance, a richer set of derivatives markets would enable private agents, including corporations, to insure themselves against a variety of risks associated with currency volatility, mitigating the need for reserves as a public insurance mechanism. A deeper and broader financial system would also reduce the risks involved with the greater capital flow volatility to which China will be exposed as the capital account becomes more open.

An analysis of China's investment position in the U.S. shows that Treasury and agency debt (issued by U.S. government-sponsored enterprises) continue to dominate in the total stock position (Figure A.1). Chinese portfolio investment in the U.S. has expanded rapidly—from $29 billion in 2007 to $330 billion in 2015. Direct investment from China to the U.S. has been growing rapidly as well

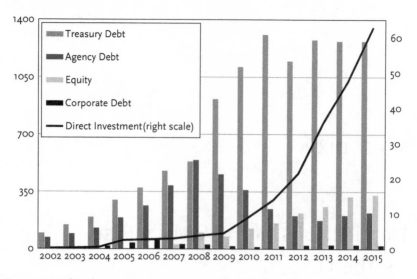

Figure A.1 China's investment position in the U.S. (in billions of U.S. dollars). This chart shows the stocks of China's direct investment and other types of securities holdings in the U.S. Except for direct investment, all other categories are based on data at the end of June each year.

Sources: U.S. Treasury International Capital System and the Rhodium Group.

but, in absolute amounts, still stands at a relatively modest cumulative total of $63 billion in 2015.

The U.S. Treasury International Capital System data suggest that the absolute amount of Treasury securities held by China remained relatively stable from 2013 to 2015 (Figure A.2), even though China's foreign exchange reserves fell by nearly $800 billion from June 2014 to January 2016. Thus, it does not appear China has been selling U.S. Treasury securities while trying to prevent RMB depreciation. Meanwhile, China's declining share of U.S. government debt ownership indicates that other investors, both domestic and foreign, are maintaining their strong demand for U.S. Treasuries. Moreover, given the U.S. federal government's substantially lower financing needs in recent years, especially relative to the period during and in the immediate aftermath of the financial crisis, it is unlikely that reduced purchases of Treasury securities by China will, by itself, have a marked effect on the U.S. Treasury yield curve.

As Chinese financial markets develop and private investors increase the international diversification of their portfolios,

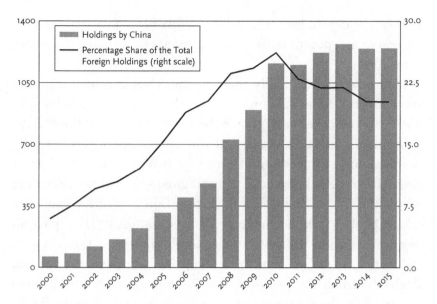

Figure A.2 China's holdings of U.S. Treasuries (in billions of U.S. dollars). This chart shows China's holdings of U.S. Treasury securities at the end of each year. *Source:* U.S. Treasury International Capital System.

the shifts in China's outward investment patterns are likely to become more pronounced. Currently, China invests a relatively modest amount in U.S. equities. This is likely to shift as capital account openness leads to more capital flowing out of China in search of divers ification and yield. This would result in rising flows into various asset markets in the U.S.—from equities to real estate.

Thus, the various policy reforms that are needed to support the international role of the RMB could also create significant changes in China's economy and the patterns of its capital inflows and out-flows, both overall and also specifically from and to the U.S.

THE RENMINBI VERSUS THE DOLLAR

While the RMB is likely to become a significant reserve currency over the next decade, it is unlikely to challenge the dollar's dominance. There is still a huge gulf between China and the U.S. regarding the availability of safe and liquid assets such as government bonds. The depth, breadth, and liquidity of U.S. financial markets will serve as a potent buffer against threats to the dollar's preeminent status.

It is nevertheless likely that, as the RMB becomes a prominent international currency, and as the costs of transacting in the RMB and other emerging market currencies falls, the dollar's prominence as a unit of account (for denominating trade transactions) and as a medium of exchange (for settling cross-border financial trade and financial transactions) will decline. This could affect the use of the dollar in international financial markets, which by itself will not necessarily have a substantial impact on the U.S. economy. However, these developments, in tandem with measures taken by China to develop its own payment system, could diminish the primacy of U.S. financial institutions. This would affect the ability of the U.S. to continue wielding the financial clout that it currently has as a result of the dollar's dominance in international finance.

It has also been argued by some that the RMB is on a trajectory to displace the dollar as the dominant global reserve currency. However, as discussed earlier, China is missing one crucial ingredient: the world's trust. To achieve currency dominance, China needs more than economic and military might; true dominance requires a broader and more credible set of public and political institutions. Indeed, the importance of such institutions was apparent in the aftermath of the global financial crisis. Even though America's financial markets nearly collapsed, its public debt levels rose sharply, and the Federal Reserve was forced to undertake massive monetary expansion to support the economy, the dollar strengthened relative to most other currencies.

Global investors seeking a safe haven still automatically turn to U.S. Treasury securities in times of global financial turmoil. Foreign investors now hold $6.2 trillion of these low-yielding securities, not to mention large quantities of other dollar assets. And the dollar's share in global foreign exchange reserves has held steady since the crisis. Indeed, recent data from the IMF suggest

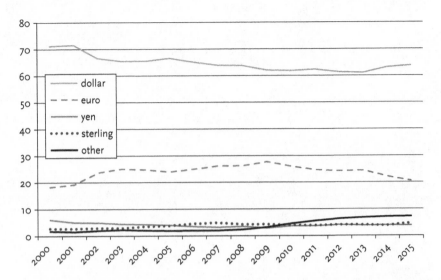

Figure A.3 Currency composition of world foreign exchange reserves (measured as a percentage).
Source: The International Monetary Fund.

that the dollar's share of global foreign exchange reserves increased slightly, to about 64 percent, in 2014 and 2015 (Figure A.3).

In short, the RMB will not contest the dollar's supremacy unless China's leaders align the country's political and legal institutions with its economic reforms.

APPENDIX B

Data Tables

This appendix provides a set of tables that present more detailed data related to some of the analysis in the book.

Table B.1. CONFIGURATION OF GLOBAL GROSS DOMESTIC PRODUCT

	Nominal GDP		GDP in PPP	
	USD billions	Percent of world total	USD billions	Percent of world total
U.S.	17,947	24.5	17,947	15.8
Eurozone	11,540	15.8	—	—
China	10,983	15.0	19,392	17.1
Japan	4,123	5.6	4,830	4.3
U.K.	2,849	3.9	2,679	2.4
Canada	1,552	2.1	1,632	1.4
Australia	1,224	1.7	1,138	1.0
Switzerland	665	0.9	482	0.4
BRICS	16,484	22.5	34,991	30.8

Notes: BRICS, Brazil, Russia, India, China, and South Africa; GDP, gross domestic product; PPP, purchasing power parity; USD, U.S. dollars. Data are for 2015. Nominal GDP converted to U.S. dollars at market exchange rates. PPP refers to purchasing power parity–adjusted measures of GDP. The 2015 nominal GDP and shares of world GDP of the BRICS economies other than China at market exchange rates are as follows: Brazil $1.8 trillion (2.4 percent), India $2.1 trillion (3 percent), Russia $1.3 trillion (1.8 percent), and South Africa $0.3 trillion (0.4 percent). At PPP exchange rates, their GDP and GDP shares are as follows: Brazil $3.2 trillion (2.8 percent), India $8.0 trillion (7.0 percent), Russia $3.7 trillion (3.3 percent), and South Africa $0.7 trillion (0.6 percent).
Source: IMF.

Table B.2. COUNTRY SHARES OF WORLD TRADE (IN PERCENTAGES)

	Exports	Imports	Total trade
A. Trade in Goods			
Eurozone	24.2	22.7	23.4
China	12.1	10.1	11.1
U.S.	8.8	13.3	11.0
Germany	8.1	6.6	7.4
Japan	3.8	4.5	4.1
U.K.	2.6	3.8	3.2
Russia	2.7	1.7	2.2
India	1.8	2.3	2.0
Switzerland	1.8	1.5	1.6
Brazil	1.2	1.3	1.3
South Africa	0.5	0.6	0.5
B. Trade in Goods and Services			
Eurozone	25.4	24.0	24.7
U.S.	9.9	12.5	11.2
China	10.5	9.6	10.1
Germany	7.5	6.7	7.1
Japan	3.7	4.4	4.0
U.K.	3.5	3.9	3.7
India	2.1	2.4	2.2
Russia	2.4	1.9	2.1
Switzerland	1.9	1.6	1.7
Brazil	1.1	1.4	1.3
South Africa	0.5	0.5	0.5

Notes: Data are for 2014. Eurozone data include trade between countries within the area. In 2015, China accounted for 12 percent of global trade in goods and 11 percent of global trade in goods and services. Data for 2015 were not available for some of the countries in the table. *Sources:* World Bank, IMF, and SAFE.

Table B.3. CHINA'S INTERNATIONAL INVESTMENT POSITION (IN BILLIONS OF U.S. DOLLARS)

	Year											
	2004	2005	2006	2007	2008	2009	2010	2011	2012	2013	2014	2015
Net position	276	408	640	1,188	1,494	1,491	1,688	1,688	1,866	1,996	1,603	1,598
Assets	929	1,223	1,690	2,416	2,957	3,437	4,119	4,735	5,213	5,986	6,438	6,215
FDI	53	64	91	116	186	246	317	425	532	660	883	1,129
Portfolio	92	117	265	285	253	243	257	204	241	259	263	261
Equity	0	0	1	20	21	55	63	86	130	153	161	162
Debt	92	117	264	265	231	188	194	118	111	105	101	99
Other investments	166	216	254	468	552	495	630	850	1,053	1,187	1,394	1,419
Reserve assets	619	826	1,081	1,547	1,966	2,453	2,914	3,256	3,388	3,880	3,899	3,406
FX reserves	610	819	1,066	1,528	1,946	2,399	2,847	3,181	3,312	3,821	3,843	3,330
Liabilities	653	816	1,050	1,228	1,463	1,946	2,431	3,046	3,347	3,990	4,836	4,617
FDI	369	472	614	704	916	1,315	1,570	1,907	2,068	2,331	2,599	2,842
Portfolio	57	77	121	147	168	190	224	249	336	387	796	811
Equity	43	64	106	129	151	175	206	211	262	298	651	591
Debt	13	13	14	18	17	15	18	37	74	89	145	220
Other investments	227	267	315	378	380	442	637	891	943	1,272	1,440	964

Notes: FDI, foreign direct investment; FX, foreign exchange. The data for 2015 are not directly comparable with those for previous years. Starting in 2015, China began reporting its IIP based on the IMF's latest Balance of Payments and International Investment Position Manual Version 6 (BPM6). A major change, according to the SAFE, is that the key IIP items are now reported using the market capitalization method rather than the historical flow accumulation method. Data through 2014 are still reported based on BPM5. It should be noted that the SAFE began reporting balance of payments (BOP) data based on BPM6 standards earlier, so those data are in fact comparable over time, although these changes also highlight the difficulty of matching flow (BOP) and stock (IIP) measures in earlier years.
Source: SAFE.

Table B.4. CURRENCY DISTRIBUTION OF GLOBAL FOREIGN EXCHANGE
MARKET TURNOVER (SELECTED CURRENCIES, IN PERCENTAGES)

	Year				
	2001	2004	2007	2010	2013
USD	89.9	88.0	85.6	84.9	87.0
Euro	37.9	37.4	37.0	39.1	33.4
Japanese yen	23.5	20.8	17.2	19.0	23.0
British pound sterling	13.0	16.5	14.9	12.9	11.8
Australian dollar	4.3	6.0	6.6	7.6	8.6
Swiss franc	6.0	6.0	6.8	6.3	5.2
Indian rupee	0.2	0.3	0.7	1.0	1.0
Russian ruble	0.3	0.6	0.7	0.9	1.6
Chinese RMB	0.0	0.1	0.5	0.9	2.2
South African rand	0.9	0.7	0.9	0.7	1.1
Brazilian real	0.5	0.3	0.4	0.7	1.1
All currencies	200.0	200.0	200.0	200.0	200.0

Notes: USD, U.S. dollar. The percentage shares of individual currencies sum to 200 percent because two currencies are involved in each transaction. Data are adjusted for local and cross-border inter-dealer double counting (i.e., "net-net" basis).
Source: BIS.

Table B.5. INTERNATIONAL BONDS AND NOTES
OUTSTANDING (SELECTED CURRENCIES)

	June 2015 (USD billions)	Share (percent of total)
USD	8,816	42.7
Euro	8,092	39.2
British pound sterling	1,988	9.6
Japanese yen	402	1.9
Swiss franc	295	1.4
Chinese RMB	98	0.5
Brazilian real	37	0.2
South African rand	29	0.1
Russian ruble	21	0.1
Indian rupee	7	0.0

Notes: USD, U.S. dollar. This table shows the breakdown of outstanding international debt securities by currency denomination.
Source: BIS.

Table B.6. INTEREST RATE DERIVATIVES BY CURRENCY

	Gross notional value		Total trade count	
	USD billions	Percent of total	Trade count	Percent of total
A. Trades Cleared through Centralized Counterparty				
Euro	80,018	33.9	628,417	25.3
USD	75,502	32.0	702,401	28.3
Japanese yen	29,271	12.4	267,440	10.8
British pound sterling	20,526	8.7	234,049	9.4
Swiss franc	2,652	1.1	32,221	1.3
South African rand	1,792	0.8	30,080	1.2
Brazilian real	776	0.3	15,658	0.6
Indian rupee	742	0.3	43,097	1.7
Chinese RMB	435	0.2	22,417	0.9
Russian ruble	1,466	0.6	6,648	0.3
Share of total	213,180	90.3	1,982,428	79.8
Total	236,185		2,483,499	
B. All Trades				
Euro	172,596	34.8	1,103,212	25.6
USD	172,099	34.7	1,320,501	30.7
Japanese yen	64,845	13.1	64,845	1.5
British pound sterling	42,325	8.5	425,289	9.9
Swiss franc	5,921	1.2	77,470	1.8
South African rand	2,387	0.5	49,975	1.2
Brazilian real	775	0.2	15,658	0.4
Indian rupee	742	0.1	43,097	1.0
Chinese RMB	435	0.1	22,417	0.5
Russian ruble	132	0.0	6,648	0.2
Share of total	462,257	93.2	3,129,112	72.7
Total	495,889		4,302,569	

Notes: USD, U.S. dollar. Any trade cleared through a central counterparty was calculated by adding the trade summary by currency for G14 and non-G14 dealers. Tri-Optima's Interest Rate Trade Repository Report no longer publishes these data. The Depository Trust and Clearing Corporation now manages the data but does not make them available to the public.
Source: Tri-Optima Trade Repository Report, 2012.

Table B.7. RECENT OFFSHORE RMB CLEARING ARRANGEMENTS
(EXCLUDING HONG KONG AND MACAO)

Country	Date signed	Bank appointed
Singapore	July 6, 2012	ICBC
Taiwan	August 31, 2012	Bank of China
Germany	March 28, 2014	Bank of China
U.K.	March 31, 2014	CCB
Luxembourg	June 28, 2014	ICBC Luxembourg
France	June 28, 2014	Bank of China Paris
South Korea	July 3, 2014	Bank of Communications
Qatar	November 3, 2014	ICBC (Qatar)
Malaysia	November 10, 2014	Bank of China (Malaysia) Berhad
Australia	November 17, 2014	Bank of China (Sydney)
Canada	November 17, 2014	ICBC (Canada)
Thailand	December 22, 2014	ICBC (Thai) Public Co. Ltd.
Switzerland	January 21, 2015	TBA
Chile	May 26, 2015	CCB (Chile)
South Africa	July 1, 2015	Bank of China (Johannesburg)
Argentina	September 17, 2015	TBA
Russia	June 25, 2016	TBA

Notes: ICBC, Industrial and Commercial Bank of China; CCB, China Construction Bank. Each offshore clearing center has only one clearing bank. The third column of the table shows official RMB clearing banks. In addition to the designated offshore clearing centers listed in the table, two special RMB centers were set up over a decade ago—Hong Kong (December 2003) and Macao (September 2004).

Table B.8. STOCKS AND TURNOVER OF GOVERNMENT AND CORPORATE
BONDS: A CROSS-COUNTRY PERSPECTIVE

	Government			Corporate		
	Amount outstanding	Turnover	Turnover ratio	Amount outstanding	Turnover	Turnover ratio
U.S.	18,902	126,815	6.7	8,158	6,706	0.8
Japan	8,274	10,260	1.2	656	39	0.1
Eurozone	8,614	—	—	3,726	—	—
China	4,306	2,153	0.6	2,199	550	0.3
Germany	1,195	5,104	4.3	301	—	—

Notes: Data shown in this table are for 2015 (U.S., Japan, and Germany) and, in some cases, for the 12-month period running to March 2016 (Eurozone, China, and Germany-corporate debt). Government bonds include both central and general government debt (including municipal bonds in the case of the U.S.). In the case of Germany, government debt data is limited to federal debt. The data do not cover debt securities issued by monetary financial institutions such as central banks. The value of government and corporate bonds outstanding and turnover are expressed in billions of U.S. dollars. Corporate bonds for China, the eurozone, Germany, and Japan include those issued by nonfinancial and financial corporations. *Sources:* Securities Industry and Financial Markets Association (SIFMA), Federal Reserve Board, European Central Bank, Bundesbank, The Federal Republic of Germany Finance Agency, AsianBondsOnline, and author's calculations.

Table B.9. CENTRAL BANK SWAP ARRANGEMENTS WITH THE PEOPLE'S
BANK OF CHINA (DECEMBER 2008–JUNE 2016)

Bank	Date	Amount (billion RMB)	USD equivalent (billion)
Bank of Korea	December 12, 2008	180	27.5
	October 26, 2014	360	55.0
Hong Kong Monetary Authority	January 20, 2009	200	30.5
	November 27, 2014	400	61.1
Bank Negara Malaysia	February 8, 2009	80	12.2
	April 18, 2015	180	27.5
National Bank of the Republic of Belarus	March 11, 2009	20	3.1
	May 11, 2015	7	1.1
Bank Indonesia	March 23, 2009	100	15.3
	October 1, 2013	100	15.3
Central Bank of Argentina	April 2, 2009	70	10.7
	July 18, 2014	70	10.7
Central Bank of Iceland	June 9, 2010	3.5	0.5
	September 1, 2013	3.5	0.5
Monetary Authority of Singapore	July 23, 2010	150	22.9
	March 7, 2016	300	45.8
Reserve Bank of New Zealand	April 18, 2011	25	3.8
	May 22, 2014	25	3.8
Central Bank of the Republic of Uzbekistan	April 19, 2011	0.7	0.1
Bank of Mongolia	April 19, 2011	5	0.8
	August 21, 2014	15	2.3
National Bank of Kazakhstan	June 13, 2011	7	1.1
	December 14, 2014	7	1.1
Bank of Thailand	December 22, 2011	70	10.7
	December 22, 2014	70	10.7
State Bank of Pakistan	December 23, 2011	10	1.5
Central Bank of the United Arab Emirates	January 17, 2012	35	5.3
Central Bank of the Republic of Turkey	February 21, 2012	10	1.5
	November 16, 2015	12	1.8
Reserve Bank of Australia	March 22, 2012	200	30.5
	April 8, 2015	200	30.5
National Bank of Ukraine	June 26, 2012	15	2.3
Banco Central do Brazil	March 26, 2013	190	29.0
Bank of England	June 22, 2013	200	30.5
	October 20, 2015	350	53.4

(continued)

Bank	Date	Amount (billion RMB)	USD equivalent (billion)
Central Bank of Hungary	September 9, 2013	10	1.5
Bank of Albania	September 12, 2013	2	0.3
European Central Bank	October 9, 2013	350	53.4
Swiss National Bank	July 21, 2014	150	22.9
Central Bank of Sri Lanka	September 16, 2014	10	1.5
Central Bank of Russian Federation	October 13, 2014	150	22.9
Qatar Central Bank	November 3, 2014	35	5.3
Bank of Canada	November 18, 2014	200	30.5
Nepal Rastra Bank	December 25, 2014	Unknown	Unknown
Central Bank of Suriname	March 18, 2015	1	0.2
Central Bank of Armenia	March 30, 2015	1	0.2
South African Reserve Bank	April 10, 2015	30	4.6
Central Bank of Chile	May 25, 2015	22	3.4
National Bank of Tajikistan	September 7, 2015	3	0.5
Central Bank of Morocco	May 11, 2016	10	1.5
National Bank of Serbia	June 17, 2016	1.5	0.2
Total amount of latest arrangements		**3,325**	**508**

Notes: USD, U.S. dollar. The table shows the dates of the initial arrangement and the latest arrangement only (if the initial arrangement has been renewed). Intermediate renewals (for instance, the Bank of Korea's and Hong Kong Monetary Authority's renewals in 2011) are not shown. The totals shown at the end of the table are based on the amount of the latest arrangement for each country. The U.S. dollar equivalent amounts are calculated using the May 30, 2016 exchange rate of 6.55 RMB per dollar.
Sources: PBC and other participating central banks.

NOTES

PREFACE

The epigraph is taken from pages xxiii–xxiv of the preface to Wilson (1868). Andrew Wilson was a Scottish journalist and traveller who lived from 1831 to 1881. The version of Wilson's book that I draw upon is a facsimile edition printed in 2005 as part of the Elibron Classics Series by Adamant Media Corporation.

Data on GDP are based on market exchange rates. At purchasing power parity–adjusted exchange rates, China accounted for 17 percent of global GDP in 2015, a larger share than that of the U.S. For more details, see Table B.1 in Appendix B. The trade shares are based on data that include within-eurozone trade for the eurozone. China's share of total trade in goods and services is 10 percent. For more details, see Table B.2 in Appendix B.

CHAPTER 1. A HISTORICAL PROLOGUE

The epigraph is from *The Travels of Marco Polo the Venetian*, translated and edited by William Marsden (1948, p. 214). The subsequent quote is from the same source, pages 149–150. Basbanes (2013) reviews the invention of paper and how its use evolved over time in China and elsewhere. For a discussion of the evolution of paper money, see Beresiner and Narbeth (1973, pp. 9–11).

For more details about the early development of paper money in China, see Reinfeld (1957, p. 8) and *A History of Chinese Currency (16th Century BC–20th Century AD)*. Xinhua Publishing House, N.C.C. Limited, M.A.O. Management Group Ltd, 1983, pp. 25, 49, 52, 58–68, 129–130, 173, 189, 198.

For more on Cai Lun, see http://www.britannica.com/biography/Cai-Lun.

For details about the history of printing, see Twyman (1998, pp. 20–21).

The timeline of major dynasties is from Bowker (2003).

Needham (1986, p. 48) describes the production and use of paper currency during the Song dynasty.

MONETARY DEBATES IN ANCIENT CHINA

Von Glahn (1996) provides a rich account of historical monetary debates in China. The description of such debates during the Song dynasty is drawn from his account.

Historian Sima Qian's views are based on his magnum opus, *Shi Ji*, published around 94 BC, and translated by Burton Watson as *Records of the Grand Historian*. Sima Qian's views on economic and monetary matters can be found in *Shi Ji 129: Biographies of the Money Makers*. Also, see Lin, Peach, and Wang (2014) for more on this topic.

THE WORLD'S FIRST FIAT CURRENCY

For more on the printing and use of Chao banknotes, see Allsen (2001, pp. 179, 183).

The key details of the Tai Ping Rebellion are summarized in http://www.britannica.com/event/Taiping-Rebellion. For an interesting historical narrative on the Tai Ping Rebellion from a very particular perspective, see Wilson (1868).

The full title of Alexander Del Mar's 1885 volume is *A History of Money in Ancient Countries: From the Earliest Times to the Present*. The quoted text is from p. 30 of a facsimile edition produced by Palala Press in 2015.

A CURRENCY WAR

For more information on Fa Bi Reform, see Coble (2003, pp. 64–66). The martial phase of the currency war is described in Coble (2003, pp. 91–97), drawing on Wakeman (1996). For a discussion of the Kuomintang gold yuan notes, see Beresiner (1977, p. 183).

Ji (2002) provides a comprehensive account of Shanghai banking and capital markets from 1842 to 1952, including the creation of the Japanese central banks and the competition between currency issued by those banks and the Kuomintang's Fa Bi currency.

THE RENMINBI APPEARS

Details about the origins of the RMB, the story of its widespread acceptance among the people, and Mao's reactions to requests that his name should be on the notes are based on Deng (2015) and the following references: "Disclose the Secrets of Renminbi." *Zheng Fu Fa Zhi [The Government Law], China Academic Journals (Qingdao Server)-Politics/Military Affairs/Law (Series G)*, 2010;8:18–19. "Why Mao Rejected Four Times to Appear on Renminbi." *Gong Chan Dong Yuan [The Communist], China Academic Journals (Qingdao Server)-Politics/Military Affairs/Law (Series G)*, 2012;6:23.

The calligraphic pursuits of Dong Biwu and other Chinese leaders are detailed in Kraus (1991, pp. 65–67). For more on Dong Biwu's role in the design of the RMB notes, see Wu, Dong Bi. 1996, "Beijing: Zhong Yang Wen Xian Chu Ban She." Central Literature Press Series 1: 76, 128, 266.

THE FACE OF THE RENMINBI

Details about successive series of RMB notes and how the images on the notes were chosen are found in the following references: "The Beginning and End of Putting Mao's Portrait on Renminbi." *Lao You [Old Friend], China Academic Journals (Qingdao Server)–Politics/Military Affairs/Law (Series G)*, 2013; 12:13–14. "The Change of the Renminbi Banknotes." *Xin Yi Dai [The New Generation], China Academic Journals (Qingdao Server)–Politics/Military Affairs/Law (Series G)*, 2012;8:48. "The Story of Renminbi." *Wen Shi Jing Hua [The Essence of Chinese History], China Academic Journals (Qingdao Server)–Politics/Military Affairs/Law (Series G)*, 2012;6:16–25. Yishuo Yang, Cornell University, provided text translations of these materials.

A ROSE BY ANY OTHER NAME?

The Wall Street Journal reporters with whom I checked are Bob Davis and Lingling Wei. Sandrine Rastello of Bloomberg channeled her newsroom's style guru. Jeff Sommer of

The New York Times graciously provided an excerpt from The New York Times style book. The Economist's style guide is available online (www.economist.com/styleguide) and its rules for good writing are entertaining and instructive.

The source for currency names is http://www.currency-iso.org/en/home/.

Sovereign countries were identified from the U.S. State Department website (http://www.state.gov/s/inr/rls/4250.htm).

CHAPTER 2. CURRENCY CONCEPTS

The epigraph is from the comic script Dilbert by Scott Adams. The two strips used here originally ran March 27 to 28, 2015. Here is more of the sequence:

> WALLY: My new hobby is explaining economics using babble talk. It sounds totally real. For instance, did you know that the bubble in commodities is creating an oversupply of interest rates?
>
> Meanwhile . . .
>
> POINTY-HAIRED BOSS: Our chief economist quit.
>
> CEO: Promote that bald guy. He sounds smart.
>
> POINTY-HAIRED BOSS: Our CEO wants to promote you to chief economist because nothing you say makes sense. He thinks that's the sign of a great economist.
>
> WALLY: It totally is.
>
> POINTY-HAIRED BOSS: Say something smart.
>
> WALLY: Whoa, I don't want to create an oversupply of wisdom.
>
> The next day . . .
>
> POINTY-HAIRED BOSS: Our new chief economist, Wally, will tell us what to expect in the coming quarter.
>
> WALLY: The exchange rate on derivatives will trigger a bubble in monetary policy and deflate the yen.
>
> CEO: I totally understand that and have no questions.
>
> POINTY-HAIRED BOSS: Wow, he's good.
>
> The next day . . .
>
> TINA: My interview with you is live on the [company] website. Nothing you said made sense, so I strung together a bunch of economic jargon and called it your forecast.
>
> One month later . . .
>
> TV ANNOUNCER: Only one economist accurately predicted when this bubble would burst.
>
> DILBERT: Uh-oh. You are being hailed as the best economist of our age because your random jargon turned out to mean something.
>
> WALLY: That's nice, but as a professional economist, I only care if there's a cash award.
>
> DILBERT: The world's greatest economist should already be rich.
>
> WALLY: It's more art than science.

The paper to which I refer here is Lucas (1982).

A BRIEF PRIMER

Obstfeld and Rogoff (1996) provide an authoritative and comprehensive overview of analytical concepts in international finance.

EXCHANGE RATE MANAGEMENT

Trade shares were calculated using data from the China General Administration of Customs and the World Trade Organization.

ONSHORE AND OFFSHORE EXCHANGE RATES

Details on and data about the CFETS are drawn from the agency's website (http://www.chinamoney.com.cn/en/index.html).

The CFETS provides trading, information, and benchmark and training facilities to the interbank lending, bond, and foreign exchange markets; monitors market transactions; provides services for the operation and transmission of the central bank's monetary policies; and engages in other businesses authorized by the People's Bank of China (PBC). The CFETS also runs an interbank market for purely RMB-related transactions. There are nearly 10,000 members on that market.

As of June 2016, the instruments traded in the foreign exchange/RMB spot market cover fifteen currency pairs with the CNY: the U.S. dollar (USD), the euro (EUR), the Japanese yen (JPY), the Hong Kong dollar (HKD), the British pound sterling (GBP), the Australian dollar (AUD), the New Zealand dollar, the Singapore dollar (SGD), the Swiss franc (CHF), the Canadian dollar (CAD), the Malaysian ringgit, the Russian ruble, the South African rand, the Thai baht, and the Kazakhstani tenge. Forwards and swaps are available for the CNY relative to thirteen of these currencies (except the Thai baht and the Kazakhstani tenge). Separately, there are nine G-7 currency pairs for which spots, forwards, and swaps can be traded without CNY involved: AUD/USD, EUR/JPY, EUR/USD, GBP/USD, USD/CAD, USD/CHF, USD/HKD, USD/JPY, and USD/SGD.

The trading hours for the spot markets are 9:30 a.m. to 11:30 p.m. Beijing time (corresponding to 9:30 p.m. to 11:30 a.m. New York time). The operating hours for trading in foreign currency pairs are 7:00 a.m. to 11:30 p.m. Beijing time.

The two exchange rates (CNY and CNH, relative to the dollar) became more closely linked after a series of developments during the last quarter of 2010 boosted RMB-denominated financial transactions. These included the approval granted to financial institutions and banks in Hong Kong to open RMB accounts and for Hong Kong banks to access the onshore interbank market, activation of a currency swap line between the PBC and the Hong Kong Monetary Authority (HKMA), and a flurry of RMB-denominated bond issuance activities. These measures have lowered transaction costs for eligible financial market participants seeking to access both markets.

For more on the integration of the CNY and CNH markets and the drivers of pricing differentials between the two, see Craig, Hua, Ng, and Yuen (2013) and Funke, Shu, Cheng, and Eraslan (2015).

THE INTERNATIONAL ROLES OF A CURRENCY

Chen, Peng, and Shu (2009) and Subramanian (2011) argue that the RMB is well on its way to becoming a major, if not dominant, reserve currency. Dobson and Masson (2009), Eichengreen (2011b), Frankel (2011), Kroeber (2011), Bowles and Wang (2013), Chinn (2015), and Yu (2015) offer more nuanced and skeptical views. Shu, He, and Cheng (2014) discuss the RMB's increasing influence in the Asia–Pacific region.

The IMF Articles of Agreement are available at https://www.imf.org/external/pubs/ft/aa/.

The commitment to currency convertibility for current account transactions is under Article VIII, "general obligations of members."

See Prasad (2014) for further discussion of these concepts.

CHAPTER 3. CAPITAL ACCOUNT OPENING

The epigraph is taken from Campbell (1991), page 161. The book is essentially a transcript of an extended interview with Joseph Campbell conducted by Bill Moyers.

For discussions of why capital account opening matters for the RMB's role in international finance, see Lardy and Douglass (2011) and Ito and Chinn (2014).

HOW OPEN IS CHINA'S CAPITAL ACCOUNT?
De Jure Financial Openness

See Chinn and Ito (2006) and updated versions of the data set posted at http://web.pdx.edu/~ito/Chinn-Ito_website.htm.

De Facto Financial Openness

Data on countries' international investment positions are from the IMF. See Ma and McCauley (2013) for a comparison of China's and India's financial openness. See Table B.3 in Appendix B for more detailed information on China's IIP over the years.

See Sam Hornblower, "Wal-Mart and China: A Joint Venture," *PBS Frontline*, November 23, 2004. For a description of the cases of Siemens and Kawasaki, see Spike Nowak, "On the Fast-Track: Technology Transfer in China," *China Briefing*, September 3, 2012. To learn more about the deals between Boeing and China, see Dominic Gates, "Boeing Near Deal to Open 737 Delivery Center in China," *Seattle Times*, September 18, 2015.

Another, earlier example of this approach of the Chinese government is that of Xinjiang Goldwind Science and Technology Company, which has become one of China's largest domestic wind-turbine manufacturers and a global wind powerhouse. It received investments as well as technology transfers from Bonus Energy of Denmark in 1989 and from Jacobs Energie of Germany in 1996. See Kenneth Jarrett and Amy Wendholt, "Transferring Technology to Transform China—Is It Worth It?" *China Business Review*, March 1, 2010. Also see Keith Bradsher and Tom Zeller, "China's Push Into Wind Worries U.S. Industry," *New York Times*, December 15, 2010, for more on Xinjiang Goldwind's push into the American market.

WHY LIBERALIZE THE CAPITAL ACCOUNT?

See Prasad, Rogoff, Wei, and Kose (2003) and Kose, Prasad, Rogoff, and Wei (2009) for analytical discussions and summaries of the views of skeptics of the benefits of capital account liberalization, a list that includes Jagdish Bhagwati, Dani Rodrik, and Joseph Stiglitz.

See Prasad (2009) for a more detailed discussion of how capital account opening could spur financial sector reforms in China, which in turn are important for more balanced and sustainable growth. Also see Prasad and Rajan (2008).

CONTROLLED CAPITAL ACCOUNT LIBERALIZATION

See Prasad and Wei (2007) for an overview of China's approach to capital account opening. Prasad and Rajan (2005) discuss the benefits of controlled capital account liberalization and suggest a scheme for controlled outflows that resembles the qualified domestic institutional investor scheme discussed later.

LIBERALIZING INFLOWS
Qualified Foreign Institutional Investor (QFII) Scheme

This section draws extensively on Sharma (2015).

For a transcript of the press conference from which the CSRC spokesperson's remarks are taken, see http://www.sipf.com.cn/en/lawsandregulations/linvestors/reguforqfii/10/6638.shtml.

The PBC statement of February 24, 2016, allowing QFIIs to invest in the interbank bond market without any quota restrictions is posted at

http://www.pbc.gov.cn/goutongjiaoliu/113456/113469/3021206/index.html   (in Chinese only). Also see Steve Johnson, "China Bond Market Shake-Up Seen to Attract Trillions of Dollars," *Financial Times*, March 2, 2016.

The steps taken in March and May 2016 are described in: "Reform QFII Foreign Exchange Administration to Further Open Up Domestic Capital Market," SAFE Press Release, March 14, 2016 (http://www.safe.gov.cn/wps/portal/english/News); "Consultation on China A-Shares Index Inclusion Roadmap," Morgan Stanley Capital International, April 2016. (https://www.msci.com/index-consultations); Kevin Yao, "China Allows Foreign Investors in Debt Market to Remit Funds Freely," *Reuters*, May 27, 2016.

Renminbi Qualified Foreign Institutional Investor (RQFII) Scheme

This section draws on the following official sources: PBC, "Implementation of the Measures for Pilot Domestic Securities Investment Made by RMB Qualified Foreign Institutional Investors." http://bit.ly/1RCfNk0; China Securities Regulatory Commission, "Measures for Pilot Domestic Securities Investment Made by RMB Qualified Foreign Institutional Investors of Fund Management Companies and Securities Companies." http://bit.ly/1TYo7tN; and SAFE, "Relevant Issues Concerning the Pilot Program on Domestic Securities Investments by Fund Management Companies and Securities Companies as RMB Qualified Foreign Institutional Investors." http://bit.ly/1ONOMcv.

RMB funds that can be remitted outward may be remitted in RMB or in foreign exchange purchased with RMB. Latest versions of the rules and regulations governing the QFII program can be found on the CSRC website at http://www.csrc.gov.cn/pub/csrc_en/OpeningUp/RelatedPolices/QFII/.

The RQFIIs with the top five quota allocations (amounting to a combined $20 billion in 2015) are all based in Hong Kong: CSOP Asset Management Limited; E-Fund Management (Hong Kong) Co., Limited; China Asset Management (Hong Kong) Limited; Harvest Global Investments Limited; and Haitong International Investments Limited.

LIBERALIZING OUTFLOWS

See "2014 Annual Report of the State Administration of Foreign Exchange." SAFE, Beijing, China.

Qualified Domestic Institutional Investor (QDII) Scheme

QDII regulations are taken from the websites of the PBC, the CSRC, and the SAFE.

Financial institutions must first apply for a QDII license from the relevant regulatory agencies (the Securities, Banking or Insurance Regulatory Commission) and then seek a quota allocation from the SAFE.

This subsection and the next draw on the following sources:

"IMFC Statement by PBC Governor Zhou Xiaochuan." https://www.imf.org/External/spring/2015/imfc/statement/eng/chn.pdf; The Report on Inter-nationalization of RMB." PBC, June 2015; The Plans on Promoting the Trials of Finance Opening and Innovation in Shanghai FTZ to Accelerate the Construction of Shanghai International Financial Center." Co-released by the PBC, the Ministry of Commerce, the China Banking Regulatory Commission (CBRC), the CSRC, the China Insurance Regulatory Commission (CIRC), the SAFE and the Government of Shanghai, October 2015.

Qualified Domestic Individual Investor Scheme

Also see "China May Let Individuals in Shanghai FTZ Invest Abroad in H1—Sources." *Reuters*, April 29, 2015. "Shanghai Trade Zone Aims for QDII2 Trial This Year—Official." *Reuters*, March 17, 2015.

See, for instance, Gabriel Wildau, "China to Allow Individuals Buy [sic] Overseas Financial Assets," *Financial Times*, May 29, 2015; and "China to Launch QDII2 Overseas Investment Scheme Soon in Six Cities." *Reuters*, October 26, 2015.

The delay in the launch of the QDII2 scheme and another program called the *Qualified Domestic Limited Partner scheme*, which was intended to allow large foreign asset managers operating in the Shanghai FTZ to sell overseas investment products directly to wealthy Chinese is reported in Don Weinland, "China Halts Overseas Investment Schemes," *Financial Times*, February 28, 2016.

LIBERALIZING TWO-WAY FLOWS
Islands of Integration: Free Trade Zones

The discussion in this subsection draws on material from China Briefing, an online resource provided by Dezan Shira & Associates. The relevant links and official documents from which the materials in this section are drawn are as follows: State Council Infographic, "Negative List on Foreign Investment in China's Free Trade Zones." http://english.gov.cn/policies/infographics/2015/04/21/content_281475093149079.htm. PBC, "Supporting Expanded Cross-Border Use of RMB in the China (Shanghai) Pilot Free Trade Zone." http://en.china-shftz.gov.cn/Government-affairs/Laws/Banking/265.shtml. State Administration of Foreign Exchange, "Issuing the Detailed Rules for the Implementation of Regulations on Foreign Exchange Management in the China (Shanghai) Pilot Free Trade Zone." http://en.china-shftz.gov.cn/Government-affairs/Laws/General/255.shtml. PBC, "Lifting the Upper Limit on Small-Amount Foreign Currency Deposit Rates in the China (Shanghai) Pilot Free Trade Zone. http://en.china-shftz.gov.cn/Government-affairs/Laws/Banking/264.shtml. China Banking Regulatory Commission, "Issues Concerning Banking Supervision in China (Shanghai) Free Trade Zone." http://en.china-shftz.gov.cn/Government-affairs/Laws/Banking/191.shtml. China Insurance Regulatory Commission, "Supporting the Construction of the China (Shanghai) Pilot Free Trade Zone." http://en.china-shftz.gov.cn/Government-affairs/Laws/Insurance/193.shtml.

A more detailed listing of the key features of the FTZs is as follows: (1) without seeking approval from the PBC, banking institutions in the zone are free to process cross-border RMB settlement under current accounts and under direct investment for entities; (2)

companies in the zone are allowed to borrow RMB offshore, although these funds cannot be used outside the FTZ and cannot be invested in securities or used for extending loans; (3) voluntary foreign exchange settlement by foreign-invested enterprises (FIEs) within the zone is permitted, allowing FIEs to convert foreign currency in their capital accounts into RMB at any time; (4) qualified foreign-invested banks are allowed to set up subsidiaries, branches, or special institutions, and to upgrade existing subbranches to branches; (5) qualified private investors can enter the banking sector in the FTZ and set up banks as well as finance leasing companies, consumer finance companies, and other finance institutions; and (6) the government has indicated its intention to support banking institutions in the FTZ to develop cross-border financing services.

The concept of a national security review was first introduced when the Chinese government released a draft for the new Foreign Investment Law. Such a review is conducted by the National Development and Reform Commission and the Ministry of Commerce, usually at the suggestion of the registration authority of the FTZ. The review considers the impact of the investment on six factors: (1) national security, including China's capacity to provide essential goods and services to that end; (2) the stability of the economy; (3) basic social order; (4) culture and social morality; (5) Internet security; and (6) sensitive technology for use in national defense.

A review is conducted when an investment is believed to touch on sensitive agricultural products, key natural and energy resources, strategic infrastructure, transport capabilities, important information technology and other technology, or investments near military facilities. Interestingly, such a review does not look merely at the equity a foreign party has in a Chinese company; it focuses in particular on the party's exercising "actual control" over a company. This appears to be a continuation of the government's recent scrutiny of FIEs. In the separate regulation that introduces a national security review, the term *actual control* is defined for the first time. It applies when one or more foreign investors, including parties affiliated with them, meet one of these criteria: holding more than 50 percent of a company's shares; having sufficient voting rights to exert significant control over the company's board of directors or shareholder's meetings; or, through other circumstances, being able to exert significant control over the company's operational decisions, staffing, finance, or technology.

During President Xi's visit to the U.S. in September 2015, China committed to limiting the scope of the national security review. However, the U.S. has continued to express concerns about how this process might impede foreign investment in the FTZs. See "Fact Sheet: U.S.–China Economic Relations." White House Office of the Press Secretary, September 25, 2015, https://www.whitehouse.gov/the-press-office/2015/09/25/fact-sheet-us-china-economic-relations. Also see the briefs by Tim Stratford and Yan Luo, "National Security Review Creates FDI Hurdle," *China Law & Practice* (Covington & Burling), July 13, 2015, https://www.cov.com/~/media/files/corporate/publications/2015/07/national_security_review_creates_fdi_hurdle.pdf; and Thomas Chou et al., "China's Draft Foreign Investment Law: A Paradigm Shift in Regulation of Foreign Investment," Morrison & Foerster LLP, February 12, 2015, http://www.mofo.com/~/media/Files/ClientAlert/2015/02/150212ChinasDraftForeignInvestment.pdf.

The Shanghai–Hong Kong Stock Connect

The quota balances are calculated at the end of each trading day on a net-buy basis: Aggregate Quota Balance = Aggregate Quota – Aggregate Buy Trades + Aggregate Sell Trades. The daily quota caps the daily net value of cross-border trades and is updated on a real-time basis. When the balance falls short of the daily quota, all buy orders on the next trading day are suspended while sell orders are still accepted. The control mechanism under the daily quota can be shown in the form of the following schematic:

	Call Auction	Continuous Auction
Balance ≤ Zero	New buy orders will be rejected until balance reaches positive level Sell orders will still be accepted	No further buy orders will be accepted for this trading day

Sources: Shanghai Stock Exchange and Hong Kong Exchanges.

Enforcement of the daily and annual quotas is managed through the structure of the settlement mechanisms. The Hong Kong Securities Clearing Corporation and the China Depository and Clearing Corporation in Mainland China are the clearing participants for each other and undertake the settlement obligations of their respective clearing participants' trades on a net basis. Importantly, settlement is undertaken on the day after a trade is executed. In addition, the stock exchanges on both sides keep themselves informed by tracking buying and selling transactions as well as daily balances. With these mechanisms in place, regulators have real-time information on the volume of trades in both directions and the quota balances.

Mutual Fund Connect

Details about the Mutual Fund Connect scheme are taken from the CSRC website. http://www.csrc.gov.cn.

THE PRICE OF VIRTUE

Data on IIP and investment income flows are from the SAFE, the U.S. Bureau of Economic Analysis, and the IMF.

China's net income flow was slightly positive in 2007 and 2008 despite the return differential between external assets and liabilities. This is because the stock of foreign assets was larger than the stock of foreign liabilities.

The U.S. IIP turned negative in 1985, although some authors have argued that, taking into account some conceptual and technical issues with the official data, the U.S. shifted to a net foreign liability position only at the end of 1988. See, for instance, Meyer (1989).

SHIFTING STRUCTURE OF CAPITAL OUTFLOWS

Balance-of-payments data are from the IMF and the SAFE.

A TROJAN HORSE

I used the metaphor of a Trojan horse to describe the PBC's strategy earlier in an op-ed article "China's Sensible Yuan Policy," *The Wall Street Journal*, February 9, 2012. It had been used independently by Bob Davis in "Were China's Leaders Conned?" *The Wall Street Journal*, June 2, 2011.

The quotes are from "Transcript of Governor Zhou Xiaochuan's Exclusive Interview with Caixin Weekly." PBC, February 14, 2016, http://www.pbc.gov.cn/english/130721/3017134/index.html.

THE END GAME

See Yam (2011).

The full text of the thirteenth Five-Year Plan is available at http://news.xinhuanet.com/fortune/2015-11/03/c_1117027676.htm.

See Mark Magnier, "China Lowers Expectations for Growth—President Xi Jinping sets 6.5% Growth as New Floor for Economy," *The Wall Street Journal*, November 3, 2015.

The statement by Li Keqiang is posted at http://english.gov.cn/premier/news/2015/03/15/content_281475071837425.htm.

The statement by Xi Jinping is posted at

http://www.wsj.com/articles/full-transcript-interview-with-chinese-president-xi-jinping-1442894700.

The IMF Committee statement by PBC Governor Zhou Xiaochuan is available at https://www.imf.org/External/spring/2015/imfc/statement/eng/chn.pdf.

CHAPTER 4. THE EXCHANGE RATE REGIME

The epigraph was taken from Milne (1991), Chapter VII, "In Which Tigger is Unbounced."

The quote by Donald Trump is from Charles Riley, "Donald Trump Slams Beijing for Crashing the Yuan," *CNN Money*, August 12, 2015. The full statement by Lindsey Graham can be found in "Senior U.S. Lawmakers Condemn 'Provocative' China Currency Devaluation." *Reuters*, August 11, 2015. Charles Grassley's statement is posted on his website at http://www.grassley.senate.gov/news/news-releases/grassley-china's-latest-currency-devaluation.

Charles Schumer's statement is reported in Keith Bradsher, "China's Currency Move Clouds Its Policy Goals," *New York Times*, August 11, 2015. Bob Casey's statement is posted at: https://www.casey.senate.gov/newsroom/releases/casey-statement-on-chinas-move-to-devalue-currency.

STABILITY AS A VIRTUE

Some authors take a narrower view, limiting the group of Asian tigers to four of the richer economies in that group: Hong Kong, Singapore, South Korea, and Taiwan.

See Corsetti, Pesenti, and Roubini (1999) for an overview of the determinants and dynamics of the Asian financial crisis.

The quote by Dai Xianglong can be found in "Statement by Mr. Dai Xianglong Governor of the People's Bank of China at the 1998 Annual Meeting of the International Monetary Fund and the World Bank," IMF, October 6, 1998.

The statement by China's Ministry of Foreign Affairs is from "Pro-Active Policies by China in Response to Asian Financial Crisis," Ministry of Foreign Affairs of the People's Republic of China.

The IMF statement appears in its 1998 annual report, p. 13. U.S. Treasury Secretary Robert Rubin's quote appears in Mark Landler, "Clinton in China: The Economy; China Tells U.S. It Won't Devalue Currency," *New York Times*, June 27, 1998. Tony Blair's statement is taken from http://www.people.com.cn/item/ldhd/zhurongj/1998/hui-jian/hj0057.html.

STABILITY BECOMES A VICE

Data on China's GDP growth, foreign exchange reserves, and trade are from the IMF and China's National Bureau of Statistics.

Frankel (2005), Prasad and Rajan (2006), and Obstfeld (2007) discuss the policy complications that arise from tight exchange rate management.

THE TRAJECTORY OF A CURRENCY (OSTENSIBLY) BREAKING FREE

For an overview of China's exchange rate policy before 2009, see Goldstein and Lardy (2009).

For the report on PBC Governor Zhou's speech, see "Central Bank Specifies Currency Basket as Reference of Renminbi Exchange Rate." *People's Daily*, August 11, 2005.

The PBC's statement regarding the May 2008 move is available (in Chinese) at http://www.pbc.gov.cn/bangongting/135485/135495/135499/809002/index.html.

The IMF's response is taken from http://www.imf.org/external/np/speeches/2007/053107.htm. The U.S. Treasury's response is at http://www.chinadaily.com.cn/china/2007-05/19/content_876149.htm. The foreign exchange trader's quote is from Andrew Batson, James Areddy, and Michael Phillips, "Beijing May Calm Stocks with Steps, Not Spur Yuan," *The Wall Street Journal*, May 19, 2007.

The RMB–dollar exchange rate was 8.2 in June 2005 and 6.84 in August 2008, implying an appreciation of 17 percent.

The June 2010 PBC announcement is available (in Chinese) at http://www.pbc.gov.cn/goutongjiaoliu/113456/113469/2845821/index.html.

The IMF comment is in "Statement by IMF Managing Director Dominique Strauss-Kahn on China's Exchange Rate Regime." IMF press release no. 10/251. June 19, 2010. President Obama's comment on the PBC's plan to increase the RMB's flexibility is taken from "Obama Welcomes China's Move Towards Flexible Yuan." *BBC*, June 20, 2010. The statement by U.S. Treasury Secretary Timothy Geithner is from "U.S.' Geithner Eyes Implementation of Yuan Move." *Reuters*, June 19, 2010.

FLEXIBILITY WELCOME, BUT ONLY ONE WAY

The statement by IMF Managing Director Christine Lagarde can be found in "Transcript of a Press Conference by International Monetary Fund Managing Director Christine Lagarde and First Deputy Managing Director David Lipton." IMF, April 19, 2012. The subsequent statement by the U.S. Treasury Department is from "China Widening Yuan Band Shows Confidence in Economy." *Bloomberg*, April 15, 2012.

The March 2014 PBC announcement is available (in Chinese) at http://www.pbc.gov.cn/zhengwugongkai/index.html.

The IMF endorsement is at http://www.imf.org/external/np/speeches/2014/032414.htm. The U.S. Treasury's endorsement is reported in Fion Li, "China Doubles Yuan Trading Band Giving Market Greater Role," *Bloomberg*, March 16, 2014.

For the U.S. Treasury's account of subsequent criticism of China's exchange rate policies, see "Report to Congress on International Economic and Exchange Rate Policies," U.S. Department of the Treasury Office of International Affairs, April 15, 2014.

From June 2005 to June 2014, the RMB's NEER appreciated by 29 percent whereas the REER appreciated by 36 percent.

THE TIDE BEGINS TO TURN

For the IMF's statement about the RMB no longer being undervalued and the U.S. Treasury's response, see Shawn Donnan and Tom Mitchell, "China Currency is 'No Longer Undervalued', says IMF," *Financial Times*, May 26, 2015.

The official estimate of valuation effects on foreign exchange reserves during 2015 appears in "SAFE Press Spokesperson Answers Press Questions on Balance of Payments for 2015," SAFE Press Release, March 14, 2016 (http://www.safe.gov.cn/wps/portal/english/News).

GOOD INTENTIONS BACKFIRE

The official PBC statement about the August 11, 2015, change in currency policy reads as follows:

> For the purpose of enhancing the market-orientation and benchmark status of central parity, the PBC has decided to improve quotation of the central parity of RMB against U.S. dollar. Effective from 11 August 2015, the quotes of central parity that market makers report to the CFETS daily before market opens should refer to the closing rate of the inter-bank foreign exchange market on the previous day, in conjunction with demand and supply condition in the foreign exchange market and exchange rate movement of the major currencies.

The full statement is posted at

http://www.pbc.gov.cn/english/130721/2941603/index.html.

"PBC Q&A." August 11, 2015,

http://www.pbc.gov.cn/english/130721/2941606/index.html.

"PBC Q&A." August 12, 2015,

http://www.pbc.gov.cn/english/130721/2941618/index.html.

The transcript of the press conference featuring Zhang Xiaohui and Yi Gang is available (in Chinese) at http://www.pbc.gov.cn/rmyh/fangtan/tu.htm. Li Keqiang's statement is reported (in Chinese) at http://news.xinhuanet.com/fortune/2015-09/09/c_128212950.htm. Ma Jun's comment is reported in "Economist: Yuan Weakening is Not Devaluation." *Xinhua*, August 11, 2015.

The statement made by the U.S. Treasury can be found in "China Devalues Yuan Currency to Three-Year Low." *BBC*, August 11, 2015.

President Obama's statement is posted at

https://www.whitehouse.gov/the-press-office/2015/09/25/remarks-president-obama-and-president-xi-peoples-republic-china-joint.

President Xi's speech in September is posted (in Chinese) at

http://www.china.com.cn/cppcc/2015-09/23/content_36662360_2.htm.

President Xi's interview with *The Wall Street Journal* is available at

http://www.wsj.com/articles/full-transcript-interview-with-chinese-president-xi-jinping-1442894700.

The State Council statement of October 18, 2015, is posted (in Chinese) at http://www.gov.cn/zhengce/2015-10/18/content_2948693.htm.

Translations from the Chinese of relevant documents, or portions of documents, in this section were provided by Yishuo Yang, Cornell University.

PLUS ÇA CHANGE ... THE BASKET REEMERGES

PBC notice by Guest Commentator of CFETS, "The Launch of RMB Index Helps to Guide Public View of RMB Exchange Rate," PBC, December 11, 2015,

http://www.pbc.gov.cn/english/130721/2988680/index.html.

The dollar's weights are as follows: 41.7 percent in the SDR basket, 26.4 percent in the CFETS index, and 17.8 percent in the BIS broad basket. In December 2015, the South African rand was not in the CFETS basket. Spot trading between the RMB and the rand commenced only in June 2016.

PBC article by Guest Commentator of CFETS, "RMB Exchange Rate Has a Solid Foundation to Remain Stable Against a Basket of Currencies," PBC, December 14, 2015, http://www.chinamoney.com.cn/fe/Info/15875909#.

The PBC Q&A about the use of the 4:30 p.m. RMB–dollar exchange rate as the closing price on the interbank market is based on a document titled "PBC Official Answers Press Questions on Extending Foreign Trading Time and Introducing Qualified Foreign Players," which was posted on the SAFE website with a date of December 30, 2015. The full statement reads as follows:

> After the extension [of trading hours], the market liquidity may still chiefly come from day trading in a fairly long time to come and will reflect to the largest extent the real supply–demand situation in China's foreign exchange market. But the liquidity in night trading will be poor and may heighten volatility in the market, making it easy for the exchange rate to be misstated and even manipulated. If the exchange rate at 23:30 is regarded as the closing price, market makers may refer to this price to quote the central parity rate for the second day, thereby weakening the representativeness of the central parity rate as a benchmark. But if the market makers quote the central parity rate for the second day without referring to the closing price due to its lack of representativeness, the authoritativeness of the central parity rate quotation mechanism will be impacted, leading to a structural deviation of the closing price from the second-day central parity rate. As a result, the strike price at 16:30 will continue to be the closing price of the interbank foreign exchange market.

See "The Central Parity of RMB Against U.S. Dollar Became More Market-Based in 2015." CFETS, January 7, 2016,

http://www.chinamoney.com.cn/fe/Info/16105127#.

NEITHER GOD NOR MAGICIAN

The quotes in this and the next section are from "Transcript of Governor Zhou Xiaochuan's Exclusive Interview with Caixin Weekly." PBC, February 14, 2016,

http://www.pbc.gov.cn/english/130721/3017134/index.html.

CHAPTER 5. THE RMB GOES GLOBAL

The epigraph is taken from page 72 of the English translation (by John E. Woods) of *Justiz*, a novel written in German by the Swiss author Friedrich Dürrenmatt and originally published in 1985.

The sanctions are summarized in Edward Christie, "Sanctions after Crimea: Have They Worked?" *Nato Review*, 2015. For the EU statement, see "Statement by President

Barroso and President Van Rompuy in the Name of the European Union on the Agreed Additional Restrictive Measures Against Russia." European Commission, July 29, 2014.

Putin's remarks can be found in "Transcript of Media Forum of Independent Local and Regional Media." April 24, 2014, http://en.kremlin.ru/events/president/news/20858.

Medvedev's remarks are reported in "Russia Set for National Payment System But Visa, MasterCard Will Stay." *Tass Russian News Agency*, May 14, 2014, http://tass.ru/en/opinions/763278.

Nabiullina's remarks are in "[President Putin's] Meeting with Governor of the Central Bank Elvira Nabiullina." The Kremlin, June 30, 2014, http://en.kremlin.ru/events/president/news/46091.

The National Payment System problem is noted in "Russia's State-Run Replacement for Visa and MasterCard Crashes." *The Moscow Times*, April 29, 2015.

The 2015 PBC Report on Internationalisation of the RMB is available (only in Chinese) at http://upload.xh08.cn/2015/0611/1434018340443.pdf. Tao Wang, Cornell University, provided translations of relevant portions of this document from Chinese to English.

HONG KONG AS A STARTER PROJECT

See Prasad and Ye (2012) for more details.

TRADE SETTLEMENT

The main data source is CEIC. Some of the data in this paragraph and the next one are taken from the HKMA's publication, "Hong Kong: The Global Offshore Renminbi Business Hub." January 2016.

DIM SUM AND PANDA BONDS

Elaine Moore and Josh Noble, "UK Takes First Orders for Debut Renminbi Bond." *Financial Times*, October 14, 2014. Jonathan Wheatley, "Russia to Issue Renminbi-Denominated Debt." *Financial Times*, December 7, 2015. Elaine Moore and Gabriel Wildau, "China Completes First London Debt Sale." *Financial Times*, October 20, 2015. Gabriel Wildau, "China Finance Ministry to Sell Offshore Renminbi Bonds in London," *Financial Times*, May 24, 2016.

For more on panda bonds, see Moonyoung Tae, Kyungji Cho, and Helen Sun, "South Korea Sells First Sovereign Bonds as China Opens Up." *Bloomberg*, December 15, 2015.

THE RMB'S ROLE AS A PAYMENT CURRENCY

Information about SWIFT is from its website (https://www.swift.com/) and various documents posted there, in particular the monthly RMB Tracker. Members of the SWIFT Institute generously shared their time and expertise to explain certain features of the data. See Society for Worldwide Interbank Financial Telecommunication (2011, 2012) for an analysis of the implications of RMB internationalization for the global financial industry.

LIMITED USE IN INTERNATIONAL FINANCIAL TRANSACTIONS

Data on foreign exchange market turnover, derivatives markets, and currency denomination of international debt securities are taken from the Bank for International Settlements. See Prasad and Ye (2012) for further discussion of the concepts and data.

Tables B.4 through B.6 in Appendix B display detailed information on some of the data cited in this section.

OFFSHORE CLEARING CENTERS

Information on offshore clearing centers is from the PBC (see Table B.7 in Appendix B for a listing). For more on China's strategy toward development of offshore financial centers, see Subacchi and Huang (2012, 2013). The joint statement from the June 2016 U.S.-China Strategic and Economic Dialogue is available at www.treasury.gov/press-center.

SETTLING ACCOUNTS DIRECTLY

Andrew Kramer, "Sidestepping the U.S. Dollar, a Russian Exchange Will Swap Rubles and Renminbi." *The New York Times*, December 12, 2015.

"Enhanced Cooperation for Financial Markets Development between China and Japan." PBC, December 25, 2011. Kosuke Takahashi, "Japan, China Bypass U.S. in Currency Trade." *Asia Times*, June 2, 2012.

Data on China–Japan trade in goods and services are from the Japan External Trade Organization. IMF data from the Coordinated Portfolio Investment and Coordinated Direct Investment Surveys indicate that China's total FDI and portfolio investment in Japan amounted to $20 billion in 2014 (up from $11 billion in 2013). Japan's corresponding investment in China amounted to $199 billion in 2014 (down from $265 billion in 2013, mainly because of a $70 billion decline in portfolio investment). The stock of Japanese FDI in China has remained stable at around $100 billion.

"People's Bank of China Welcomes Direct Trading between RMB and Australian Dollar Launched by the China Foreign Exchange Trade System." PBC, April 9, 2013. Lu Jianxin and Gabriel Wildau, "China and Australia to Launch Direct Currency Trading—Source." *Reuters*, April 3, 2013.

Joonhee Yu and Yena Park, "South Korea Launches Yuan/Won Trading." *Reuters*, December 1, 2014. "New Progress in China–Korea Financial Cooperation," PBC, October 30, 2015. Grace Zhu, "China, South Korea in Currency Pact." *The Wall Street Journal*, October 31, 2015.

See "Direct Trading between Renminbi and Swiss Franc Launched." Swiss National Bank press release, November 10, 2015. Also, see Fion Li, "China to Allow Direct Conversion between Yuan and Swiss Franc." *Bloomberg*, November 9, 2015.

CROSS-BORDER INTERNATIONAL PAYMENT SYSTEM

More information about the Cross-Border International Payment System is available from the PBC website, http://www.pbc.gov.cn/english/130721/2963649/index.html.

Premier Li Keqiang's remarks were made in speech at a World Economic Forum event in Dalian, China, on September 11, 2015, http://www.weforum.org/agenda/2015/09/chinese-premier-li-keqiangs-speech-at-amnc15/.

The remarks by Ma Jun and lawyer Gerard Comizio are reported in Gabriel Wildau, "China Launch of Renminbi Payments System Reflects SWIFT Spying Concerns." *Financial Times*, October 8, 2015.

Information about UnionPay is taken from its website: http://en.unionpay.com.

CHAPTER 6. RESERVE CURRENCY

The epigraph is from the story "There are More Things" in *Collected Fictions* by Jorge Luis Borges, translated by Andrew Hurley, NY: Penguin Press, 1998.

Premier Li Keqiang also said: "China wishes to join the SDR, not just for making the RMB more internationalized, but also for fulfilling China's due international responsibilities as a big developing country." His quotes are from a transcript of his meeting with business leaders at Summer Davos (http://english.cri.cn/12394/2015/09/10/2982s895402.htm).

"China Pledges Targeted Reform to Help RMB Included in SDR." *Xinhua*, March 23, 2015, http://news.xinhuanet.com/english/2015-03/23/c_134090847.htm.

See Ben Blanchard, "China's Premier Asks IMF to Include Yuan in SDR Basket." *Reuters*, October 23, 2015.

Lagarde's quote is taken from "IMF Managing Director Meets Senior Chinese Officials, Speaks at 2015 China Development Forum." IMF press release no. 15/131. March 23, 2015. For the IMF's statement, see "IMF's Executive Board Completes Review of SDR Basket, Includes Chinese Renminbi." IMF press release no. 15/540. November 30, 2015.

THE BIG BOYS CLUB

Figures on U.S. currency in circulation are from the Federal Reserve Board website (https://www.federalreserve.gov/paymentsystems/coin_data.htm). Estimates of the share of U.S. banknotes held outsides the U.S. are based on Goldberg (2010), Judson (2012), and Williams (2012). Figures on euro banknotes and coins in circulation, both in total and outside the euro zone, are from the European Central Bank website (https://www.ecb.europa.eu/stats/money/euro/circulation/html/index.en.html). At the end of 2015, euro banknotes in circulation amounted to €1,083.4 billion and coins in circulation amounted to €26 billion. The euro–U.S. dollar exchange rate at the end of 2015, 1.09, was used to convert these figures into dollar amounts.

For a useful description of what the exorbitant privilege has meant for the dollar and the international monetary system, see Eichengreen (2011a).

NOT ALL ROSES

The statement by Otmar Emminger was reported in *Frankfurter Allemaigne Zeitung*, September 27, 1979. For subsequent discussion of Germany, and for Tietmeyer's statement, see *Germany: A Country Study*, edited by Eric Solsten, Library of Congress Federal Research Division, 1995.

McKinnon and Schnabl (2014) discuss the potential policy complications related to the RMB's rise as an international currency.

The Triffin Dilemma

See Prasad and Ye (2012) and Prasad (2014) for more details on the current account balances of reserve currency economies and the analytical arguments made in this section. Lago, Duttagupta, and Goyal (2009) argue that the Triffin dilemma does not necessarily apply in the context of large gross capital flows across countries.

WHAT DOES IT TAKE?

Angeloni et al. (2011) note that, in addition to strong financial markets, a reserve currency should be backed up by (1) the reliability of rules and institutions, (2) the quality and predictability of fiscal and monetary policies, (3) the ability of policymakers to respond to unexpected shocks, and (4) political cohesion. Some authors also argue that network externalities are important because they generate economies of scale and scope. See, for instance, Chinn and Frankel (2007). There is related empirical evidence on strong persistence effects in international investment patterns. See "The International Role of the Euro." Frankfurt, Germany: European Central Bank, Appendix C, July 2013. Also see Li and Liu (2008) and McCauley and Chan (2014) for alternative perspectives.

Economic Size

See Table B.2 in Appendix B for details on trade shares. The trade openness ratio is based on data from the IMF and the SAFE.

See Errico and Massara (2011). In the data set used in this study, the U.S. ranks first in size and nineteenth in terms of interconnectedness, giving it the rank of sixth in systemic trade importance. The Netherlands has the highest rank in terms of interconnectedness; it is a small but very open economy with extensive trade linkages. The systemic trade importance ranks of some other countries are as follows: Germany, second; Korea, seventh; Japan, ninth; India, fourteenth; Russia, nineteenth; and Brazil, twentieth.

Macroeconomic Policies

Statements about public deficits and debt are based on "People's Republic of China: Staff Report for the 2015 Article IV Consultation." IMF, July 2015.

See Prasad and Ye (2012) for the calculations related to inflation.

Financial Market Development

On the importance of home country financial market development for attaining reserve currency status, see Tavlas (1991), Chinn and Frankel (2007), and Forbes (2009).

See Prasad and Ye (2012) for additional cross-country comparisons.

With government approval, Chinese companies can also list on the Hong Kong exchange, where their share prices are quoted in Hong Kong dollars. These instruments are called *H-shares*, as noted earlier.

The number of listed companies on the Shanghai and Shenzhen exchanges—1,098 and 1,770, respectively—is taken from their websites as of May 11, 2016 (http://english.sse.com.cn/ , http://www.szse.cn/main/en/). The companies listed on the New York Stock Exchange and NASDAQ can be found at http://www.nasdaq.com/screening/company-list.aspx. The reported numbers are based on data as of March 15, 2016.

See Eswar S. Prasad, "China's Fitful Economic Reforms." *The International New York Times*, December 2, 2015.

See Table B.8 in Appendix B for details on bond market size and turnover in different countries. Data on the size of China's and Japan's fixed-income markets are from Asian Bonds

Online (https://asianbondsonline.adb.org/). Turnover data are from the same source; the reported turnover numbers are averages for the most recent four quarters for which data are available (ending in September 2015). Data for the U.S. are from the Securities Industry and Financial Markets Association. Turnover statistics for U.S. bond markets are constructed using data on average daily trading volumes, scaled up to the annual level. For more details on these data and international comparisons, see Prasad (2016).

SCORECARD

For other assessments of the RMB's ascendancy, see the essays in the book edited by Eichengreen and Kawai (2015). Eichengreen and Kawai (2014) provide a useful summary and overview. Also see Huang, Wang, and Fan (2014).

WINNING A MEDAL BEFORE REACHING THE FINISH LINE

Details about country holdings of RMB in reserve portfolios are as follows: Banco Central de Chile, *Monetary Policy Report*, September 2015. "Nigeria Approves Inclusion of Chinese Renminbi in External Reserves." Central Bank of Nigeria press release. September 5, 2011. Denis McMahon, "Malaysia Looks to Invest in China," *The Wall Street Journal*, June 22, 2009. Kevin Brown, Robert Cookson, and Geoff Dyer, "Malaysian Bond Boost for Renminbi." *Financial Times*, September 19, 2010.

The OeNB press release is "People's Bank of China and Oesterreichische Nationalbank Sign Important Agreement Today." Oesterreichische Nationalbank, November 10, 2011.

The SNB official's statement is in Fritz Zurbrugg, "The SNB's Investment Policy: Some Topical Issues." November 20, 2014.

The IMF estimate of the share of global foreign exchange reserves held in RMB is from Table 4 in "Review of the Method of the Valuation of the SDR: Initial Considerations." IMF, August 2015. This section draws heavily on the text in that report.

The IMF statement about identifying the RMB separately in the Composition of Official Foreign Exchange Reserves (COFER) reports is "Chinese Renminbi to be Identified in the IMF's Currency Composition of Foreign Exchange Reserves." IMF press release no. 16/90, March 4, 2016. The press release begins with the following: "The International Monetary Fund (IMF) will separately identify the renminbi (RMB) in its official foreign exchange reserves database starting October 1, 2016. The change will be reflected in the survey for the fourth quarter of 2016 that will be published at the end of March 2017."

SWAP LINES

Details about the bilateral swap arrangements between foreign central banks and the PBC are from press releases issued by the PBC and relevant foreign central banks. Table B.9 in Appendix B contains a full list of these arrangements, including amounts, as of June 2016.

The extent to which these swap lines have been drawn upon appears to be limited. The HKMA activated its bilateral swap line with the PBC in October 2010, more than a year and a half after the swap line was set up. At the end of 2010, the amount of bilateral swaps outstanding for the HKMA was 20 billion yuan, or about $3 billion (HKMA Annual Report, 2010). The PBC mentions in its 2010 Annual Report that "at end-2010, overall volume of currency swap agreements reached 803.5 billion yuan. The PBC also conducted 30 billion yuan of local currency swap operations at the request of a number of monetary authorities." This suggests that RMB 10 billion, about $1.5 billion, was drawn outside of Hong Kong.

The PBC's 2014 Report on RMB Internationalization claims that the substantive use of the swap arrangements has increased significantly. The report seems to indicate that 38 billion yuan (about $6 billion) were actually drawn by other central banks during 2014, with the cumulative amount used by the end of 2014 adding up to 80.7 billion yuan (about $12.6 billion). There is also an intriguing statement in this report to the effect that the PBC itself conducted swap transactions, with its use of other currencies amounting to 1.6 billion yuan (about $250 million).

THE IMF ELEVATES THE RMB

Technically, the SDR basket consists of the major currencies that (1) are issued by IMF members (or monetary unions that include IMF members) that are the largest exporters and (2) have been determined by the IMF to be "freely usable." The latter condition was added as a formal criterion only in 2000 and is clearly open to interpretation, as is the number of countries with currencies in the SDR basket. The IMF's operational definition of a freely usable currency requires that it be (1) widely used to make payments for international transactions and (2) widely traded in the principal exchange markets. That is, a freely usable currency is one that is liquid, convertible, and used for the settlement of international transactions. The objective of the freely usable currency concept in the context of IMF financing is to ensure that a member purchasing another member's currency under an IMF arrangement will be able to use it, directly or indirectly, to meet its balance of payments needs.

How the RMB Staked Its Claim on SDR Inclusion

The paper referred to here is by Zhou (2009).

This is based on a stock of about 204 billion SDRs converted to U.S. dollars at the March 1, 2016, exchange rate of 0.72 SDRs per dollar. Foreign exchange reserve stocks data are from the IMF.

"IMF Executive Board Completes the 2010 Review of SDR Valuation." IMF public information notice 10/149.

The documents summarizing the IMF's official positions are as follows: "IMF Executive Board Completes the 2010 Review of SDR Valuation." IMF public information notice 10/149; and "IMF Executive Board Discusses Criteria for Broadening the SDR Currency Basket." IMF public information notice 11/137. For more details on the underlying analysis, see "Criteria for Broadening the SDR Currency Basket." IMF, September 2011.

See "China FX Head Proposes Adding BRICS Currencies to SDR." *Reuters*. May 5, 2011.

For PBC Governor Zhou's statement, see "Statement by the Honorable Zhou Xiaochuan to the Thirty-First Meeting of the International Monetary and Financial Committee." IMF, April 18, 2015, http://www.imf.org/External/spring/2015/imfc/statement/eng/chn.pdf.

See "Review of the Method of the Valuation of the SDR: Initial Considerations." IMF, August 2015. This section draws heavily on the text in that report.

The report summarized the requirements for the RMB's inclusion in the SDR basket as follows:

> Availability of representative market-based exchange and interest rates is essential for the proper functioning of the SDR basket and the Fund's financial operations, and the ability to hedge SDR-denominated positions is important to many Fund members and other SDR users. Restrictions

on access to onshore markets pose difficulties in these areas, although some potential mitigating measures have been identified and the Chinese authorities have begun to implement such measures.

Approval of the decision to delay implementation of the new SDR basket until October 2016 is in "IMF Executive Board Approves Extension of Current SDR Currency Basket Until September 30, 2016," IMF press release no. 15/384, August 19, 2015.

A Step in the Right Direction Turns into a Stumble

For a discussion of the discrepancy between the CNH and CNY exchange rates and the implications of that discrepancy for the IMF's SDR decision, see: Lingling Wei, "China's Two-Yuan Dilemma." *The Wall Street Journal*, August 31, 2015.

See "Statement by the Honorable Yi Gang to the Thirty-Second Meeting of the International Monetary and Financial Committee." October 9, 2015, https://www.imf.org/External/AM/2015/imfc/statement/eng/chn.pdf.

President Xi Jinping's statement is excerpted from "China's Yuan to Be Included in IMF's SDR Basket of Currencies." *MercoPress*, November 23, 2015.

Lagarde's statement is in IMF press release no. 15/513. November 13, 2015.

"Readout from a Treasury Spokesperson of Secretary Lew's Meeting with Chinese Vice Premier Wang Yang and Finance Minister Lou Jiwei at the G-20 Leaders Summit in Antalya." U.S. Department of the Treasury, November 15, 2015.

Lagarde's statement is in IMF press release no. 15/540. November 30, 2015.

Shifting Weights

The previous formula essentially involved summing up the country's exports and the stock of global foreign exchange reserves held in assets denominated in its currency. The weights under the new formula are as follows: 41.7 percent for the U.S. dollar, 30.9 percent for the euro, 10.9 percent for the RMB, 8.3 percent for the Japanese yen, and 8.1 percent for the pound sterling. The U.S. dollar's weight remains almost the same even after the inclusion of the RMB in the SDR basket, whereas the weight of the euro has fallen by 7 percentage points. The weights of the four currencies in the previous SDR basket were as follows: 41.9 percent for the U.S. dollar, 37.4 percent for the euro, 9.4 for the Japanese yen, and 11.3 percent for the pound sterling. See "Review of the Method of Valuation of the SDR." IMF policy paper. November 2015.

Not an Immediate Game-Changer

The statement from the IMF is taken from a Q&A about its SDR decision, posted at http://www.imf.org/external/np/exr/faq/sdrfaq.htm.

CHAPTER 7. THE MIRAGE OF SAFETY

The epigraph is taken from the Alix G. Mautner Memorial Lectures delivered by Richard Feynman (1985, p. 10).

The values of the S&P 500 on January 3, 2005, and April 29, 2016, were 1,202 and 2,065, respectively—an increase of 72 percent. The values of the Shanghai composite index on those dates were 1,267 and 2,938—an increase of 132 percent. The dollar–RMB exchange rates (dollars per RMB) on those two days were 0.121 and 0.155, respectively, implying a 28 percent appreciation of the RMB. This is the relevant exchange rate because, at the end of the period, the international investor would convert RMB back into dollars and cares about how many dollars she would have after this conversion. Note that, if the exchange rate were stated in terms of RMB per dollars, the RMB's appreciation during this period would amount to 22 percent (8.278 to 6.459).

Data on the currency composition of foreign exchange reserves are taken from the IMF's COFER, based on data through the end of 2015. The COFER database indicates that, relative to total official foreign exchange holdings of $10.9 trillion, only $6.8 trillion (62 percent) can be allocated to holdings of specific currencies. The remainder, referred to as *unallocated reserves*, constitutes reserves with currency composition not reported to the IMF even on a confidential basis. China started providing information on the currency composition of a portion of its reserves in 2015 and probably still accounts for a large fraction of the "unallocated" reserves in COFER.

See Wolf (2014) for an insightful description of the financial crisis and its aftermath. Bernanke (2015) and El-Erian (2016) discuss the role of central banks during the crisis and the postcrisis period.

THE CONVOLUTED QUEST FOR SAFETY

In the U.S., gross federal public debt includes intragovernmental holdings, including U.S. Treasuries held by the Social Security trust funds (which are required to hold their surpluses in Treasuries). Net debt excludes intragovernmental holdings but does include the Federal Reserve's holdings of government debt. Technically, the Federal Reserve is not part of the U.S. government. Rather, it is described as "an independent entity within the government, having both public purposes and private aspects." See http://www.factcheck.org/2008/03/federal-reserve-bank-ownership/.

Data on U.S. federal government debt is from the U.S. Treasury. A breakdown of this debt into separate categories is provided in the U.S. Treasury Bulletin, which is available at https://www.fiscal.treasury.gov/fsreports/rpt/treasBulletin/treasBulletin_home.htm. Data on foreign holdings of Treasury securities are from the U.S. Treasury's table on "Major Foreign Holders of Treasury Securities." The reported data were taken in March 2016 from http://ticdata.treasury.gov/Publish/mfh.txt. A useful public source for historical data on U.S. debt is https://research.stlouisfed.org/fred2/series/FDHBPIN.

See Prasad (2014) for a more detailed description of the episodes described in this section.

THE ATTRIBUTES OF A SAFE HAVEN

The seminal work of Douglass North (1982) emphasized the growth-enhancing role of institutions that support private contracting arrangements but also limit the possibility of expropriation by the government or other politically powerful groups.

It has become an article of faith among academic economists that economic, legal, and political institutions, along with social norms, are important determinants of a country's long-term economic success. See, for instance, Acemoglu and Robinson (2012).

Doidge, Karolyi, and Stulz (2007, 2009) provide evidence in support of the bonding hypothesis.

POLITICAL REFORMS

See Mao Zedong, "On the People's Democratic Dictatorship." June 30, 1949. The full text of a translated version can be found at https://www.marxists.org/reference/archive/mao/selected-works/volume-4/mswv4_65.htm.

For Xi's quotes, see Clifford Coonan, "Democracy Not for China, Says Xi Jinping." *Irish Times*, April 2, 2014.

A translation of Document No. 9 is available at http://www.chinafile.com/document-9-chinafile-translation, where *Mingjing Magazine* is cited as the source for the full text of the document. For more on this document, see "Tilting Backwards." *The Economist*, June 24, 2013. See also Chris Buckley, "China Takes Aim at Western Ideas." *The New York Times*, August 19, 2013. Although summaries of the document are reported to have been posted even on government wesbites, a Chinese journalist was subsequently arrested for disclosing the full document. See Chris Buckley, "Chinese Journalist Sentenced to 7 Years on Charges of Leaking State Secrets." *The New York Times*, April 16, 2015.

For a discussion of Document No. 30, see Chris Buckley and Andrew Jacobs, "Maoists in China, Given New Life, Attack Dissent." *The New York Times*, January 4, 2015.

THE PARTY AND THE CONSTITUTION

Quotes from Xi Jinping's speech can be found in "Xi Jinping Pledges to Implement Rule of Law." *China Daily*, December 5, 2012.

The *People's Daily* quotes are reported in Chris Buckley, "China Takes Aim at Western Ideas." *The New York Times*, August 19, 2013.

See Michael Forsythe, "Magna Carta Exhibition in China Is Abruptly Moved from University." *The New York Times*, October 14, 2015.

See Tom Mitchell, "Book by Prominent Chinese Academic 'Banned.'" *Financial Times*, December 3, 2015.

The prologue of the 2014 book indicates that it is an edited version rather than a simple compilation of speeches:

> In order to facilitate understanding by the entire Party of President Xi's main goals and spirits, the Propaganda Department of the CPC Central Committee organizes and edits the collection. The structure of the book is based on the deep understanding of President Xi's important speeches. The main ideas and arguments in the book are loyal to the original speeches. It is an important supplementary material for the CPC members to study President Xi's spirit.

The book does include some ideas from a February 2013 speech by Xi that touches on themes similar to those of the December 2012 speech, but the language in the latter speech is less direct and forceful about the primacy of the Constitution. See http://news.xinhuanet.com/politics/2014-10/13/c_127090941_7.htm.

CHINA'S APPROACH TO LEGAL REFORMS

For a description of legal reforms in China during the 1980s and 1990s, see Lubman (2000). He argues that Chinese leaders have traditionally harbored a basic ambivalence toward law that makes their commitments to the rule of law partial at best. He also makes the case that legal reforms are unlikely to lead to political reform. Lubman (2012) and He (2012) provide critical perspectives on recent legal reforms in China.

Official biographies of China's leaders can be found at http://news.xinhuanet.com/rwk/2013-02/01/c_114586554.htm.

The communiqué of the fourth plenary session of the 18th Central Committee of the CPC is available at http://www.china.org.cn/china/fourth_plenary_session/2014-12/02/content_34208801.htm.

See "Outline of the Fourth Five-Year Reform of the People's Courts (2014–2018): Opinion of the Supreme People's Court on Deepening Reform of the People's Courts Comprehensively." SPC release no. 32015. Supreme People's Court, 2015, http://news.xinhuanet.com/legal/2015-02/26/c_127520462.htm. The translation taken from China Law Translate is available at http://chinalawtranslate.com.

For Zhou Qiang's quotes, see http://news.china.com.cn/2015-02/26/content_34888966.htm (in Chinese) and Josh Chin, "Don't Call It Western: China's Top Court Unveils Vision for Reform." *The Wall Street Journal*, February 26, 2015.

President Xi's quotes are translations from the official website of the CPC, http://cpc.people.com.cn/xuexi/n/2015/0511/c385475-26978527.html. The first statement is based on his talk given on February 2, 2015, to provincial- and ministerial-level cadres regarding the spirit of the fourth plenary session of the eighteenth CPC Central Committee. The second quote is based on a document dated October 23, 2014, and used by the website on May 11, 2015.

The *People's Daily* article is posted at http://paper.people.com.cn/rmrb/html/2015-07/12/nw.D110000renmrb_20150712_2-02.htm (in Chinese). See also "China's 'Rule by Law' Takes an Ugly Turn." *Foreign Policy*, July 14, 2015.

CENTRAL BANK INDEPENDENCE

Some of the statements about the institutional structure of the PBC are taken from its website, which states:

> The People's Bank of China (PBC) was established on December 1, 1948 based on the consolidation of the Huabei Bank, the Beihai Bank, and the Xibei Farmer Bank. In September 1983, the State Council decided to have the PBC function as a central bank. The Law of the People's Republic of China on the People's Bank of China adopted on March 18, 1995 by the 3rd Plenum of the 8th National People's Congress has since legally confirmed the PBC's central bank status.

> With the improvement of the socialist market economic system, the PBC, as a central bank, will play an even more important role in China's macroeconomic management. The amended Law of the People's Republic of China on the People's Bank of China, adopted by the 6th meeting of the Standing Committee of the 10th National People's Congress on December 27, 2003, provides that the PBC performs the following major functions:

> 1. Drafting and enforcing relevant laws, rules and regulations that are related to fulfilling its functions;
> 2. Formulating and implementing monetary policy in accordance with law;
> 3. Issuing the Renminbi and administering its circulation;
> 4. Regulating financial markets, including the inter-bank lending market, the inter-bank bond market, foreign exchange market and gold market;

5. Preventing and mitigating systemic financial risks to safeguard financial stability;
6. Maintaining the Renminbi exchange rate at adaptive and equilibrium level; Holding and managing the state foreign exchange and gold reserves;
7. Managing the State treasury as fiscal agent;
8. Making payment and settlement rules in collaboration with relevant departments and ensuring normal operation of the payment and settlement systems;
9. Providing guidance to anti-money laundering work in the financial sector and monitoring money-laundering related to suspicious fund movement;
10. Developing statistics system for the financial industry and responsible for the consolidation of financial statistics as well as the conduct of economic analysis and forecast
11. Administering credit reporting industry in China and promoting the building up of credit information system;
12. Participating in international financial activities in the capacity of the central bank;
13. Engaging in financial business operations in line with relevant rules;
14. Performing other functions prescribed by the State Council.

See Chiu and Lewis (2006) and Pissler (2015) for a discussion of China's central banking law and sources of some of the statements from that law. See Bell and Feng (2013) for more details on the origins and functioning of the PBC and its relationship with the CPC. Goodfriend and Prasad (2007) discuss the importance of operational independence for the PBC's effective functioning and also sketch the details of an independent monetary policy framework for China.

MIND THE INSTITUTIONAL GAP

See Prasad (2014) for a more detailed discussion of some of these ideas.

CHAPTER 8. HOUSE OF CARDS?

The epigraph is from Gould (1989, p. 51). The full paragraph reads as follows:

> The reconstructed Burgess fauna, interpreted by the theme of replaying life's tape, offers powerful support for this different view of life: any replay of the tape would lead evolution down a pathway radically different from the road actually taken. But the consequent differences in outcome do not imply that evolution is senseless, and without any meaningful pattern; the divergent route of the replay would be just as interpretable, just as explainable *after* the fact, as the actual road. But the diversity of possible itineraries does demonstrate that eventual results cannot be predicted at the outset. Each step proceeds for cause, but no finale can be specified at the start, and none would even occur a second time in the same way, because any pathway proceeds through thousands of improbable stages. Alter any early event, ever so slightly and without apparent importance at the time, and evolution cascades into a radically different channel.

For a useful overview of the economic risks that China faces, see Wolf (2016). For an earlier analysis, the main points of which still remain relevant, see Prasad (2009).

THE CAPITAL ACCOUNT

See Justin Yifu Lin, "Why I Oppose Opening Capital Account." August 18, 2013, China. org.cn. Also see Lin (2015).

See Yu Yongding, "The Temptation of China's Capital Account." *Project Syndicate*, March 27, 2013.

A Matter of Sequence

For a discussion of sequencing capital account liberalization in the context of China, see Prasad, Rumbaugh, and Wang (2005) and references therein. Also see Eichengreen (2015).

Data on China's external debt are from the SAFE.

Until July 2013, there had also been a floor (lower limit) on bank lending rates, resulting in comfortable net margins for banks. The cap on deposit rates was liberalized progressively until October 2015, when it was scrapped altogether.

Capital Outflows

According to SAFE data, China's foreign currency external debt declined from $896 billion at the end of 2014 to $760 billion at the end of 2015.

Foreign exchange reserves data are from the IMF.

The official estimate of valuation effects on foreign exchange reserves during 2015 appears in "SAFE Press Spokesperson Answers Press Questions on Balance of Payments for 2015," SAFE Press Release, March 14, 2016 (http://www.safe.gov.cn/wps/portal/english/News).

For measures of reserve adequacy, see "People's Republic of China: Staff Report for the 2015 Article IV Consultation." IMF, July 2015, pp. 7–8 and Table 3. For an overview of the IMF's composite metric for reserve adequacy, see "Assessing Reserve Adequacy: Specific Proposals." IMF, April 2015.

Capital Flight

Strictly speaking, the current account is the sum of (1) the trade balance (exports less the imports of goods and nonfactor services), (2) net factor income (income earned abroad by the home country's labor and capital less the income earned in the home country by foreign labor and capital), and (3) current transfers (private and government transfers inward less private and government transfers outward). Private transfers include workers' remittances whereas government transfers include aid, donations, and official assistance. Usually, the trade balance tends to dominate the current account balance.

Trade Misinvoicing

The formal name of the agency that collects China's trade statistics is the *General Administration of Customs*. For more analysis of the phenomenon of trade misinvoicing, see Buehn and Eichler (2011).

Macanese Roulette

See Gordinho (2013) for more details.

"Monetary Authority of Macao and People's Bank of China Entered into MOU on Prevention of Money Laundering and Terrorist Financing." PBC press release. August 21, 2015, http://bit.ly/1YDAKwP. "Mainland, Macao Ink Pact to Fight Money Laundering." The State Council, August 22, 2015, http://bit.ly/1Tgjom9.

Banking Dens

"Press Conference on SAFE's Policies for 2015 Q3." SAFE, 2015, www.safe.gov.cn (News). Mark Magnier, "China Police Reveal Busted Illegal Banking Operation." *The Wall Street Journal*, November 20, 2015, p. XX. "China Arrests 75 in Crackdown on Underground Banks." *Reuters*, September 30, 2015.

Capital Outflows in Search of Soft and Hard Assets

Laura Kusisto and Alyssa Abkowitz, "Chinese Pull Back from U.S. Property Investments." *The Wall Street Journal*, November 27, 2015.

For an analysis of the effects of official and illegitimate capital flows from Mainland China on equity and property market prices in Hong Kong, see Cheung, Chow, and Yiu (2015).

See Institute of International Education, "Top 25 Places of Origin of International Students." http://www.iie.org/Research-and-Publications/Open-Doors/Data/International-Students/Leading-Places-of-Origin/2013-15.

These figures are based on government data compiled by CNNMoney. See "U.S. Runs out of Investors Again as Chinese Flood Program." *CNNMoney*, April 15, 2015.

See "People's Bank of China and Monetary Authority of Macau Memorandum of Understanding on Prevention of Money Laundering and Terrorist Financing." August 21, 2015.

THE FINANCIAL SYSTEM

See Lardy (2011, 2014) for an overview of China's financial system.

Growing Mountain of Debt

See Reinhart and Rogoff (2011).

The debt data for the U.S. are from the U.S. Congressional Budget Office.

The IMF measures of augmented public deficits and debt are taken from "People's Republic of China: Staff Report for the 2015 Article IV Consultation." IMF, July 2015, pp. 6 and 8, and Table 5. The augmented debt figure does not include estimates of contingent liabilities in the state-owned banking system.

See "Debt (and Not Much) Deleveraging." McKinsey Global Institute, February 2015. The IMF's estimate that corporate debt is 145 percent of GDP is reported in: Shawn Donnan and Tom Mitchell, "IMF Sounds Warning on China's Corporate Debt." *Financial Times*, June 12, 2016. An alternative estimate that corporate debt amounts to 160 percent of GDP is in: Patti Waldmeir, "China Bank Governor Warns Over Corporate Debt." *Financial Times*, March 30, 2016.

Banking System

The official increase in NPAs during 2015 is described in "China's Bad Loans Rise to Highest in a Decade as Economy Slows." *Bloomberg*, February 15, 2016.

For a summary of private analysts' views about China's nonperforming asset ratio, see "Credit Sleuths in China Uncover Bad Debt Dwarfing Official 1.5%." *Bloomberg*,

October 29, 2015; and Katherine Lei, "China Banks: Are Bad Loan Fears Overplayed." *Barron's*, February 29, 2016. The IMF estimates of bank loan losses are from its April 2016 *Global Financial Stability Report*.

Shadow Banking

The definition of shadow banking is from the Financial Stability Board. The discussion and data in this section draw on various IMF sources and also Douglas J. Elliott, Arthur R. Kroeber, and Yu Qiao, "Shadow Banking in China: A Primer." Brookings Institution, 2015; and Wei Jiang, "The Future of Shadow Banking in China." Chazen Institute, Columbia University, 2015.

The State Council document is an internal document (Circular No. 107) issued in December 2013. A selected set of key regulatory measures instituted following the issuance of the State Council guidelines is listed here and is based on various circulars issued by the CIRC and the CBRC.

- Commercial banks are required to establish a specific department for WMPs and to set up a specific accounting system for these products. Funds raised by WMPs are not to be used to invest in own lending assets.
- Trust companies are (1) forbidden from conducting "fund pools" business, a common practice that enabled these companies to finance cash payouts by selling new WMPs; (2) required to reduce lending when their capital levels fall as a result of losses; and (3) required to establish a mechanism for managing crises, including delaying executives' incentive compensation, restricting dividend payouts, and disposing of some businesses.
- The CBRC imposed a minimum asset requirement of RMB 3 billion (about $460 million); restricted the scope of trust funds that can be invested in by insurance companies; and imposed system restrictions on interbank operations, such as repos and interbank borrowing/lending, and also set capital, accounting, and maturity requirements on interbank operations.
- Commercial banks are required to report WMP operations to the CBRC, starting at the end of July 2014.
- The CBRC assigns grades to trust companies and implements discretionary regulation rules depending on their grades.
- The CIRC highlights the risks of insurance investment in trust funds and requires insurance companies to comply with the regulation rules.
- The trust industry insurance fund company is established jointly by the China Trustee Association and thirteen trust firms, with registered capital of nearly RMB 10 billion (about $1.5 billion). Trust companies are required to subscribe to the insurance fund in an amount equal to 1 percent of assets under management. The fund is to be used in emergencies for providing short-term liquidity and assisting in the restructuring of a distressed trust company.
- Commercial banks are barred from bearing credit risks for entrusted loans. Entrusted loan investments in securities, futures, stocks, and financial derivatives are prohibited.

Stock Market Swings

Cheerleading the Stock Market

Xinhua's interview with CSRC spokesperson Deng Ge is posted at http://news.xinhuanet.com/fortune/2014-09/02/c_1112333072.htm (in Chinese). The *People's Daily* quote is from the article available at http://finance.people.com.cn/stock/n/2015/0421/c67815-26880528.html (in Chinese). Chinese translations were provided by Wang Tao of Cornell University. Another example of the numerous articles in official media that echoed a similar theme is http://news.xin-huanet.com/finance/2014-08/31/c_1112297540.htm (in Chinese).

The Tumble

See, for instance, "China Security Ministry to Probe 'Malicious' Short Selling." *Bloomberg*, July 8, 2015; "China Rolls Out Emergency Measures to Prevent Stock Market Crash." *Reuters*, July 5, 2015; "China Central Bank Pledges Liquidity Support to Stock Market." *Bloomberg*, July 7, 2015; "China Stock Exchanges Step Up Crackdown on Short-Selling." *Reuters*, August 4, 2015; Edward Wong, "China Punishes Nearly 200 Over 'Rumors' About Stocks, Blasts and Parade." *The New York Times*, August 31, 2015; Patti Waldmeir, "China Reporter Confesses to Stoking Market 'Panic and Disorder.'" *Financial Times*, August 31, 2015.

Official documents include "Notice on Modifying Article 15 of 'SSE Detailed Rules for Implementation of Margin Trading and Securities Lending (Revised in 2015),'" Shanghai Stock Exchange, August 3, 2015; "SZSE Amends Rules for Margin Trading and Securities Lending." Shenzhen Stock Exchange, August 4, 2015.

Time-out Measure Intended to Calm, Instead Stokes Panic

For details on the NYSE's circuit breakers, see https://www.nyse.com/markets/market-model.

For details on India's circuit breaker mechanism, see http://www.nseindia.com/products/content/equities/equities/circuit_breakers.htm.

The actual operation of the circuit breakers in the U.S. and India is slightly more complicated than described in the text. In both countries, there are three trigger levels and their implementation depends on the time of the day they are activated. The U.S. also has a limit up-limit down mechanism intended "to address market volatility by preventing trades in listed equity securities when triggered by large, sudden price moves in an individual stock." See http://www.sec.gov/investor/alerts/circuitbreakersbulletin.htm.

See Kit Tang, "China's Latest Step to Curb Stocks' Wild Ride: Circuit Breakers." *CNBC. com*, January 4, 2016. "China Suspends Stock Circuit Breaker Days After Introduction." *Bloomberg*, January 7, 2016.

Xiao Gang's quote is reported in "China's Stock Market Regulator 'Resigns' After Circuit-Breaker Fiasco." *Reuters*, January 18, 2016. His actual firing is reported in Keith Bradsher, "Xiao Gang, China's Top Securities Regulator, Ousted Over Market Tumult." *The New York Times*, February 19, 2016.

See "China Has More Than 100 mln Stock Market Investors." *Xinhua*, January 30, 2016.

MORE FUNDAMENTAL CONCERNS ABOUT ECONOMIC AND POLITICAL STABILITY
Growth Prospects

Robert Fogel, "$123,000,000,000,000. China's Estimated Economy by the Year 2040. Be Warned." *Foreign Policy*, January 2010.

See Perkins and Rawski (2008).

See Pritchett and Summers (2014).

See "Prasad, Pettis Lock Horns on China Growth Prospects." *Bloomberg Brief Economics Asia*, March 2015. For a discussion of China's efforts to rebalance its growth away from an investment- and export-led growth model, see Prasad (2009, 2011). In related work that has implications for growth rebalancing, Chamon and Prasad (2010) and Chamon, Liu, and Prasad (2013) analyze the determinants of household savings in China.

The capital-to-labor ratio comparison between China and the U.S. is based on the following calculations using Penn World Tables data posted at http://www.rug.nl/research/ggdc/data/pwt/pwt-8.1. In China, the capital-to-output ratio was 3.2 in 2011 and had been growing by 0.1 percentage point a year. In the U.S., the capital output ratio was 3.1 in 2011 and has stayed in a narrow range in recent years. Extrapolating the capital-to-output ratio for China to 3.6 in 2015, and assuming this ratio for the U.S. remains unchanged at 3.1, this ratio would be 1.16 times that of the U.S. China has output that is about two-thirds that of the U.S. Its labor force is roughly five times that of the U.S. (800 million vs. 160 million, according to the World Bank). This yields a capital-to-labor ratio that is roughly one-sixth that of the U.S. ($1.16 \times 2/3 \times 1/5 = 0.155$).

Political and Social Instability

See Cheng Li, "Xi Jinping's Inner Circle: The Shaanxi Gang." *China Leadership Monitor*, January 2014.

The resistance to reforms, the scholar's quote, and the admonitions by state media are reported in the following articles: Keira Lu Huang, "Xi Jinping's Reforms Encounter 'Unimaginably Fierce Resistance,' Chinese State Media Says in 'Furious' Commentary." *South China Morning Post*, August 21, 2015; Michael Forsythe and Jonathan Ansfield, "Fading Economy and Graft Crackdown Rattle China's Leaders." *The New York Times*, August 22, 2015; Austin Ramzy, "In Chinese Media, a Rebuff to Officials Who Won't Fully Retire." *The New York Times*, August 11, 2015.

David Shambaugh, "The Coming Chinese Crackup." *The Wall Street Journal*, March 6, 2015. His earlier views can be found in Shambaugh (2009). In a similar vein, Pei (2016) makes a forceful argument that China's expanding prosperity is a façade that, for now, papers over the vulnerabilities of a state apparatus controlled by corrupt public elites and in an advanced stage of decay. Also see Wallace (2015).

Michael Forsythe, "Roderick MacFarquhar on Xi Jinping's High-Risk Campaign to Save the Communist Party." *The New York Times*, January 30, 2015.

Policy Instability: One Step Forward, Two Steps Sideways

The CSRC quote about the market is from Tom Mitchell, "China Markets Regulator Warns Media on 'Market Disturbance.'" *Financial Times*, July 30, 2015.

The quote by Yi Gang is reported in "China's Central Bank Gives Verbal Support to Yuan." *Bloomberg*, August 12, 2015.

The threat against Soros is reported in Gabriel Wildau, "China Mouthpiece Warns Soros against Shorting Renminbi." *Financial Times*, January 26, 2016.

On the need for state enterprise reforms, see Eswar Prasad, "Ownership is Key to Fixing China's SOEs." *The Wall Street Journal*, June 21, 2016.

CHAPTER 9. RISING GLOBAL INFLUENCE

The epigraph is from Robert M. Pirsig's 1974 classic *Zen and the Art of Motorcycle Maintenance: An Inquiry into Values*. The text appears on p. 70 of the paperback version printed by Bantam Press (New Age Edition) in 1981.

For more information on the TPP, see http://www.brookings.edu/blogs/brookings-now/posts/2015/05/20-trade-terms-explained.

See "Statements by the President on the Trans-Pacific Partnership." Washington, DC: The White House, October 5, 2015.

See Mark Magnier, "Trans-Pacific Trade Deal a Setback for China." *The Wall Street Journal*, October 5, 2015.

The *Study Times* article is summarized in "China Communist Party Paper Says Country Should Join U.S.-led Trade Pact." *Reuters*, October 24, 2015.

Ma Jun's and Sheng Laiyun's views are reported in Tom Mitchell, "China Lays Out 'Countermeasures' to Offset Exclusion from TPP." *Financial Times*, October 19, 2015.

The arguments that TPP accession could benefit China are summarized by David Pilling, "The 'Anyone But China' Club Needs a Gatecrasher." *Financial Times*, October 7, 2015.

The RCEP is mentioned in this article: Ben Blanchard, "China Communist Party Paper Says Country Should Join U.S.-Led Trade Pact." *Reuters*, October 24, 2015.

President Xi's quote from his speech at the meeting of the Asia-Pacific Economic Cooperation forum in Manila in November 2015 is reported by Elaine Kurtenbach, "Pacific Trade Pact Praised, Panned as Obama Urges Approval," *Associated Press*, November 18, 2015.

FLEXING ECONOMIC MUSCLES

See Derek Scissors, "The Double-Edged Sword of China's Global Investment Success." American Enterprise Institute, January 2016. The interactive China Global Investment Tracker is available at the institute's website, www.aei.org/china-global-investment-tracker. For a broader discussion of China's outward investment strategy, see Rosen and Hanemann (2009) and Scissors (2011).

See Clifford Krauss and Keith Bradsher, "China's Global Ambitions, Cash and Strings Attached." *The New York Times*, July 24, 2015.

See "Spokeswoman: China's Aid to Africa Never Offers Blank Promises." *China Daily*, December 10, 2015.

See Moisés Naím, "Rogue Aid." *Foreign Policy*, October 15, 2009.

For more about the relationship between Chinese aid and political violence in Africa, see the University of Sussex study by Kishi and Raleigh (2015).

To learn more about the differences between Chinese and Western Official Development Assistance, see the AidData study by Axel Dreher et al. (2015). The Brookings Institution study is Dollar, Tang, and Chen (2015). See Brautigam (2010).

For more details on Zimbabwe's relationship with China, see the following articles: Adam Taylor, "Zimbabwe's Curious Plan to Adopt China's Currency." *The Washington Post*, December 23, 2015; Sheila Rule, "Dalai Lama Wins the Nobel Peace Prize." *The New York Times*, October 6, 1989; Adam Taylor, "Zimbabwean Strongman Robert Mugabe Wins China's Version of the Nobel Peace Prize." *The Washington Post*,

October 22, 2015; and Edward Wong, "President Robert Mugabe of Zimbabwe Turns Down Confucius Peace Prize." *Sinosphere–The New York Times,* October 27, 2015.

For the official statement at the end of the China–Africa summit, see http://www.focac.org/eng.

China's funding support of $60 billion for Africa comprises $5 billion in grants and interest-free loans, $35 billion in preferential loans and export credit, $5 billion in additional capital each for the China–Africa Development Fund and the Special Loan for the Development of African Small and Medium Enterprises, and a China–Africa production capacity cooperation fund with an initial capital of $10 billion.

The full text of President Xi Jinping's speech at the Johannesburg Summit of the Forum on China–Africa Cooperation in December 2015 is available at

http://english.cri.cn/12394/2015/12/05/4083s906994.htm. The relevant paragraph from the speech reads as follows: "Development holds the key to solving all problems. China supports the settlement of African issues by Africans in the African way. We are of the view that in resolving security issues, both the symptoms and the root causes must be addressed in a holistic way."

A NEW APPROACH

For a historical perspective on China's approach to foreign affairs, see Kissinger (2012).

CHANGING EXISTING INSTITUTIONS

The quoted figure is based on the IMF's capital base of SDR 477 billion converted into U.S. dollars at the March 1, 2016, exchange rate of SDR 1 = $1.38. (see http://www.imf.org/external/np/exr/facts/quotas.htm). For the voting shares of various countries after the approval of the 2010 governance reforms, see

http://www.imf.org/external/np/sec/pr/2010/pdfs/pr10418_table.pdf.

Information about the ADB, including voting shares and capital, is from its annual report and website (http://www.adb.org).

See "Agreement Establishing the European Bank for Reconstruction and Development." European Bank for Reconstruction and Development (EBRD), 1991. For more details on the values of the EBRD, see http://www.ebrd.com/our-values.html.

See "China Voice: Why Should China Say No to 'Wrong Western Values?'" *Xinhua,* February 13, 2015.

THE ASIAN INFRASTRUCTURE INVESTMENT BANK

See Jane Perlez, "U.S. Opposing China's Answer to World Bank." *The New York Times,* October 9, 2014.

Information about the capital, members, voting shares, and speeches of officials are from the AIIB website (http://www.aiib.org).

The AIIB website indicates that twenty-two countries, including China, signed the memorandum of agreement on October 24, 2014. However, news reports, including from official Chinese sources, indicate that only twenty-one countries signed the initial memorandum of agreement. An article in *Xinhua* reports that Indonesia signed the memorandum of agreement on November 25, 2014. The article is posted at http://news.xinhuanet.com/2014-11/25/c_1113401983.htm.

The statement by Jin Liqun is from "China Creates a World Bank of Its Own, and the U.S. Balks." *New York Times*, December 4, 2015.

The Grand Kowtow

Osborne's statement is from "UK Announces Plans to Join Asian Infrastructure Investment Bank." *Gov.UK*, March 12, 2015.

The White House response to the U.K.'s joining the AIIB can be found in the article "UK–China Trade Bromance a Blow to White House." *CNN Money*, March 13, 2015. The statement made by the White House National Security Council is from "U.S. Anger at Britain Joining Chinese-Led Investment Bank AIIB." *Guardian*, March 12, 2015.

See "European Giants Side with UK in Chinese World Bank Row with U.S." *Telegraph*, March 16, 2015.

The statements by Japan's Finance Minister Taro Aso and Prime Minister Shinzo Abe are from Martin Fackler, "Japan, Sticking with U.S., Says It Won't Join China-Led Bank." *The New York Times*, March 31, 2015.

To read more about the joint U.S.–China agreement on the AIIB, go to "Fact Sheet: U.S.–China Economic Relations." Washington, DC: White House Press Office, September 25, 2015.

The press conference at which Takehiko Nakao and Lou Jiwei spoke was reported on *China Business News* and is available at http://finance.sina.com.cn/hy/20150322/141021777641.shtml.

The speech by AIIB President Jin Liqun can be found in "The Asian Infrastructure Investment Bank Inaugural Ceremony." January 16, 2016. For his subsequent remarks, see: Li Xiang, "AIIB Will Have 100 Countries as Members by Year-End: Jin Liqun." *China Daily*, May 31, 2016; "AIIB President Says Bank to Have 100 Members by Year End." *Xinhua*, June 1, 2016.

BONDING AMONG THE BRICS

For more information on the BRICS New Development Bank, see http://ndbbrics.org/index.html.

The joint statement by country leaders at the first BRICS summit is posted at

http://brics.itamaraty.gov.br/category-english/21-documents/114-first-summit-2.

For more information on the Treaty for the Establishment of a BRICS Contingent Reserve Arrangement, see http://brics.itamaraty.gov.br/media2/press-releases/220-treaty-for-the-establishment-of-a-brics-contingent-reserve-arrangement-fortaleza-july-15.

SILKEN GIFT OR NOOSE?

The statements by Ibn Battuta are taken from Battuta (1829, p. 209).

For more information about the Silk Road and its history, see Hansen (2012).

For a compendium of information on the Silk Road, see Daniel Waugh's website, http://faculty.washington.edu/dwaugh/srehist.html.

More information about the Silk Road Fund is available at http://www.silkroadfund.com.cn.

The Q&A item quoted in the text can be found at http://www.silkroadfund.com.cn/enweb/23819/23770/index.html.

See also http://www.pbc.gov.cn/english/130721/2973830/index.html.

See "Vision and Actions on Jointly Building Silk Road Economic Belt and 21st-Century Maritime Silk Road." National Development and Reform Commission, 2015.

See Francis Fukuyama, "Exporting the Chinese Model." *Project Syndicate*, January 12, 2016. See also the following report: Simeon Djankov and Sean Miller, "China's Belt and Road Initiative: Motives, Scope, and Challenges." Peterson Institute for International Economics, March 2016.

Some of the material in this section is drawn from Scott Kennedy and David A. Parker, "Building China's One Belt, One Road." Center for Strategic and International Studies, April 3, 2015.

For one view about the U.S. motivation behind the Marshall Plan, see Cohen, Iriye, LaFeber, and Weeks (2013).

Chinese investment in Pakistan and comparisons with U.S. financial assistance to Pakistan are reported in Katherine Houreld, "Chinese President Xi Is Making a $46 billion Move in Pakistan." *Reuters*, April 20, 2015. Statements in this paragraph are from that article and also from the following articles: "Editorial: Welcome China." *The News*, April 21, 2015; and "Spotlight: Foreign Media, Experts Praise Xi's State Visit to Pakistan as Historically Significant" *Xinhua*, April 22, 2015. The full text of Pakistani Prime Minister Nawaz Sharif's speech to the joint session of Parliament during Xi Jinping's visit is posted at http://www.dawn.com/news/1177312.

For more on the origin, history, and details of the Marshall Plan, see http://marshall-foundation.org/marshall/the-marshall-plan/history-marshall-plan/.

The four principles of China's periphery diplomacy were articulated by President Xi in October 2013. See http://news.xinhuanet.com/world/2013-11/08/c_118063342.htm.

OTHER ARMS OF THE OCTOPUS

The China Development Bank's official website is http://www.cdb.com.cn/english/index.asp. For 2015 data, see Zhang Yangpeng, "China Development Bank Overseas Loan Hits $328.2 billion." *China Daily*, December 16, 2015.

Information about China's Export-Import Bank is from its official website, http://english.eximbank.gov.cn/en/.

CHAPTER 10. CONCLUSION

The epigraph is taken from the last paragraph of the British astronomer and physicist Sir Arthur S. Eddington's (1882–1944) 1927 book *Stars and Atoms*. I first came across material from Eddington's book in Subrahmanyan Chandrasekhar's (1987) book *Truth and Beauty: Aesthetics and Motivations in Science*.

REFERENCES

Acemoglu, Daron, and James Robinson. 2012. *Why Nations Fail: The Origins of Power, Prosperity, and Poverty*. New York, NY: Crown Publishing Group.

Allsen, Thomas. 2001. *Culture and Conquest in Mongol Eurasia*. Cambridge, UK: Cambridge University Press.

Angeloni, Ignazio, Agnès Bénassy-Quéré, Benjamin Carton, Zsolt Darvas, Christophe Destais, Jean Pisani-Ferry, André Sapir, and Shahin Vallée. 2011. "Global Currencies for Tomorrow: A European Perspective." CEPII Research Report. Paris: CEPII.

Basbanes, Nicholas. 2013. *On Paper: The Everything of Its Two-Thousand-Year History*. New York, NY: Alfred A. Knopf.

Battuta, Ibn. 1829. *The Travels of Ibn Battuta*. Cambridge, UK: The Oriental Committee. [Translated by Samuel Lee in 2012; reprinted by Cambridge University Press.]

Bell, Stephen, and Hui Feng. 2013. *The Rise of the People's Bank of China: The Politics of Institutional Change*. Cambridge, MA: Harvard University Press.

Beresiner, Yasha. 1977. *A Collector's Guide to Paper Money*. New York, NY: Stein and Day.

Beresiner, Yasha, and Colin Narbeth. 1973. *The Story of Paper Money*. New York, NY: Arco Publishing.

Bernanke, Ben S. 2015. *The Courage to Act: A Memoir of a Crisis and Its Aftermath*. New York, NY: Norton.

Borges, Jorge Luis. 1998. *Collected Fictions*. Translated by Andrew Hurley. New York, NY: Penguin Press.

Bowker, John. 2003. *The Concise Oxford Dictionary of World Religions*. New York, NY: Oxford University Press.

Bowles, Paul, and Baotai Wang. 2013. "RMB Internationalization: A Journey to Where?" *Development and Change* 44(6): 1363–1385.

Brautigam, Deborah. 2010. *The Dragon's Gift: The Real Story of China in Africa*. New York, NY: Oxford University Press.

Buehn, Andres, and Stefan Eichler. 2011. "Trade Misinvoicing: The Dark Side of World Trade." *World Economy* 34(8): 1263–1287.

Campbell, Joseph. 1991. *The Power of Myth*. Interviewed by Bill Moyers. New York, NY: Anchor Books.

Chamon, Marcos, Kai Liu, and Eswar S. Prasad. 2013. "Income Uncertainty and Household Savings in China." *Journal of Development Economics* 105: 164–77.

Chamon, Marcos, and Eswar S. Prasad. 2010. "Why Are Saving Rates of Urban Households in China Rising?" *American Economic Journal: Macroeconomics* 2(1): 93–130.

Chandrasekhar, Subrahmanyan. 1987. *Truth and Beauty: Aesthetics and Motivations in Science*. Chicago, IL: University of Chicago Press.

Chen, Hongyi, Wensheng Peng, and Chang Shu. 2009. "The Potential of the RMB as an International Currency." Manuscript. Hong Kong Monetary Authority.

Cheung, Yin-Wong, Kenneth K. Chow, and Matthew S. Yiu. 2015. "The Nexus of Official and Illicit Capital Flows: The Case of Hong Kong." HKIMR Working Paper no. 25/2015. Hong Kong, China: Hong Kong Institute for Monetary Research.

Chinn, Menzie. 2015. "Emerging Market Economies and the Next Reserve Currencies." *Open Economies Review* (26): 155–174.

Chinn, Menzie, and Jeffrey A. Frankel. 2007. "Will the Euro Eventually Surpass the Dollar as Leading International Reserve Currency?" In *G7 Current Account Imbalances: Sustainability and Adjustment*, edited by Richard Clarida. Chicago, IL: University of Chicago Press, 283–338.

Chinn, Menzie, and Hiro Ito. 2006. "What Matters for Financial Development? Capital Controls, Institutions, and Interactions." *Journal of Development Economics* 81(1): 163–192.

Chiu, Becky, and Mervyn Lewis. 2006. *Reforming China's State-Owned Enterprises and Banks*. Northampton, MA: Edward Elgar Publishing.

Coble, Parks. 2003. *Chinese Capitalists in Japan's New Order: The Occupied Lower Yangzi, 1937–1945*. Oakland, CA: University of California Press.

Cohen, Warren, Akira Iriye, Walter LaFeber, and William Earl Weeks. 2013. *The New Cambridge History of American Foreign Relations*. Cambridge, UK: Cambridge University Press.

Corsetti, Giancarlo, Paolo Pesenti, and Nouriel Roubini. 1999. "What Caused the Asian Currency and Financial Crisis? Parts I and II." *Japan and the World Economy* (11): 305–373.

Craig, Sean, Changchun Hua, Philip Ng, and Raymond Yuen. 2013. "Development of the RMB Market in Hong Kong SAR: Assessing Onshore–Offshore Market Integration." IMF Working Paper no. 13/268. Washington, DC: International Monetary Fund.

Del Mar, Alexander. 1885. *A History of Money in Ancient Countries: From the Earliest Times to the Present*. London, UK: George Bell and Sons.

Deng, Jiarong. 2015. "The Story of Renminbi's Birth." *Chinese Book Review Monthly*, China Academic Journals (Qingdao Server)-Politics/Military Affairs/Law (Series G) 13: 114–121.

Dobson, Wendy, and Paul R. Masson. 2009. "Will the RMB Become a World Currency?" *China Economic Review* 20(1): 124–135.

Doidge, Craig, G. Andrew Karolyi, and René M. Stulz. 2007. "Why Do Countries Matter So Much for Corporate Governance?" *Journal of Financial Economics* 86: 1–39.

———. 2009. "Has New York Become Less Competitive Than London in Global Markets? Evaluating Foreign Listing Choices over Time." *Journal of Financial Economics* 91: 253–277.

Dollar, David, Heiwai Tang, and Wenjie Chen. 2015. "Why Is China Investing in Africa? Evidence from the Firm Level." Washington, DC: Brookings Institution.

Dreher, Axel, Andreas Fuchs, Bradley Parks, Austin M. Strange, and Michael J. Tierney. 2015. "Apples and Dragon Fruits: The Determinants of Aid and Other Forms of State Financing from China to Africa." AidData Working Paper no. 15. Williamsburg, VA: AidData.

Dürrenmatt, Friedrich. 1989. *The Execution of Justice*. Translated from German by John E. Woods. New York, NY: Random House.

Eddington, Arthur S. 1927. *Stars and Atoms*. Oxford, UK: Oxford University Press.

Eichengreen, Barry. 2011a. *Exorbitant Privilege: The Rise and Fall of the Dollar and the Future of the International Monetary System*. New York, NY: Oxford University Press.

———. 2011b. "The RMB as an International Currency." Manuscript. University of California, Berkeley.

———. 2015. "Sequencing RMB Internationalization." CIGI Paper no. 69. Ontario, Canada: Centre for International Governance Innovation.

Eichengreen, Barry, and Masahiro Kawai, editors. 2014. "Issues for RMB Internationalization: An Overview." ABDI Working Paper no. 454. Tokyo, Japan: Asian Development Bank Institute.

———. 2015. *RMB Internationalization: Achievements, Prospects, and Challenges*. Washington, DC: Brookings Institution Press.

El-Erian, Mohamed A. 2016. *The Only Game in Town: Central Banks, Instability, and Avoiding the Next Collapse*, New York, NY: Random House.

Elliott, Douglas, Arthur Kroeber, and Yu Qiao. 2015. "Shadow Banking in China: A Primer." Washington, DC: The Brookings Institution.

Errico, Luca, and Alexander Massara. 2011. "Assessing Systemic Trade Interconnectedness: An Empirical Approach." IMF Working Paper no. 11/214. Washington, DC: International Monetary Fund.

Feynman, Richard. 1985. *QED: The Strange Theory of Light and Matter*. Princeton, NJ: Princeton University Press.

Forbes, Kristin. 2009. "Financial Network Effects and Deepening." In *The Euro at Ten: The Next Global Currency?* edited by Jean Pisani-Ferry and Adam Posen. Washington, DC: Peterson Institute of International Economics, 41–52.

Frankel, Jeffrey. 2005. "On the RMB: The Choice between Adjustment under a Fixed Exchange Rate and Adjustment under a Flexible Rate." NBER Working Paper no. 11274. Cambridge, MA: National Bureau of Economic Research.

———. 2011. "Historical Precedents for the Internationalization of the RMB." Paper prepared for workshop organized by Council on Foreign Relations and China Development Research Foundation, Beijing, China, November 1.

Funke, Michael, Chang Shu, Xiaoqiang Cheng, and Sercan Eraslan. 2015. "Assessing the CNH-CNY Pricing Differential: Role of Fundamentals, Contagion and Policy." *Journal of International Money and Finance* 59: 245–262.

Goldberg, Linda. 2010. "Is the International Role of the Dollar Changing?" In *Current Issues in Economics and Finance* 16(1). New York, NY: The Federal Reserve Bank of New York.

Goldstein, Morris, and Nicholas Lardy. 2009. *The Future of China's Exchange Rate Policy*. Washington, DC: Peterson Institute for International Economics.

Goodfriend, Marvin, and Eswar S. Prasad. 2007. "A Framework for Independent Monetary Policy in China." *CESifo Economic Studies* 53(1): 2–41.

Gordinho, Jorge A. F. 2013. "The Prevention of Money Laundering in Macau Casinos." Manuscript. University of Macau.

Gould, Stephen Jay. 1989. *Wonderful Life*. New York, NY: Norton.

Hansen, Valerie. 2012. *The Silk Road: A New History*. New York, NY: Oxford University Press.

He, Weifang. 2012. *In the Name of Justice: Striving for the Rule of Law in China*. Washington, DC: Brookings Institution Press.

Huang, Yiping, Daili Wang, and Gang Fan. 2014. "Paths to a Reserve Currency: Internationalization of the RMB and Its Implications." ABDI Working Paper no. 482. Tokyo, Japan: Asian Development Bank Institute.

Ito, Hiro, and Menzie Chinn. 2014. "The Rise of the 'Redback' and the People's Republic of China's Capital Account Liberalization: An Empirical Analysis of the Determinants of Invoicing Currencies." ADBI Working Paper no. 473. Tokyo, Japan: Asian Development Bank Institute.

Ji, Zhaojin. 2002. *A History of Modern Shanghai Banking: The Rise and Decline of China's Financial Capitalism*. New York, NY: Routledge.

Jiang, Wei. 2015. "The Future of Shadow Banking in China." Manuscript. Chazen Institute, Columbia University.

Judson, Ruth. 2012. "Crisis and Calm: Demand for U.S. Currency at Home and Abroad from the Fall of the Berlin Wall to 2011." International Finance Discussion Papers. Washington, DC: Board of Governors of the Federal Reserve System.

Kishi, Roudabeh, and Clionadh Raleigh. 2015. "Chinese Aid and Africa's Pariah States." Manuscript. University of Sussex.

Kissinger, Henry. 2012. *On China*. New York, NY: Penguin.

Kose, M. Ayhan, Eswar S. Prasad, Kenneth Rogoff, and Shang-Jin Wei. 2009. "Financial Globalization: A Reappraisal." *IMF Staff Papers* 56(1): 8–62.

Kraus, Richard. 1991. *Brushes with Power: Modern Politics and the Chinese Art of Calligraphy*. Berkeley, CA: University of California Press.

Kroeber, Arthur. 2011. "The Chinese Yuan Grows up Slowly: Fact and Fiction about China's Currency Internationalization." Policy paper. Washington, DC: New America Foundation.

Lago, Isabelle Mateos, Rupa Duttagupta, and Rishi Goyal. 2009. "The Debate on the International Monetary System." IMF Staff Position Note no. 09/26. Washington, DC: IMF.

Lardy, Nicholas. 2011. *Sustaining China's Growth after the Global Financial Crisis*. Washington, DC: Peterson Institute for International Economics.

———. 2014. *Markets Over Mao*. Washington, DC: Peterson Institute for International Economics.

Lardy, Nicholas, and Patrick Douglass. 2011. "Capital Account Liberalization and the Role of the RMB." Working Paper no. 11-6. Washington, DC: Peterson Institute for International Economics.

Li, David, and Linlin Liu. 2008. "RMB Internationalization: An Empirical and Policy Analysis." *Journal of Financial Research* 11: 1–16.

Lin, Cheng, Terry Peach, and Wang Fang. 2014. *The History of Ancient Chinese Economic Thought*. New York, NY: Routledge.

Lin, Justin Yifu. 2015. "Why I Do Not Support Complete Capital Account Liberalization." *China Economic Journal* 8(1): 86–93.

Lubman, Stanley B. 2000. *Bird in a Cage: Legal Reform in China after Mao*. Stanford, CA: Stanford University Press.

———, editor. 2012. *The Evolution of Law Reform in China: An Uncertain Path*. London, UK: Edgar Elgar.

Lucas, Robert E., Jr., 1982. "Interest Rates and Currency Prices in a Two-Country World." *Journal of Monetary Economics* 10(3): 335–359.

Ma, Guonan, and Robert McCauley. 2013. "Is China or India More Financially Open?" Bank of International Settlements Working Paper no. 410. Basel, Switzerland.

Marsden, William, ed., trans. 1948. *The Travels of Marco Polo the Venetian*. Garden City, NY: Doubleday.

McCauley, Robert, and Tracy Chan. 2014. "Currency Movements Drive Reserve Composition." *BIS Quarterly Review* (December 2014): 23–36.

McKinnon, Ronald, and Gunther Schnabl. 2014. "China's Exchange Rate and Financial Repression: The Conflicted Emergence of the RMB as an International Currency." CESifo Working Paper no. 6469. Munich, Germany: Center for Economic Studies and Ifo Institute.

Meyer, Stephen A. 1989. "The U.S. as a Debtor Country: Causes, Prospects, and Policy Implications." *Federal Reserve Bank of Philadelphia Business Review*, November/December: 19–31.

Milne, Alan Alexander. 1991. *The House at Pooh Corner*. London, UK: Puffin Books.

Needham, Joseph. 1986. *Science and Civilisation in China: Volume 5, Chemistry and Chemical Technology—Part 7: Military Technology; The Gunpowder Epic*. Cambridge, UK: Cambridge University Press.

North, Douglass C. 1982. *Structure and Change in Economic History*. New York, NY: Norton.

Obstfeld, Maurice. 2007. "The Renminbi's Dollar Peg at a Crossroads." *Monetary and Economic Studies* 25(S1): 29–56. Tokyo, Japan: Institute for Monetary and Economic Studies, Bank of Japan.

Obstfeld, Maurice, and Kenneth Rogoff. 1996. *Foundations of International Macroeconomics*. Cambridge, MA: MIT Press.

Pei, Minxin. 2016. *China's Crony Capitalism: The Dynamics of Regime Decay*. Cambridge, MA: Harvard University Press.

Perkins, Dwight, and Thomas G. Rawski. 2008. "Forecasting China's Economic Growth to 2025." In *China's Great Economic Transformation*, edited by Loren Brandt and Thomas G. Rawski. Cambridge, UK: Cambridge University Press, 829–886.

Pirsig, Robert M. 1974. *Zen and the Art of Motorcycle Maintenance: An Inquiry into Values*. New York, NY: William Morrow.

Pissler, Knut. 2015. "History and Legal Framework of the People's Bank of China." In *Central Banking and Financial Stability in East Asia*, edited by Frank Rövekamp, Moritz Bälz, and Hanns Günther Hipert. London, UK: Springer, 11–24.

Prasad, Eswar S. 2009. "Is China's Growth Miracle Built to Last?" *China Economic Review* 20(1): 103–23.

———. 2011. "Rebalancing Growth in Asia." *International Finance* 14(1): 27–66.

———. 2014. *The Dollar Trap: How the U.S. Dollar Tightened Its Grip on Global Finance*. Princeton, NJ: Princeton University Press.

———. 2016. *China's Efforts to Expand the International Use of the Renminbi*. Washington, DC: Brookings Institution and U.S.–China Economic and Security Review Commission.

Prasad, Eswar S., and Raghuram G. Rajan. 2005. "Controlled Capital Account Liberalization: A Proposal." IMF Policy Discussion Paper no. 05/7. Washington, DC: IMF.

———. 2006. "Modernizing China's Growth Paradigm." *American Economic Review* 96(2): 331–336.

———. 2008. "A Pragmatic Approach to Capital Account Liberalization." *Journal of Economic Perspectives* 22(3): 149–172.

Prasad, Eswar S., Kenneth Rogoff, Shang-Jin Wei, and M. Ayhan Kose. 2003. "Effects of Financial Globalization on Developing Countries: Some Empirical Evidence." Occasional Paper no. 220. Washington DC: IMF.

Prasad, Eswar S., Thomas Rumbaugh, and Qing Wang. 2005. "Putting the Cart before the Horse? Capital Account Liberalization and Exchange Rate Flexibility in China." IMF Policy Discussion Paper no. 05/1. Washington, DC: IMF.

Prasad, Eswar S., and Shang-Jin Wei. 2007. "The Chinese Approach to Capital Inflows: Patterns and Possible Explanations." In *Capital Controls and Capital Flows in Emerging Economies: Policies, Practices and Consequences*, edited by Sebastian Edwards. Chicago, IL: University of Chicago Press for National Bureau of Economic Research, 421–480.

Prasad, Eswar S., and Lei Ye. 2012. "The Renminbi's Role in the Global Monetary System." Brookings Institution report. Washington, DC: Brookings Institution.

Pritchett, Lant, and Lawrence H. Summers. 2014. "Asiaphoria Meets Regression to the Mean." NBER Working Paper no. 20573. Cambridge, MA: National Bureau of Economic Research.

Reinfeld, Fred. 1957. *The Story of Paper Money*. New York, NY: Sterling Publishing.

Reinhart, Carmen, and Kenneth Rogoff. 2011. *This Time Is Different: Eight Centuries of Financial Folly*. Princeton, NJ: Princeton University Press.

Rosen, Daniel H., and Thilo Hanemann. 2009. "China's Changing Outbound Foreign Direct Investment Profile: Drivers and Policy Implications." Policy Brief no. 09-14. Washington, DC: Peterson Institute for International Economics.

Scissors, Derek. 2011. "Chinese Outward Investment: More Opportunity Than Danger." Heritage Foundation Backgrounder no. 2579. Washington, DC: The Heritage Foundation.

Shambaugh, David. 2009. *China's Communist Party: Atrophy and Adaptation*. Los Angeles, CA: University of California Press.

Sharma, Parul. 2015. "How Does Capital Market Opening Affect Investment Choices? Evidence from China's Qualified Foreign Institutional Investor Scheme." Manuscript. Cornell University.

Shu, Chang, Dong He, and Xiaoqiang Cheng. 2014. "One Currency, Two Markets: The RMB's Growing Influence in Asia–Pacific." *China Economic Review* 33: 163–178.

Sima Qian. Circa 94 BC. *Shiji*. Translated by Burton Watson as *Records of the Grand Historian: Han Dynasty II (Volume 2)*. Reprinted in 1993. New York, NY: Columbia University Press.

Subacchi, Paola, and Helena Huang. 2012. "The Connecting Dots of China's RMB Strategy: London and Hong Kong." Chatham House Briefing Paper, IE BP no. 2012/02. London, UK: Chatham House.

———. 2013. "Taipei in the RMB Offshore Market: Another Piece in the Jigsaw." Chatham House Briefing Paper, IE BP no. 2013/01. London, UK: Chatham House.

Subramanian, Arvind. 2011. *Eclipse: Living in the Shadow of China's Economic Dominance*. Washington, DC: Institute of International Economics.

Society for Worldwide Interbank Financial Telecommunication. 2011. *RMB Internationalisation: Implications for the Global Financial Industry*. La Hulpe, Belgium.

Society for Worldwide Interbank Financial Telecommunication. 2012. *RMB Internationalisation: Perspectives on the Future of RMB Clearing*. La Hulpe, Belgium.

Tavlas, George. 1991. "On the International Use of Currencies: The Case of the Deutsche Mark." Essays in International Finance no. 181. Princeton, NJ: Princeton University Press.

Twyman, Michael. 1998. *The British Library Guide to Printing*. Ontario, Canada: University of Toronto Press.

Von Glahn, Richard. 1996. *Fountain of Fortune: Money and Monetary Policy in China, 1000–1700*. Oakland, CA: University of California Press.

Wakeman, Frederic, Jr. 1996. *The Shanghai Badlands: Wartime Terrorism and Urban Crimes, 1937–1941*. Cambridge, UK: Cambridge University Press.

Wallace, Jeremy. 2015. "The New Normal: Reform, Information, and China's Anti-Corruption Crusade in Context." Department of Government Working Paper. Ithaca, NY: Cornell University.

Williams, John. 2012. "Monetary Policy, Money, and Inflation." *Presentation to the Western Economic Association International*. San Francisco, CA: Federal Reserve Bank of San Francisco.

Wilson, Andrew. 1868. *The 'Ever-Victorious Army': A History of The Chinese Campaign Under Lt.-Col. C.G. Gordon and of the Suppression of the Tai-Ping Rebellion*. London, UK: William Blackwood and Sons.

Wolf, Martin. 2014. *The Shifts and the Shocks: What We've Learned and Have Still to Learn from the Financial Crisis*. New York, NY: Penguin.

————. 2016. "The Great Stall: The Chinese Slowdown." *The American Interest* 11(4): 5–9.

Yam, Joseph. 2011. "A Safe Approach to Convertibility for the RMB." Working Paper no. 5. Hong Kong, China: Chinese University of Hong Kong, Institute for Global Economics and Finance.

Yu, Yongding. 2015. "How Far Can RMB Internationalization Go?" In *RMB Internationalization: Achievements, Prospects, and Challenges*, edited by Barry Eichengreen and Masahiro Kawai. Washington, DC: The Brookings Institution Press, 53–84.

Zhou, Xiaochuan. 2009. "Reform the International Monetary System." Beijing, China: People's Bank of China.

ACKNOWLEDGMENTS

This book incorporates research I have conducted on China for the past decade and a half. During this period, I have had the privilege of working with a remarkable group of co-authors, particularly on topics related to China, but also more broadly on international finance. This book draws on collaborative work with Marcos Chamon, Menzie Chinn, Marvin Goodfriend, M. Ayhan Kose, Kai Liu, Raghuram Rajan, Kenneth Rogoff, Thomas Rumbaugh, Qing Wang, Shang-Jin Wei, and Lei Ye.

Yusuke Horiguchi first gave me the opportunity to work on China at the IMF. I learned a great deal from numerous colleagues there, and continue to benefit from the institution's knowledge and research conducted by its staff.

Cornell University and the Brookings Institution have been wonderful places to continue my research on China, and my colleagues at both institutions have deepened my understanding of the subjects explored in this book. I am particularly grateful for the encouragement and support I have received over the years from Deans Susan Henry and Kathryn Boor at Cornell, and Lael Brainard, Kemal Derviş, and Strobe Talbott at Brookings.

There is a long list of people in (or from) China whose knowledge and advice has helped me to understand its economy better. I am particularly grateful to Fang Xinghai, Hu Xiaolian, Huang Haizhou, Huang Yiping, Jin Liqun, Li Ruogu, Lin Yifu Justin, Liu He, Luo Ping, Ma Jun, Wang Xiaoyi, Wu Xiaoling, Yi Gang, Yu Yongding, Zhou Xiaochuan, and Zhu Min. I have also benefited from conversations with David Dollar, Arthur Kroeber, Nicholas

Lardy, and Li Cheng, whose work has informed mine throughout the years.

Basia Kamińska read through early drafts of the manuscript and provided many thoughtful comments and suggestions that greatly improved the exposition. James Daniel, Mengjie Ding, David Dollar, Karim Foda, Christina Golubski, Yusuke Horiguchi, Saori Katada, Nicholas Lardy, Markus Rodlauer, and Jeremy Wallace read through various parts of the manuscript and offered useful comments.

Audrey Breitwieser, Wentong Chen, Karim Foda, Ritesh Shinde, Tao Wang, and Yishuo Yang provided superb research assistance. Each of them worked long hours, helping with the data and background research for this book and also reading through and commenting on various chapters. Tao Wang and Yishuo Yang also translated many original source materials from Chinese. William Barnett provided very useful editorial assistance. Shraddha Anand and Nathalie Abigail Budiman also helped with editing. Erika Rose provided administrative support for my research.

Scott Parris was the commissioning editor for this book (and also gave the book its title). Anne Dellinger of OUP and Alphonsa James of NewGen helped shepherd it through to its publication. Howard Benson suggested the title of one of the chapters.

This book builds on analytical work I did for a report commissioned by the U.S.–China Economic Security and Review Commission ("China's Efforts to Promote the International Use of the Renminbi," Brookings Institution, February 2016). Katherine Koleski, Nargiza Salidjanova, and their colleagues at the Commission offered a number of substantive and editorial comments on that report.

I am forever indebted to my late parents, Parvathi and Shanker, and my sisters, Shanti and Jayanthi, for all that they have done for me.

My faithful dog Mozart kept me company during intense writing sessions, and long walks with him helped clear my mind. Finally, and most importantly, I owe an immense debt to my wife, Basia, and my daughters, Berenika and Yuvika, for their unfailing support and love. They make it all worthwhile.

SUBJECT INDEX

Note: Page numbers followed by *f* or *t* denote figures or tables, respectively. The letter *b* stands for box.

Bonds, 105–107, 132–133, 258*t*, 260*t*
Border tensions, 236
Bo Xilai, 207–208
Boys clubs, 122–123
Brazil, 256*t*, 279. *See also* BRICS
Brazilian real, 258*t*–259*t*
Bribery, 207–208
BRICS (Brazil, Russia, India, China,
    and South Africa), 142, 234–238,
    247–248, 255*t*
BRICS New Development Bank, 236
Britain. *See* United Kingdom
British Columbia (Canada), 106
British pound sterling, xiv, 20
    global foreign exchange market
        turnover shares, 258*t*
    interest rate derivatives, 259*t*
    international bonds and notes
        outstanding, 258*t*
    as payment currency, 108
    as reserve currency, 136, 151–152,
        252–253, 253*f*
    SDR weight, 148, 282
    trade with RMB, 113
Bronze coin, 2, 4–5, 7
Brunei, 213, 228–229
B-share, 43
Bubbles, 200

Cai Lun, 1–2
Caixin, 97
Calligraphy, 16
Cambodia, 228–229
Canada, 79, 100–101, 111, 187–188, 213,
    255*t*, 260*t*
Canadian dollar, 35, 136, 151–152
Capital-to-labor ratios, 206, 291
Capital-to-output ratios, 291
Caribbean Development Bank, 223
Casino operations, 185–186
Central Bank of Argentina, 261*t*
Central Bank of Armenia, 262*t*
Central Bank of Chile, 262*t*
Central Bank of China, 11
Central Bank of Hungary, 262*t*
Central Bank of Iceland, 261*t*
Central Bank of Nigeria, 135
Central Bank of Russia, 262*t*
Central Bank of Sri Lanka, 262*t*
Central Bank of Suriname, 262*t*

Central Bank of the Republic of Turkey,
    261*t*
Central Bank of the Republic of
    Uzbekistan, 261*t*
Central Bank of the United Arab
    Emirates, 261*t*
Central parity, 79–80, 96–97
Central Reserve Bank, 13
Chao (Zhi Yuan Tong Xing Bao Chao),
    5–7, 7*f*
Cheng (earnestness), 243
Chengdu, China, 3
Chiang Kai-shek, 11, 16, 159
Chile, 111, 135, 213, 260*t*
China. *See* People's Republic of China
China–Africa Development Fund, 293
China–Africa production capacity
    cooperation fund, 293
China Asset Management (Hong Kong)
    Limited, 268
China Bank (Huabei Bank), 14
China Banking Regulatory Commission
    (CBRC), 197–198, 289
China Briefing, 269
China Construction Bank, 115, 260*t*
China Cross-Border International
    Payment System (CIPS), 114–118
China Customs Agency, 183
China Depository and Clearing
    Corporation, 59, 271
China Development Bank, 243, 295
China Development Forum, 231
China Foreign Exchange Trading System
    (CFETS), 30–31, 93–97, 113–114,
    266
China Global Investment Tracker, 292
China Insurance Regulatory Commission
    (CIRC), 269, 289
China Investment Corporation, 65
China National Advanced Payment
    System (CNAPS), 114
China-Pakistan Economic
    Corridor, 240
China Reserve Bank, 11–12
China Securities Finance
    Corporation, 201
China Securities Index Company, 202
China Securities Regulatory
    Commission (CSRC), 48–49,
    200–203, 211

Chinese Nationalist Party (Kuomintang), 2*b*, 11–14, 159
Chinese students, 187
CIRC. *See* China Insurance Regulatory Commission
Circuit breakers, 201–203, 290
Citadel money *(Hui Zi)*, 3
Citigroup, 115
Clearing House for Interbank Payments System (CHIPS), 116
CNH (offshore) exchange rates, 30–32, 92, 144–145, 266
CNY (onshore) exchange rates, 30–32, 92, 96, 144–145, 266
"Communiqué on the Current State of the Ideological Sphere" (Document Number 9) (CPC), 161–162
Communist Party of China (CPC), 11, 14, 158–159, 162–165
  Central Committee, 170
  Central Committee Fourth Plenum, 165–167
  Central Committee Third Plenum, 165
  Central Party School, 214–215
  Central Propaganda Office, 164
  Document Number 9 ("Communiqué on the Current State of the Ideological Sphere"), 161–162
  Document Number 30, 162
  economic management by, 171–172
  leadership, 166–168, 207–210
Competition, 118–119
Composition of Foreign Exchange Reserves (COFER), 136–137, 283
Confucius, 19
Confucius Peace Prize, 219–220
Constitution (China), 162–165
Constitutional democracy, 164
Constitutionalism, 163
Constitution Day (China), 164
Consumer price index inflation, 129
Contingent Reserve Arrangement (BRICS), 236–237
Corporate bonds, 260*t*
Corporate debt, 132, 190–191
Corruption, 181, 207–209
Counterfeiting, 19
CPC. *See* Communist Party of China
Credit instruments, 195. *See also* Bank loans

Crimea, 100–101
Cross-Border International Payment System (CIPS) (China), 114–118
Cross-border payment systems, 102–103, 114–118
Cross-border trade and financial transactions, 103–105, 246
CSI 300, 202–203
CSOP Asset Management Limited, 268
Currency. *See also specific currencies*
  appreciation of, 24–25
  concepts, 23–36
  fiat, 5–10
  freely usable, 281
  international roles of, 32–36
  management of, 78–87
  mother, 4–5
  payment, 107–109
  reserve, 34, 122–133, 278–280
  safe haven, 150–172
  swap arrangements, 138–140, 139*f*, 261t–262t, 280–281
  vehicle, 104
Currency agreements, 113
Currency famines *(qianhuang)*, 3
Currency reserves, 34–35, 136
Currency status, 122–123
Currency war, 10–14
Current accounts, 32, 181–182, 287. *See also specific countries*

Dai Xianglong, 76
Dalai Lama, 219–220
Da Ming Tong Xing Bao Chao, 8–10, 9*f*
Data, 255t–262t
Debt securities (fixed-income markets), 132
De facto financial openness, 39–44
De jure financial openness, 39–40
Democracy, 164, 225
Deng Xiaoping, 16–17, 78
Denmark, 152
Deposit rates, 287
Deutsche Bank, 115
Deutsche Bundesbank, 124
Deutsche mark, 124
Development finance, 217–219
Dilbert, 23, 265
Dim sum bonds, 105–107
Dirty floats, 88

Document Number 9 ("Communiqué on the Current State of the Ideological Sphere") (CPC), 161–162
Document Number 30 (CPC), 162
Dollar. *See* U.S. dollar
Dong Biwu, 15*f*, 16

East-West trade, 238
EB-5 immigrant visas, 187–188
Economic corridors, 240
Economic sanctions, 100–102, 117
Economic stability, 204–212
The Economist, 21
Ecuador, 217
E-Fund Management (Hong Kong) Co., Limited, 268
Empty money *(kongqian),* 4–5
Entrusted loans, 195
Equity markets, 45, 131
Eurasian Land Bridge, 240
Euro, xiv
  banknotes in circulation, 122–123
  euro–U.S. dollar exchange rate, 278
  global foreign exchange market turnover shares, 258*t*
  international bonds and notes outstanding, 258*t*
  as payment currency, 108
  as reserve currency, 136, 151–152, 252–253, 253*f*
  SDR weight, 148, 282
  trade with RMB, 113
European Bank for Reconstruction and Development (EBRD), 223–224
European Central Bank (ECB), 84, 138–140, 139*f*, 169–170, 262*t*
European Union (EU), 79, 100–101, 122–123, 223
Eurozone, 124–125, 152–155, 255*t*, 256*t*, 260*t*
Evergreening, 192–193
Evil speculators, 201
Exchangeable money *(Jiao Zi),* 3
Exchange rate indexes, 95
Exchange rates, 24, 73–99
  CNH (offshore), 30–32, 92, 144–145, 266
  CNY (onshore), 30–32, 92, 96, 144–145, 266
  effective, 29

elastic, 90
euro–dollar, 278
fixed, 90, 99
flexible, 134
floating, 35–36, 79–83, 88–89, 91–92, 95
management of, 26–30, 77–83, 88–99, 275
nominal effective exchange rate (NEER), 29
official, 78–79
purchasing power parity (PPP), 128
real effective exchange rate (REER), 29
RMB-dollar, 24, 28, 78–79, 83, 84*f*, 88, 93–96, 179, 273, 282–283
terminology for, 25
Export-Import Bank of China, 243–244, 295

Fa Bi (legal tender), 11, 12*f*, 13
Fa Bi Reform, 11
Fear of floating, 249
Federal Reserve System, 84, 116, 153, 169–170, 283
Federal Reserve Wire Network (Fedwire), 109, 116
Fei Qian, 2
Fiat currency, 5–10
Financial centers
  competition among, 118–119
  offshore, 111–112
Financial institutions. *See also specific institutions*
  Chinese, 243–244
  debt owed by, 190
  international (IFIs), 109–111, 222–226
Financial markets, 130–134
Financial openness
  capital account, 32, 37–72, 176–178, 246–247
  de facto, 39–44
  de jure, 39–40
Financial sanctions, 100–102, 117
Financial Times, 21
Five-Year Plan (China), 69–70
Fixed-income markets (debt securities), 132
Flexible exchange rates, 134
Flying money, 2
Foreign currency reserves, 34–35, 136

People's Republic of China. *See also* BRICS;
　　People's Bank of China (PBC)
ADB share, 222
aid outflows, 217–218, 220–221, 241,
　　293
AIIB share, 228–229, 231–234
ancient, 3–5
augmented fiscal deficit, 190
bank deposit rates, 188–189
bank deposits, 180
banking system, 191–195
bond markets, 133
border tensions with India, 236
budget deficit, 190
capital account, 32–33, 35–72,
　　133–134, 175–188, 246–247
capital controls, 38–39, 72
capital flows, 52–60, 65–67, 66f,
　　157–158, 178–188, 248, 249–251
capital-to-labor ratio, 206, 291
capital-to-output ratio, 291
Constitution, 162–167
Constitution Day, 164
contributions to IFIs, 225–226
contributions to IMF, 222
corporate debt, 132, 190–191
cross-border trade, 246
currency agreement with Australia,
　　113
currency management, 78–87
currency policy, 89
current account surplus, 85, 85f, 182
debt owed by financial
　　institutions, 190
debt owed by nonfinancial
　　corporations, 190
democracy, 225
domestic debt market value, 132
EBRD membership, 223–225
economic growth, 85, 128–129, 133,
　　173–174, 204–207, 247–248
economic stability, 76, 151, 204–212
economic strength, 216–221, 244
end game, 69–72
equity markets, 131
establishment of, 15, 15f, 17, 158
exports, 77
external assets and liabilities, 40–42,
　　41f, 61–65, 177–178, 180
financial assets, 86

financial institutions, 243–244
financial markets, 130–134
financial reforms, 247, 253, 267
financial risks, 173–212
financial system, 130–131, 188–204
fixed-income markets (debt
　　securities), 132
foreign currency external debt,
　　177–178
foreign direct investment (FDI),
　　41–44, 172, 177
foreign exchange derivatives markets,
　　184–185
foreign exchange rate management,
　　26–30, 77–83, 88–93
foreign exchange reserves, xiii, xivf,
　　43–44, 53, 66–67, 77–78, 86, 86f,
　　92–93, 177–180
Foreign Investment Law, 270
foreign investment policy, 46
free trade zones (FTZs), 56–58
General Administration of Customs,
　　287
global influence, 213–244
government bonds, 132
government debt, 129, 189–190
gross domestic product (GDP), xiii,
　　xivf, 255t
historical development of, 1–22, 2b
household debt, 190
IMF share, 222–223
income tax rates, 42
index value, 40
inflation rate, 129–130
institutional framework, 157–158,
　　171–172
international investment position
　　(IIP), 40–41, 257t
international trade, xiii, xivf
investment in Japan, 277
investment in U.S., 249–250,
　　250f, 251
Japanese investment in, 277
key regulatory measures, 291
leadership, 165, 168, 284
leadership of BRICS, 236–237
legal reforms, 165–168, 253, 284
manufacturing sector, 77
market-oriented reforms, 210–212
merchandise trade, 28–29, 128–129

SAFE. *See* State Administration of
    Foreign Exchange
Safe assets, 150–172
Safe havens, 150–172, 247
Salt and Iron Debates, 3
Sang Hongyang, 4
Sanusi, Lamido, 135
Sarkozy, Nicolas, 142
Schumer, Charles, 74
SDR. *See* Special Drawing Rights
Second Opium War, 10
Securities and Exchange Commission
    (SEC) (U.S.), 157
Seigniorage revenue, 122
Shadow banking, 195–198
Shanghai free trade zone, 57
Shanghai–Hong Kong Stock
    Connect, 58–60
  Northbound investment quotas, 59,
      270–271
  Southbound investment quotas, 59,
      270–271
Shanghai Stock Exchange, 43, 59, 131,
    150–151, 199–201, 199*f*, 281
Sharif, Nawaz, 241
Sheng Laiyun, 215–216
Shenzhen Stock Exchange, 43, 131,
    199–201, 199*f*, 281
ShiJiaZhuang, China, 14
Shi Ji [Records of the Grand Historian]
    (Sima Qian), 4
Shinzo Abe, 230
Short selling, malicious, 200–201
Siemens, 42
Silk Road, 238–243
  new, 239–240, 239*f*
Silk Road Economic Belt, 239–240, 239*f*
Silk Road Fund, 240, 243
Sima Qian, 4
Singapore, 74–75
  and AIIB, 228–229
  RMB clearing arrangements,
      111, 260*t*
  RMB payment transactions, 108
  as tiger, 272
  as trade partner, 79
  Trans-Pacific Partnership (TPP), 213
Social financing, 196
Social instability, 207–210
Socialism, 160–161, 163, 166–167

Social Security Trust Funds, 189, 283
Society for Worldwide Interbank
    Financial Telecommunication
    (SWIFT), 107–109, 116, 144, 276
Song dynasty, 2–3, 2*b*, 4–5, 7
South Africa, 136, 256*t*. *See also* BRICS
South African rand, 258*t*, 259*t*
South African Reserve Bank, 262*t*
South America, 217–218
South Korea, 74–75
  currency pact with China, 113
  global trade importance rank, 281
  panda bonds, 107
  reserve portfolio, 135
  RMB clearing arrangements, 111, 260*t*
  RQFII quota, 52
  as tiger, 272
Southbound investment, 58–59
S&P 500, 202, 282
Spain, 154–155
SPC. *See* Supreme People's Court
Special Drawing Rights (SDR), 120–121,
    141–149, 246, 281–282
Special Loan for the Development
    of African Small and Medium
    Enterprises, 293
Special mention loans, 192–194
Speculators, evil, 201
Spot markets, 266
Sri Lanka, 228–229
Stability, 74–76, 76–78
Standard Chartered, 115
State Administration of Foreign
    Exchange (SAFE), 37, 49–50
State Bank of Pakistan, 261*t*
State-owned enterprises (SOEs),
    190–191
Stock Connect, 58–60, 178
Stock Exchange of Hong Kong, 59
Stock markets, 198–204
Strategic investors, 46
Students, 187
Study Times, 214–215
Sun Yat-sen, 11, 158–159
Supreme People's Court (SPC) (China),
    167–168
Swap arrangements, 138–140, 139*f*,
    261*t*–262*t*, 280
Sweden, 152
Swedish krona, 136

Swiss franc, 35, 113–114, 124–125, 136,
 155, 258*t*, 259*t*
Swiss National Bank (SNB), 113–114,
 124–125, 136, 169–170, 262*t*
Switzerland
 current account surplus, 126
 foreign assets, 126
 gross domestic product (GDP), 128,
  255*t*
 policy interest rates, 152
 reserve currency, 126, 128
 RMB clearing arrangements, 111,
  260*t*
 as safe haven, 155
 world trade shares, 256*t*

Ta-Ching Government Bank, 10
Tai Ping Rebellion, 10
Taiwan, 74–75, 111, 218, 260*t*, 272
Tang dynasty, 2, 2*b*
Tanzania, 136
Taro Aso, 230
Terminology, 20–22
 exchange rates, 25
 QFII vs QDII, 54
Thai baht, 74–75
Thailand, 74–75, 79, 111, 135, 228–229,
  260*t*
Tianjin free trade zone, 57
Tibet, 242
Tietmeyer, Hans, 124
Tigers, Asian, 74–75, 272
Tong Shang Bank (Commercial Bank of
 China), 10
Total social financing (TSF), 197
Trade, 103–105, 256*t*. *See also specific*
 partners
 global, xiii, xiv*f*, 256*t*, 279
Trade arrangements, 112–114. *See also*
 specific arrangements
 currency agreements, 113
 Silk Road, 238–243, 239*f*
Trade misinvoicing, 183–185
Trans-Pacific Partnership (TPP),
 213–215
Transparency, 95, 97–98, 156, 166, 168
Triffin dilemma, 125–127, 278
Trump, Donald, 73
Trust companies, 197–198
Trust loans, 195

Tuition-paying Chinese students, 187
21st-Century Maritime Silk Road, 239–
 240, 239*f*
Type, movable, 1–2

Ukraine, 100–102
UnionPay, 117–118
United Kingdom
 and AIIB, 229–230
 and China, 229
 currency swap arrangements,
  139*f*, 140
 foreign liability, 125
 global foreign exchange market
  turnover, 110
 gross domestic product (GDP), 255*t*
 reserve portfolio, 136
 RMB clearing arrangements, 260*t*
 RMB-denominated bond sales, 106
 RMB payment transactions, 108
 as trade partner, 79
 world trade shares, 256*t*
United States, 249–253
 ADB share, 222
 and AIIB, 227–231, 234
 bond markets, 133
 capital-to-output ratio, 291
 Chinese investment in, 249–250,
  250*f*, 251
 circuit breakers, 201–203, 290
 corporate debt, 132
 currency notes in circulation,
  122–123
 federal debt, 153–154, 156, 189–190,
  283
 fiscal policy, 153
 foreign investments in, 64
 foreign liability, 126
 global foreign exchange market
  turnover, 110
 government debt, 132, 190
 green cards, 188
 gross domestic product (GDP), xiii,
  255*t*
 household debt, 190
 IMF share, 222, 226, 233
 interbank payment systems, 116
 international investment position
  (IIP), 271
 investments abroad, 64